T0065769

CASH IN ON CASH *Flow*

How to Make Full-Time Income

with Part-Time Effort

in America's Hottest New Business

LAURENCE J. PINO

SIMON & SCHUSTER

SIMON & SCHUSTER
Rockefeller Center
1230 Avenue of the Americas
New Yqrk, NY 10020

Designed by

Manufactured in the United States of America

10 9 8 7 6 5 4 3 2 1

Library of Congress Cataloging-in-Publication Data

ISBN-13: 978-0-7432-8859-0
ISBN-10: 0-7432-8859-9

For information regarding special discounts for bulk purchases, please contact Simon & Schuster Special Sales
1-800-456-6798 or business@simonandschuster.com

To my wife, Janet, and my little son, Jordan,
whose influence on my life has been more profound
than I ever would have imagined.

Contents

Introduction 9

Part I ✦ Welcome to the Cash Flow Business

1. What Is the Cash Flow Business? 15
2. How It All Began 25
3. Why Cash Flow Is *the* Business of the Future 32

Part II ✦ How You Can Profit in This Business

4. Fifty-Plus Ways to Make Money Without Using Your Own 45
5. The Basics of Every Cash Flow Transaction 64
6. Use Collateral to Create Your Fortune 79
7. Target Businesses and "Factor" Your Way to Profits 132
8. When Bad Debt Is a Good Investment 176
9. Win a Share of the Lottery Without Even Playing 187
10. Turn Your Neighbor's Insurance Policy into Profit 196

Part III ✦ Techniques for Success

11. Why the Entire Industry *Wants You* to Succeed 215
12. Going from Well-Off to Wealthy: "The Perpetual Money Machine" 220
13. How to Get from *Here* to *There* 230
14. Seven Attributes of a Millionaire 238

Part IV ✦ Resources

Sources of Additional Information 255
Glossary of Cash Flow Terms 266
Debt Instruments by Category and Estimated Inventory 268
Documents That Secure Real Estate 271
Tax Lien Certificate and Tax Deed States 273
Statute of Limitations for Collecting Delinquent Debt 275
Lottery States 277
Acknowledgments 279
Index 281

Introduction

Richard and Sandy, both schoolteachers, retired two years ago and put their home on the market. They looked forward to building their dream house in the Smoky Mountains. It took them a year and a half to find a buyer. Once they did, the buyer couldn't get a loan for the full price that Richard and Sandy were asking, so the couple had to finance $40,000 of the sale themselves, allowing the buyer to pay them several hundred dollars a month. Because they couldn't get the lump sum of cash they needed to build another home, it now looks as if their dream house may be only that—a dream.

Barbara recently sold her San Francisco catering business, with big plans to open a five-star restaurant. Unfortunately, her buyer couldn't pay cash up front. Small business loans, the buyer argued, aren't easy to come by. Now Barbara's stuck receiving small payments each month, and her restaurant idea seems hopelessly out of reach.

Scott owns a successful printing business in Cincinnati, Ohio. Two months ago, he finished a $30,000 print job for a major account, but the client hasn't paid the invoice yet, maintaining that "internal accounting procedures" are holding up payment. They promise to pay him within three weeks. Scott's getting nervous. He knows that a promise won't cover his payroll.

Joyce won $5 million in the Florida lottery last year. After the euphoria wore off, reality set in. She discovered that her $5 million prize is actually $250,000 a year—minus taxes—paid out over twenty years. Joyce doesn't know how to budget that kind of money. She's a lot better at spending it than planning for the day the payments stop.

✦ ✦ ✦

What do all of the individuals I've just described have in common?

All of these people are owed payments that are due sometime in the future. And given the choice, all would prefer to have their cash *now* rather than wait for those payments to be made months or years hence.

Thousands of individuals and business owners across America are in the same situation. In every community, in every state, and in every type of business, people just like those I've described are owed cash—from an individual, a customer, a business, an insurance company, or the government. Regardless of *who* owes them, the money isn't available. And that means they don't have the freedom to use it. The need or desire for individuals and businesses to get the money they're owed now, rather than over time, has given birth to a whole new sector of finance. It's called the *cash flow industry*. From this industry has emerged an entirely new professional: the cash flow specialist. Cash flow specialists connect people who need cash and people who have cash.

Millions of individuals like Richard, Sandy, Barbara, Scott, and Joyce are expecting future payments they would eagerly sell for cash, if they only knew that the buyers for their owed payments were out there. Thousands of investors would happily buy those future payments, if they only knew they were for sale. Cash flow specialists bridge that gap.

That's why the demand for cash flow specialists is exploding at the rate of 100 percent per year. New opportunities are opening up every minute of every day in this young but booming industry.

Every time someone uses a credit card, joins a health club, or visits a doctor's office, a new opportunity arises in cash flow. Every time someone finances a car, sells a business, or wins the lottery, a new chance emerges to take advantage of cash flow. Every time someone sells a boat, plane, or mobile home, a cash flow opportunity presents itself. In fact, every minute of every day, more than $1 million of new opportunities hits the public records.

My goal with this book is to introduce you to the cash flow business and show you how to make extra spending money or a six-figure income as a cash flow specialist. Anyone who has the interest and motivation to succeed can carve out an incredibly lucrative niche in this thriving new industry.

Whatever your financial goals, cash flow is an ideal business. Consider the benefits:

- **Overhead costs are low.** You can work from your home, if you like. And other than business cards, stationery, and envelopes, there are few up-front costs.
- **You don't need employees.** With no employees, you won't have to worry about payroll, vacation days, sick leave, or other personnel concerns.
- **You don't need fancy equipment.** To get a cash flow business started, all you need is a desk or table, telephone line, and access to a copier and fax machine.
- **You don't need a license.** Once you're trained, you can go to work in most areas of cash flow immediately, with few bureaucratic hassles.
- **You don't need your own capital.** If you don't have capital to invest, you can operate as a broker and generate substantial fees. If you do have capital to invest, you can function as an investor and earn remarkable yields.
- **There's little competition.** Few people know about the cash flow industry. The niche you service will be yours to conquer.
- **It doesn't require selling.** In the cash flow business, there is nothing to sell to your friends, relatives, or neighbors. When you approach potential clients, it's not for the purpose of selling anything; they either need your service, or they don't.

- **Your earnings don't have to be a one-time source of income.** You can structure your cash flow profits as a stream of income that you receive over ten, twenty, or even thirty years.
- **You don't need a financial background.** You don't even need a college education. In the cash flow business, you can use the skills and experience you've worked hard for to begin a successful new career—no matter what field you're in right now. You can learn the basic skills required to start a successful cash flow business in one week or less.

Maybe you're content with your job, but looking for a part-time source of income. Maybe you're a parent checking out work-at-home possibilities. Perhaps you're a retiree seeking a better return on your investments. Or maybe you've burned out working in Corporate America and are looking for a full-blown self-employment opportunity. Regardless of your background or goals, you can find a niche in cash flow.

Many people just like you are already prospering in the cash flow business. You can, too. Every cash flow transaction involves the same basic system. Simply learn that system, work it consistently, continue to develop your skills, and you'll be on the road to a brand-new career—a lot sooner than you could ever imagine.

This book is the starting point. It could change the way you think, work, make your living, plan, and invest for the future. I'll show you how to get in on the ground floor of the cash flow business, working on a part-time or full-time basis, right from your own home. I'll teach you how to help people and businesses solve their cash flow concerns—and earn a lucrative profit for yourself in the process.

However, let me warn you in advance: This book is not intended to describe a get-rich-quick scheme, nor a multi-level marketing opportunity. It is not about profiting from situations in which you win, but others lose. It *is* about a way to find self-fulfillment, personal satisfaction, and even self-employment, in a *real* industry that meets *real* needs for *real* people.

Enjoy the book. Perhaps one day I can shake hands with you as a new participant in this exciting and fulfilling career opportunity—the cash flow business.

PART I

WELCOME TO THE CASH FLOW BUSINESS

CHAPTER ONE

What Is the Cash Flow Business?

The Concept of Cash Flow

Every day you encounter the concept of cash flow without even realizing it. If you've ever deposited a paycheck or paid a bill, you've dealt with cash flow. Money comes in, money goes out—that's cash flow. **Cash flow simply means getting income in the front door in time to pay expenses out the back door.**

Have you ever written a check, knowing full well that the funds needed to cover that check wouldn't be in your account until the next day? It's okay, you can admit it. Most of us have. Someone (maybe your employer) owed you money, but it wasn't available yet to pay the bills. I'll bet you were holding your breath, hoping your deposit would go through without a hitch so your check wouldn't bounce.

Or maybe you've had to wait for a tax refund. You sent all your forms to the IRS in April, expecting to get a June refund that you could use for a summer vacation. Someone—the government, in this case—owed you money, but it wasn't yet available for you to spend. And if you had already promised your kids a trip to Disney World, I'm sure you were anxiously checking your mailbox every day.

In both of those cases, someone owed you money, but that money wasn't available yet to pay your bills or spend on things you wanted. The problem that arises when money is owed, but not yet available, is called a **cash flow concern.**

What is a cash flow concern? Sometimes it's a need, like the need to pay rent. Other times it's a want, like the desire to take a vacation. *Cash flow concerns occur any time people owed payments due in the future have needs or desires they want to fulfill today.*

Businesses face the same types of cash flow concerns individuals face, but on a much larger scale. Cash flow means life or death—basic survival—to a business. Lose a customer, and your business probably won't collapse. But miss payroll a few times (or payroll taxes!) and your business will go down the drain faster than you can spell "IRS."

I learned about cash flow concerns the hard way about twenty years ago. In the late 1970s, fresh out of law school, I started investing in real estate. I bought numerous properties over an eight-year period. That was during the glory days of real estate, when everything you bought went up in value, and nothing went down. You could buy a piece of property for no money down and expect it to increase in value 10 percent to 15 percent per year. You could leverage the appreciation on your invested capital as much as 100 percent or more annually.

The only problem was that you could rarely collect enough rent on your properties to cover your mortgage payments. That created negative cash flow. Buy one piece of property, and you'd end up with a little negative cash flow. Buy a number of properties, like I did, and you'd get stuck with *a lot* of negative cash flow.

If you could hang on to your properties long enough, the appreciation would certainly be worth enduring the negative cash flow, assuming (1) you had the ability to cover the negative cash flow in the meantime; and (2) appreciation continued in the future the way it had in the past. Unfortunately, a lot of investors in the 1970s didn't have the means to support the negative cash flow.

At the same time I was investing in real estate, I was also trying to operate a law firm. By 1983, my real estate was draining cash from the firm. My properties were going up in value more than I had ever hoped, but appreciation couldn't pay the bills. And it certainly couldn't cover payroll!

My father, born and raised in South Philadelphia during the Depression, handled the accounting for my law firm and real estate investments. Dad kept warning me that I was getting into rougher and rougher cash flow waters. That didn't stop me, of course. I kept on buying real estate as often as I could.

It's not that I ignored his warnings. It was just that I knew my real estate had real value, and it was appreciating far faster than the negative cash flow. What I didn't count on, however, was how long it could take to sell a piece of real estate at that appreciated price—especially if I *needed* the money. Eventually the day of reckoning arrived. I remember that desperate day in June, when Dad came to me and said that we had spent every last dime we had to make payroll for that Friday. We had no cash left to operate the law firm or cover anyone's paycheck the following week.

I had assets, of course. I just didn't have any cash. I looked around at the real estate I owned and realized that even if I got lucky, it would take me sixty to ninety days to sell enough to put cash back in the bank. However, one asset I had bought about six months earlier—a private mortgage note—stared back at me as I frantically picked apart my financial statement. It was the only mortgage note I owned, and I had come across it casually through a referral from an acquaintance of mine.

There were nine years of payments left on the note, and it was providing me an income of $1,000 a month. A nice investment for sure, but I needed a whole lot more than $1,000 to cover payroll and expenses that next week.

Uncertain of what to do, I contacted someone I thought could help. I didn't really know if I could sell my mortgage note, and I wasn't sure what kind of price it would fetch even if I could. At any rate, I told my friend what I was holding, then kept my fingers crossed and hoped for the best. The next morning, that person made me an offer that knocked my socks off. He gave me $53,000 for the note *by the following Friday*—the same day I had to cut the payroll checks.

As Dad and I walked away from that deal (and I'm not sure which one of us was gloating more) several things occurred to me. First, I discovered, probably for the first time, how vital cash flow is to a business.

Second, I realized that *having assets* and *having cash* are two very different things. And third, I figured that hundreds, if not thousands, of other business owners like me had experienced the same problems I had with cash flow.

Ever since that day, I have been fascinated with the concept of cash flow. Thirteen years later, I'm intrigued with the business that has evolved to meet cash flow needs and how it offers a win-win-win situation for everyone involved.

THE CASH FLOW BUSINESS

The cash flow business is all about solving cash flow concerns. It's about getting cash into people's hands sooner rather than later. The way the business does that is by *buying payments that are owed in the future for a lump sum of cash today.*

Suppose you own a construction company. You win a $50,000 government contract to build city tennis courts, under the condition that you won't be paid until the courts are complete. Those are the terms, take it or leave it. However, you need at least $25,000 of cold hard cash immediately in order to buy materials for the courts, lease the equipment you need, and pay your employees each week while they're working. And you simply don't have $25,000 sitting in the bank.

You've got a serious cash flow concern.

Now, suppose someone offered to give you $25,000 in cash today, plus $20,000 when you finish the courts (for a total of $45,000), in exchange for the $50,000 you will receive when the city takes possession of them. Would you accept the offer?

Of course you would. With $25,000 in cash today, you could buy materials, lease equipment, and pay your employees. And out of the $20,000 you would get later, you could collect your profit.

You would accept that offer because it would give you the means to accept the city contract without going in debt. You would—and other people would too—because it just makes sense.

It makes so much sense, as a matter of fact, that individuals and companies throughout the country are doing business exactly this way. Transactions like the one I just described are occurring every day in the

United States. Individuals and businesses are opting to collect future payments sooner, rather than later, by selling their future payments to a third party. While the people and circumstances may vary, the principle is fundamentally the same. That principle—the buying and selling of future payments—is the basis of the entire cash flow industry.

The Definition of the Cash Flow Industry

The textbook definition of the cash flow industry is the "buying, selling, and brokering of privately held income streams in the secondary market." If that sounds complicated, it really isn't. By the end of this chapter, you'll know exactly what I'm talking about.

Let's consider each part of the definition in the context of another example.

Suppose you have a boat for sale. You're asking $10,000 for the boat, and I decide to buy it. I write you a check for $10,000 and sign it. Once you own the $10,000 check, you can do whatever you want with it. (If you don't know me very well, you'll probably take it to the bank and cash it right away!) The bank will require only that you endorse the check on the back. Then, provided I actually have $10,000 in my account, you can walk out of the bank with ten grand in cash.

Now let's change the scenario a bit.

You have a boat for sale, and I want to buy it. However, instead of giving you a check for $10,000, I write you a note that says, "I owe you $10,000. I'll pay you $475 a month, including interest, for the next two years." By signing this IOU note, I make a promise that you are going to get your money, plus interest, over time. Now I have a debt, and you have an **income stream.**

An income stream is simply another word for a future payment or series of payments. Essentially, an income stream is money that one individual or business is receiving from another individual or business as a result of a debt. For that reason, we often refer to income streams specifically as debt instruments.

The income stream created when I buy your boat is **privately held,** because the IOU is held by you, a private individual, not by a bank or lending institution.

In the second scenario, you will receive a series of future payments. You will get $475 a month for the next two years, for a total of $11,400. Not a bad deal, considering that you will receive your $10,000 asking price plus $1,400 in interest over those two years.

However, suppose that after holding on to this "IOU" note for a few months, you decide you want cash immediately in order to buy a new car. Could you take my "IOU" to the bank and cash it in? Of course not. Your local banker would laugh at you if you tried.

However, there is a place where you could get cash for your boat note. That place is called the **secondary market.**

The secondary market refers to individuals and companies that are set up to buy notes just like the IOU you're holding and not just notes secured by boats, but notes secured by homes, airplanes, mobile homes, cars, and even businesses. In the secondary market, we don't deal with banks. We deal with private investors and investment companies, which we call **funding sources.** Funding sources *buy* future payments for hard cash.

At a bank, you can cash a check you own today, earn interest on money you own today, and—if you're lucky—get a loan based on collateral you own today. But in the secondary market, you can get cash today *for payments owed to you in the future.*

Here's how it works.

In the secondary market, a funding source would give you cash in exchange for your boat IOU. The amount the funding source would give you would depend on the likelihood that I would continue to make the payments on the boat (in addition to several other factors, which I'll discuss later). The important thing to note is that the funding source wouldn't really buy the *balance on the note;* it would purchase the *value of the payments due in the future.*

In this example, you would walk away with a lump sum of cash today that you could use to pay your bills or reinvest. I would continue to make my $475 payments, only now they would go to the funding source. And finally, the funding source would earn a yield on the note over the next two years as I continue to pay it off.

A boat note (in the business, we actually call it a *marine note*) is just one type of debt instrument that can be bought and sold in the secondary market. Almost any income stream—whether it is an invoice to be paid in 30 days, or lottery winnings to be paid over 20 years—can be sold to a third party for cash.

In the cash flow industry, we recognize more than fifty income streams, or debt instruments, that can be transacted for a profit. The most well known are private mortgage notes and business invoices. Dozens of other debt instruments are lesser-known, but even more profitable. A handful of acknowledged instruments have never been transacted to date, but could be under the right conditions. In Chapter Four, I'll list and describe the more than fifty specific debt instruments we have identified to date.

Why do people sell income streams?

Individuals sell income streams for three basic reasons. The first is **access.** People need or want access to their cash. Sometimes they have a serious need—to pay off credit cards, finance long-term medical care, or to settle a divorce. Other times, they simply have a desire—to purchase a dream home, take a vacation, buy a new car, finance a wedding, or start a business, for example.

In some cases, people want access to their cash just for peace of mind. They no longer want to worry about liquidity issues, collection hassles, or the financial strength of the person who owes the debt.

In the case of my law firm, I needed access to cash in order to make payroll, and $1,000 a month income from a mortgage note wasn't going to cover it. Yes, it would have been more profitable to have held on to that note for the next nine years and collect the interest. But I needed immediate access to cash, and selling my note was the perfect solution.

The bottom line is this: People sell income streams because they need or want access to their cash immediately, not months or years from now.

The second reason people sell income streams is **interest** or **yield.**

If I gave you a choice of receiving $100 today, or $100 next year, which would you choose? The logical answer is $100 today, even if you don't need access to the money. Why? Because of interest or yield. Interest or yield is what gives you the ability to invest money this year and turn it into an even larger amount of money next year. When we talk about interest or yield, we're talking about the earning power of your cash. When you have cash, you can produce income on it. When you don't, you can't. It's that simple.

If you received $100 today, and invested it at a rate of 10 percent, you would end up with $110 next year. But if you waited until next year to receive your $100, you couldn't earn interest or yield on it until the following year.

When you're dealing with the choice of investing $100 today and earning 10 percent interest on it, versus receiving $100 next year, you're talking about a difference of only $10.

But what if you were to add three zeros to that? The difference between investing $100,000 today at a 10 percent interest rate versus receiving $100,000 a year from now is *$10,000*. And what if I had the opportunity to earn a yield of 30 percent on my money? Now we're talking about a difference of $30,000! Clearly, one year can make all the difference in the world.

People will sell their income streams—even for less than face value—because they know that with cash in hand today, they can start earning interest or yield.

The third reason people sell income streams is **inflation.** Inflation eats away at the future value or "buying power" of money. I don't think anyone would dispute that you can buy more with a dollar today than you will be able to five, ten, or twenty years from now.

When my Dad retired from the Air Force in 1963, our family moved to New Jersey. I remember as a young child being told that the house we were buying was a newly constructed, split-level home on a lot in a subdivision. From the way my parents were talking, money was going to be tight. What did our new house cost? The princely sum of $14,999.

Obviously, $14,999 won't get you a home today—it will barely get you a new car. And thirty-five years from today, who knows if $100,000 will still get you a decent home? Inflation eats away at the buying power of money.

People sell their income streams because they realize that, over time, the payments they receive will drop in real value.

When you consider access, interest or yield, and inflation, it's a whole lot easier to see why an individual or company is often eager to receive a lump sum of cash today instead of a series of payments due in the future. They can count on cash; they can't always count on the promise of cash.

Why do people buy income streams?

It's clear why individuals or businesses would want to *sell* their income streams, but what about the other side of the coin? Why would anyone want to *buy* them? The answer is simple enough: Profit. *Buying future payments is a form of investing, and it's incredibly profitable.*

If I am an investor with a lump sum of cash in my hands, my objective is to get the highest rate of return I possibly can. What are my options? I can buy T bills. I can buy Certificates of Deposit. I can invest in mutual funds, stocks, bonds, real estate, and so on. In short, I can do any number of things with my cash.

My objective, however, is not to discuss the pros and cons of each of those investments. My point is that, as an investor, I want to maximize the amount of income my investment generates. Buying income streams is one way I can do that—and do it very well. When I buy future payments, I earn pure, unadulterated yield on my investment. And I know in advance exactly what that yield will be, provided the payments continue.

Investors and investment companies buy income streams because it's a profitable way to invest their money.

BRINGING SELLERS AND INVESTORS TOGETHER: THE CASH FLOW SPECIALIST

On one hand, individuals and businesses clearly are motivated to sell their income streams. And on the other, investors or investment companies have good reasons for buying them. But the backbone of the cash flow business is the *cash flow specialist,* who bridges the gap between buyers and sellers.

Cash flow specialists are professionals whose sole purpose is to solve cash flow concerns. They accomplish this in two ways. First, they operate as brokers, or "middlemen," connecting buyers and sellers and earning a fee in the process. We call these specialists **cash flow brokers.** Second, they operate as investors, using their own capital (or their companies') to buy income streams, earning a hefty yield (12 percent to 48 percent) for their effort. We call these cash flow specialists **funding sources.**

Some cash flow specialists solve cash flow concerns for individuals; others solve cash flow concerns for businesses. Either way, their goal is to locate people and companies with an income stream to sell. Then they either broker the income stream to a funding source (as a cash flow broker) or buy the income stream themselves (as a funding source).

By the end of this book, I would venture a guess that you will want to become a part-time or full-time cash flow specialist—working either as a broker, connecting buyers and sellers, or as an investor, buying income streams for your own account. In either case, you can make a great deal of money in this business—as you'll shortly learn.

REMEMBER THESE HIGHLIGHTS

- Cash flow, in this business, refers to the movement of cash from an individual or business that owes a payment to an individual or business collecting a payment. The cash flow business involves the buying, selling, and brokering of privately held income streams in the secondary market.
- A *cash flow concern* exists when money is owed but is not yet available to spend.
- A cash flow specialist is a professional who solves cash flow concerns. Some cash flow specialists operate as brokers. Others operate as investors, or as funding sources.
- People sell income streams for three main reasons: access, interest or yield, and inflation.
- People buy income streams because they can earn a high yield on their investment.

CHAPTER TWO

How It All Began

As we have learned, the cash flow industry consists simply of professionals turning income streams into cash for individuals or businesses who have a current need or desire to use that cash.

Now, let's get some background on where the industry came from. After all, few people are even aware the cash flow industry exists, despite the fact that more than fifty different debt instruments—amounting to over $3.8 trillion of inventory—are currently available for transacting in the U.S. economy. Chances are strong that if you had not picked up this book, heard about it from one of your friends, or seen one of my television shows, you would not have known about the industry, either.

The cash flow industry has its roots in two seemingly unrelated methods of finance: **owner financing** and **factoring,** which we'll learn more about in Chapters Six and Seven. For now, let's look briefly at how these two methods of finance influenced the development of the cash flow industry as a whole.

Owner Financing

The first method of finance that led to the emergence of the cash flow industry was owner financing. Owner financing originated in the early twentieth century as a method of accelerating the sale of real estate. In an owner-financed sale, a real estate seller accepts a promissory note as a portion of the purchase price. The note is then secured by the real estate being sold.

Suppose, for example, that Brad is interested in selling his house for $135,000, and Alice is prepared to buy it, but she only has $55,000 in cash. If Brad is willing to accept a downpayment of $55,000 and a promissory note for the remaining $80,000, he can sell his real estate to Alice with little fuss or inconvenience. Brad would end up holding a *private mortgage note* for $80,000, and Alice would end up owning Brad's home. Alice would write monthly mortgage checks directly to Brad until the $80,000 note was paid off. The private mortgage note Brad holds would be secured by the house itself.

Homeowners and commercial real estate investors in this country have used owner financing as a method of purchasing property since the early 1900s; however, it wasn't until much later that it became popular. During the high-interest-rate periods of the 1970s and 1980s, home buyers found it difficult to obtain affordable financing from banks. You may remember that time, when interest rates and inflation skyrocketed to double digits, making it almost impossible for people to sell their real estate. If a real estate seller was willing to take a downpayment from the buyer and hold on to a mortgage note for the remaining balance, the transaction was much more feasible for the buyer—and certainly more convenient.

By the time inflation drifted back down to earth, hundreds of thousands of individuals were holding private mortgage notes. In fact, the total dollar amount of privately held notes amounted to just over $400 billion. Individual investors and investment companies recognized a tremendous profit opportunity in those notes, and they began to buy them directly from sellers.

Today, owner financing is quite common, with approximately 7 percent to 11 percent of all real estate transactions resulting in a seller holding a note. About 1.8 million notes are presently in private hands. These privately held mortgage notes turned into a commonplace investment nationwide. In fact, private mortgage notes are even securitized and sold to the public.

FACTORING

The second method of finance that impacted the development of the cash flow industry was factoring, also called accounts receivable purchasing. When a business sells a product or service to another business, it sends the second business an invoice in order to collect the money due. The first business can either wait for the invoice to eventually be paid, or it can sell the invoice to a third party for a reduced amount. The latter transaction is called factoring. Businesses use factoring to stimulate cash flow.

Remember the example of the tennis court contract in Chapter One? That was an example of a factoring transaction. As the contractor, you had the opportunity to sell for cash today amounts owed to you at a future date. A more typical factoring transaction would involve a company that has already delivered goods to a business and is awaiting payment.

Suppose a furniture store has delivered office furniture to a local business, and now the furniture store is waiting to be paid. In a factoring transaction, the store would sell its business invoice, minus a fee, to a factor. The store would get cash within 48 hours; the factor would collect a fee when the invoice was finally paid.

According to historians, factoring dates back to the ancient Phoenicians, when merchants used factoring to settle their trade debts. It has survived as a way for manufacturers and merchants to do business. Prior to the 1980s, factoring was used primarily in the garment, textile, and furniture industries and was available only to large companies. That all changed with the rise of the independent broker.

The rise of the broker network

During the 1980s, private mortgage investors operated in their own exclusive sphere. They focused on mortgage notes, and for the most part didn't pay attention to other "income streams" available for purchase. They also tended to target only notes in their local areas. Investors based in Houston, for example, would market primarily for mortgage notes on homes in Houston. Investors located in Chicago would look for notes in Chicago.

In addition, investors usually worked *directly* with private mortgage note sellers. Once in a while, an investor would come across a note too large to buy and would broker it to one of the larger investment companies. But by and large, transactions were governed by direct relationships between buyers and sellers.

That was about the time I got involved with private mortgage investing. When I purchased my first note in the early 1980s, I was aware of very few people who either brokered or bought mortgage notes. Back then, fewer than 200 people in the United States made a living with privately held mortgage notes.

Over time, more and more individuals discovered the income potential in brokering private mortgage notes. A private mortgage broker could earn a good living simply by locating private notes and placing them with investors. A few seminars, such as my own training organization's program, cropped up to teach adults how to broker private mortgage notes for a commission.

As more people got trained to take advantage of the income opportunity in brokering, the number of brokers multiplied. The availability of brokers, in turn, provided more investment opportunities for investors. Rather than tracking down notes directly, investors could simply put up investment capital and rely on brokers to bring them transactions. In addition, investors could do business nationwide rather than just in their neighborhoods.

The broker/buyer relationship created a profitable situation for everyone involved. Today, most major private investors rely on brokers to bring them transactions. About 9,000 cash flow brokers currently manage private mortgage notes around the nation on a full- or part-time basis. Even though the number of brokers has expanded dramatically from the mid-1980s, there still is little competition. Private mortgage brokers represent a small fraction of the financial services market when you consider the 5 *million* individuals in the country working in other areas of finance, such as insurance, securities, and real estate.

The same movement toward brokering that was occurring in the private mortgage business was occurring simultaneously in the factoring industry. Traditionally, factoring had been provided by major factoring companies, often subsidiaries of large banks, and was available only to companies with annual sales in excess of $100 million per year. For smaller companies, factoring and accounts-receivable financing remained elusive.

A small group of companies recognized that an opportunity existed to provide factoring for mid-sized companies and emerged as factors, targeting businesses with annual sales below $100 million. But, just like private mortgage investors, their activities were restricted at first to the geographic areas in which they functioned. Factors in South Florida serviced businesses in South Florida; factors in Detroit serviced companies in Detroit. And again, in most cases, factors dealt directly with the businesses, not with brokers.

Eventually, some companies—my organization included—began to examine *factoring brokerage* as a career possibility. In 1993, my organization started offering training in factoring brokerage in addition to private mortgage brokerage. In these courses, we taught adults how to identify businesses with cash flow concerns and refer them to factoring funding sources. Training programs like ours helped to popularize the factoring broker as an occupational category.

Today, many factoring companies that in the past dealt directly with businesses now depend exclusively—or at least significantly—on brokers. As a result, the **factoring broker** is a thriving profession.

THE LINK BETWEEN PRIVATE MORTGAGES, INVOICES, AND OTHER INCOME STREAMS

The recognition that brokers specializing in private mortgages and brokers specializing in factoring were essentially doing the same thing—brokering future payments—laid the foundation for what we now call the cash flow industry.

When pioneering cash flow specialists started seeking out individuals and businesses with mortgage notes and invoices to sell, they came across other types of income streams that offered similar opportunities for brokering. After all, whether people are owed payments on real estate or workers' compensation checks, the same concept applies: they have income due in the future, but have a need or desire for cash now.

Cash flow is cash flow, regardless of which debt instrument created it.

Hence, brokers started actively seeking new income streams to broker and funding sources eagerly began to buy them. The search was on for alternative income streams that could be brokered or bought.

THE BIRTH OF THE CASH FLOW INDUSTRY

With brokers bringing income streams to the table, and funding sources bringing capital to the table, the stage was set by the early 1990s for an encompassing new industry. The only thing remaining to mobilize this new industry was an infrastructure that would bring the players together. That infrastructure emerged with the inception of the American Cash Flow Association.

Through the Association's efforts, brokers and funding sources from many different segments of the market obtained the opportunity to communicate with each other.

The Association currently publishes a monthly newspaper called the *American Cash Flow Journal*, hosts an annual Cash Flow Convention, offers industry-based certifications for trained brokers, provides benefits to its members, and maintains a database of national funding sources available to certified members. (For more information on the American Cash Flow Association, see the Resources section at the end of this book.)

Since the establishment of the Association, growth in the cash flow industry has accelerated rapidly. By 1993, our training organization had identified six different debt instruments that could be transacted in the secondary marketplace. By 1995, we were tracking and teaching 28 different instruments. By 1996, we had pinpointed 43. By mid-1997, we had identified more than 50 distinct debt instruments, totaling $3.8 trillion in combined inventory. And, by the time this book goes to print, we will be teaching more than 60 debt instruments valued at over $5 trillion that can be transacted for a profit in the secondary market.

THE CASH FLOW INDUSTRY TODAY

Today the cash flow industry is exploding into mainstream America. The industry is currently growing at a rate of 100 percent per year. The more than fifty different debt instruments we recognize today account for about $3.8 trillion of available inventory. Yet less than *2 percent* of the inventory is being transacted annually, by fewer than 20,000 full- or part-time individuals nationwide. Did you catch that? *Less than 20,000 people are homesteading their share of the cash flow gold mine.*

The cash flow industry *needs* qualified and trained brokers to expand cash flow opportunities to consumers and businesses across the country. And this book may well be your first opportunity to see if the business is right for *you*.

Remember These Highlights

- The cash flow industry has its roots in two seemingly unrelated methods of finance: owner financing and factoring.
- Owner financing is a type of sale in which a real estate seller accepts a private mortgage note secured by the real estate being sold.
- Factoring is a type of financing businesses use to stimulate cash flow. In a factoring transaction, a business sells its invoices for a reduced amount of cash.
- In the beginning, private mortgage note investors and factors worked directly with note sellers and invoice sellers in their immediate geographic areas.
- Eventually, *private mortgage brokers* and *factoring brokers* emerged. Brokers located transactions for investors and factors in exchange for a fee.
- Over time, brokers discovered other types of income streams that could be bought, sold, and brokered in the same manner as private mortgage notes and invoices.
- Private investors, investment companies, and factors that bought income streams came to be known as funding sources.
- The inception of the American Cash Flow Association created an infrastructure for the cash flow industry by connecting brokers with funding sources that provide capital for particular types of transactions.

CHAPTER THREE

WHY CASH FLOW IS *THE* BUSINESS OF THE FUTURE

EQUITY INVESTING VERSUS DEBT INVESTING

When we compare the cash flow business to other forms of income production, it becomes clear why cash flow is a breakthrough wealth-building opportunity you can act on today.

Equity investing has enjoyed widespread popularity during the past two decades. Nearly every individual and corporation has invested money in equities. What are equities? Stocks, bonds, mutual funds, real estate—investments in which you actually own a piece of the thing you're buying, even if it's only a small piece.

Back in the 1980s, equity investing was strongest in real estate. High inflation drove up values, and investors made a killing. It was tough *not* to. More recently, equity investing has been concentrated in stocks and mutual funds. Thanks to a bull market, the Dow has risen high enough to break all past records, and once again, investors have done exceedingly well.

Equities clearly were the rage of the 1980s and 1990s. The trend of the future, however, is not investing in equities. It's investing in *debt*.

If you invest in equities on a small scale—buying stocks and mutual funds, for example—you probably aren't involved in the actual management of your investment. There's a good side to that and a bad side. The good side is that you're not involved. The bad side is—you're not involved!

When you're not involved in your investment, anything that happens occurs outside of your control. As investors discovered on October 19, 1987, the infamous Black Monday, it was possible to wake up one morning to find 25 percent of your asset value wiped out—because of events you had no power to influence.

I don't know about you, but I look for more control over my financial future. Investing in something that is totally in the hands of others, dependent on an unpredictable economy, is disconcerting, to say the least.

But what about equity investments you *do* control? Real estate was probably the arena that so many self-employed investors—working full- or part-time—made a lot of money in during the 1980s. I was one of them. The problem with real estate, however, is that you have too much control and too much exposure.

Suppose you are a self-employed real estate investor. You purchase a piece of property for little or no money down. From a time standpoint, you have a problem at the very beginning—you own the property. What does owning it mean? It means you have to manage it. You have to spend time responding to calls, making repairs, finding tenants, and so forth. What if you then buy another piece of real estate? You now have two pieces of real estate to manage. That takes more time. And what about a third piece of real estate? That takes even more time.

When I began investing in single-family residences in the early 1980s, I had a heyday. I loved every minute of it, buying as much as I could. In fact, I bought fourteen residential real estate rentals in a three-month period of time. Suddenly—to my horror—I realized I had to *manage* all of that real estate or hire someone to manage it for me.

Either way, I was going to take a bath. If I managed it myself, I would have to spend more time managing my real estate than my law practice—for a whole lot less profit! If I hired someone to manage the real estate for me, I would do nothing but increase my negative cash flow. Manage it myself, I lose. Manage it through someone else, I lose even more. Neither option was acceptable.

When you own and manage real estate, it's only a matter of time before tenant problems and property improvements, not to mention maintenance hassles, leave you with neither the time nor the money to pursue your investmenting.

For years, I've been amused by the late-night infomercials hawking books and tapes about "how to become rich through real estate." The financial guru of the day remarks on how easy it is to buy real estate with little or no money down. He proceeds to show a parade of individuals who have become proud owners of real estate by listening to a few short audiotapes.

The joke, of course, is that virtually anyone can buy real estate with little or no money down. That's not the problem. The problem is knowing what to do with it once you've got it.

This is the real issue. In short, when you invest in real estate, you put yourself in an awkward position. *The more you own, the poorer you get!* Not only that, but when you invest in real estate, you are completely exposed. As investors in Texas, California, and Massachusetts during the booms in those states in the early 1980s know all too well, just because a piece of real estate sells for $100,000 today, that doesn't mean it's going to sell for $100,000 tomorrow. As an attorney and business advisor, I've counseled numerous investors on what to do with properties they had purchased for $300,000 but could resell for only a fraction of that cost. When you own real estate, and the value goes down, you lose, *dollar for dollar.*

In the 1980s, investing in real estate was appropriate for two reasons. First, inflation was driving up appreciation. Any time inflation rages, hard assets like real estate increase in value. Second, Congress was subsidizing real estate investing through very favorable tax treatment. (When I was investing in real estate in the 1980s, I rarely, if ever, had to pay income taxes!)

But those days are gone. Raging inflation is barely within the memory of my generation and is not even a memory at all for the newest crop of investors. In addition, the Tax Reform Act of 1986 made the favorable tax treatment of real estate just a footnote in our history books. And even though real estate values nationwide have firmed up and probably will produce predictable income by the middle of 1999, *real estate, as a significant investment opportunity for middle-class Americans, is tenuous today.*

But there's good news. Regardless of whether you made money in real estate in the 1980s—or wish you had—it's a brand-new game now. A whole new generation of wealth-building strategies awaits you. *That generation has spawned the cash flow industry.*

Investing in Debt Instruments Is Different

Like real estate, you can invest in debt with little or no money down. If you don't have the money to buy a debt instrument, you can broker it to institutions that do. If you do have the money, you can buy it yourself and enjoy the earnings. But unlike real estate, there's little or no management involved.

When you invest in debt, you don't own a piece of something (like a share of stock) or a whole something (like a piece of property). You simply own a stream of payments. See the advantage? You can focus all of your attention on seeking out your next investment opportunity, which, in turn, will deliver more income and the opportunity to buy even more.

If you invest in real estate, you've got to locate tenants, interview them, check their backgrounds and credit, contact their references, and negotiate a lease. Then you have to deal with collecting rents, fixing leaky faucets, paying property taxes, and a dozen other details. When you invest in debt, you don't have to be a manager. You don't have to repair or maintain anything. *You're buying paper—not properties, but notes.* That means someone else has ownership of the asset. When you own mortgages on real estate, for example, other people own the real estate. They insure it, fix it, and pay taxes on it. They're the ones with the headaches. You're the one with the income.

My own portfolio of debt instruments is pages long. Yet I spend almost no time managing it, other than the time it takes me (through an accounting clerk in the office) to deposit checks into the bank and keep track of them in a notebook.

Likewise, when you invest in debt, you're not at the mercy of Wall Street. You don't have to hire a money manager or check your investments every day to see how they're doing. You know in advance the long-term yield your investment will generate for as long as the income stream is coming in. This new trend—investing in debt—is what the cash flow business is all about.

HOW A CASH FLOW BUSINESS DIFFERS FROM A START-UP BUSINESS OPPORTUNITY

If real estate investing was one of the primary ways middle-class families expanded their wealth during the 1980s, start-up business was the other. And this option has become even more popular during the 1990s.

Multi-level marketing has graduated into "network marketing" and more recently into "direct selling." We can buy everything from cosmetics to long-distance service to cleaning products through a network. Book and tape distributors are promoting everything from 900 numbers to pre-paid calling cards to "mail order out of your home." Many of these start-up businesses are viable income opportunities. But many are merely fads. And like every other fad, it's just a matter of time before they *fade* out of existence.

Take virtually any start-up business and contrast it with a cash flow business, and you will understand why no other income opportunity can compete. Here's why:

- **A cash flow business doesn't require inventory.** That means no garage full of shaving cream, vitamins, facial cleansers, or anything else. You need no up-front money to purchase products, and no warehouse in which to store them.
- **A cash flow business doesn't require special equipment.** You can do all of your business using only a telephone and a fax machine. There's no need to have an office unless you prefer it. And a fax machine isn't absolutely necessary. *Access* to a fax machine is all you need.
- **A cash flow business doesn't require employees.** The work you do can be done by you and you alone. Of course, you may join up with other cash flow specialists and work together, but you

don't have to. You don't have to hire anyone, pay payroll taxes, cover health insurance premiums, buy workers' compensation policies, or anything of the like. And you don't have to "sign up representatives" to work underneath you.

- **Cash flow specialists need no capital.** When you locate a seller who needs or wants cash for an income stream, you'll need capital to buy it. But it doesn't have to be your own capital. Funding sources all over the country with billions of combined dollars will line up to buy deals you come across.
- **Cash flow specialists can work from home.** You can work right out of your kitchen, or create a home office in a basement or spare bedroom. If you like, you can team up with a spouse, brother, sister, or other family member to operate your business. (Over the years of teaching people to work in the cash flow business, I've often had the opportunity to train a husband, then his wife, or a mother, then her son.)
- **Cash flow specialists don't have to sell anything.** You don't have to peddle products to your friends, relatives, co-workers, or neighbors. You don't have to give "parties" or "home demonstrations" in order to make a profit. When you approach potential clients, you're not asking for a check, *you're giving them a check.* Most people don't even know about cash flow services. You simply explain what you do. They either need your service, or they don't. And if they don't need it today, they probably will some time in the future.

In the table that follows, I've summarized the differences between what other income opportunities involve and what a cash flow business involves.

HOW OTHER OPPORTUNITIES STACK UP AGAINST CASH FLOW

Other Income Opportunities Involve	A Cash Flow Business Involves
Inventory	No inventory
Property management	No property management

Storage space	No storage space
Employees	No employees unless you want them
Office space	No office space
Special equipment	Telephone
Computer	Typewriter or computer
Fax machine	Access to a fax machine
Selling to your friends and family	No selling to friends and family
Time away from family	Opportunity to include family
A large capital investment	No capital investment

As you can see, no other start-up business or multi-level marketing opportunity can match the benefits of cash flow. You need no inventory, employees, office, equipment, or capital to run a successful cash flow business. *All you need is the willingness to succeed and the desire to learn the strategies to get you there.*

THE CASH FLOW INDUSTRY CAN ACCOMMODATE ANYONE

At the 1997 Cash Flow Convention, I had the chance to speak with Diane Lampe, who had only recently graduated from our Diversified Cash Flow Institute training program. In less than two months' time, she had already brokered a factoring transaction worth $350,000, and she had nine more deals on the drawing board. Diane made a comment that confirmed what I had long believed.

"Larry," she said, "I've found that the cash flow business will fit anybody. You just have to decide what route to go."

Diane said it better than I could. Because it's so diverse, the cash flow industry can accommodate any background, objective, or life circumstance.

The cash flow industry is comprised of more than fifty different debt instruments in which you can specialize. Many of those instruments, like private mortgage notes, are owned by individuals who are no different than the people who live next door to you. Other instruments, like invoices, are owned by businesses. Some instruments, like insurance policies and corporate donations, involve critical social issues. Others, like retail installment contracts, result from everyday consumer transactions. Some debt instruments involve thousands of dollars, like automobile notes. Others deal with millions of dollars, like lottery prizes.

The point is, no matter what your background, objective, or life circumstance, there's a niche in the cash flow industry that's appropriate for *you*.

All Backgrounds

The cash flow business is a refuge for what I call "corporate expatriates"—people who have grown tired of the rat race and are looking for something more fulfilling.

One former student of mine, Mike Hilton, left a successful career as a financial officer at a New York City brokerage firm to start his own cash flow business. Not only did he leave the firm, he left the big city altogether. He and his partner moved to a small, quiet New England town and set up shop as a factor. Now he runs his business according to *his* pace—not Wall Street's.

The cash flow industry is also haven for what I call "professionals in transition."

Howard Levitan, for example, shut down his law practice in Kansas after learning about the cash flow industry. Today he and his wife, Sharon, operate a successful cash flow business out of their basement—with no overhead, no employees, and none of the problems associated with running his old law office. Besides the benefits of working from home, Howard enjoys the personal satisfaction his cash flow business offers. As a lawyer, he was always "against" someone; now, he's always helping someone.

Jeff Callender, a former minister from Washington State, was seeking an income opportunity that would satisfy three requirements. First, he wanted the business to allow him plenty of time with his family. Second, he wanted to provide a valuable service to the community. And third, he wanted to produce a higher income than he was as a minister. Jeff found all three in the cash flow industry, and he made the transition from minister to full-time cash flow specialist within a few short weeks.

Even retirees have found plenty of room in the cash flow business.

Bill Shaw discovered the industry after retiring from a German company, where he had spent thirteen years in sales and marketing. Initially, he decided to work as a factoring broker part-time to supplement his retirement income. To his surprise, he now has a full-fledged factoring brokerage business and even funds small accounts himself.

Ron Provart retired from the insurance business after twenty-five years of service. He knew he wanted to start a home-based business—something he could do on his own time. He wanted to be his own boss and work when *he* wanted to. The cash flow industry fit his needs perfectly. I recently saw Ron at an industry convention. He told me his factoring business provides him not only a substantial income, but a whole lot more.

"You can make a lot of money in this business," he said, "but my thrill is not making money. My job is in helping people and helping companies."

All Objectives

In addition to accommodating all backgrounds, the cash flow industry can accommodate virtually all income and career objectives. Whether you are working full- or part-time, a cash flow business allows you to direct your efforts according to your goals.

My friend Rick Jowers, who operates the very successful Southland Equities in Atlanta, emphasizes how significantly his cash flow business has improved his lifestyle—not just in terms of money, but in terms of flexibility. When you call Rick's office in Atlanta, more often than not your call will be transferred to a cell phone at his cabin in the hills of North Georgia. The first time I met Rick, he had just packed up his briefcase and cell phone and taken his father on a cross-country train ride through Canada. The trip gave him a chance to get closer to his father, he told me, and his business didn't suffer one bit.

Dow Stanley of Conway, South Carolina, has used his cash flow business as a springboard to other career opportunities that have enabled him to prosper in his community. When Dow first learned about the cash flow industry, he was making a living as a lumber broker. He noticed the same dynamic at work in brokering cash flows as in brokering lumber: locating sellers and matching them with buyers. He also recognized another similarity between the two—both required only a telephone and a makeshift desk.

As Dow became more involved in the cash flow business, he gravitated toward mobile home notes. From investing in mobile home notes, he moved to investing in mobile homes. This year, Dow is developing a mobile home park. Now only about one-fourth of his time is devoted to the cash flow business. Still, he attributes his cash flow business with his incredible success in other related fields.

Ben Patterson got into the cash flow industry simply as a means of economic survival. Ben was involved in real estate when the closing of a Navy base left his hometown of Idaho Falls in economic ruin. Ben trained in brokering private mortgages and earned $10,000 on his first transaction. Since then, he's completed more than $1 million of cash flow transactions. He credits his cash flow business with "turning his life around."

All Life Circumstances

Backgrounds and objectives aside, the cash flow industry can accommodate all life circumstances.

My friend Dee Jones, from Texas, started her cash flow business for very personal reasons. Her husband had been diagnosed with cancer, and she needed a way to stay home and care for her him while he was going through chemotherapy. Her cash flow business not only allowed her to work from home, but it provided her with enough income to take her husband on a long-planned vacation. Since then, her husband has recovered, and Dee's income now offers them even more opportunities for travel.

A cash flow business can give working parents the freedom to devote more time to their families. Cindy Irish, for example, got into the cash flow industry because she missed her young son terribly when she dropped him off at day care every day en route to her corporate job. Her cash flow business allowed her to generate the income she was accustomed to without missing out on watching her son grow up.

Scott and Joyce Jooston, from Arizona, told me several years ago that their primary reason for getting into the cash flow industry was to spend more time with their kids. Now, their cash flow business allows them to work from home without suffering a loss of earning potential.

THE CASH FLOW REVOLUTION

Regardless of your age, education, occupational or professional background, lifestyle, or income objective, the cash flow industry has a niche for you. You are in *exactly the right place at exactly the right time* to profit from an industry that is taking America by storm.

In the next few years, the cash flow industry will revolutionize the way debt is handled in America. As more cash flow specialists emerge, the industry's heightened visibility will generate even more opportunities. And the more people who know they can get cash today for an income stream, the more *you* can profit.

Your interest in this business is not only understandable, but appreciated. It will assist me in my personal objective—to make the cash flow industry as well known by the end of this decade as the real estate industry is today.

REMEMBER THESE HIGHLIGHTS

- Equity investing—mainly in real estate and mutual funds—was the rage of the 1980s and 1990s. The trend of the future, however, is not investing in equities. It's investing in debt.
- Investing in debt is what the cash flow industry is all about. The cash flow industry involves brokering and buying debt instruments, also called cash flow instruments.
- When you buy real estate, you have to manage it as well. When you buy debt instruments, you manage nothing. When you invest in stocks, you have no control over your investment. When you invest in income streams, you maintain control over your investment.
- The cash flow industry can accommodate any background, objective, or life circumstance. No matter what your interests or goals, there is a niche of the cash flow industry in which you can profit.

PART II

How You Can Profit in This Business

CHAPTER FOUR

Fifty-Plus Ways to Make Money Without Using Your Own

MOST SIGNIFICANT CAREER CHANGES require months or years of retraining. Some even require a new degree. If you decide in mid-life to become a lawyer, you're looking at a minimum of three years of law school. If you want to become a doctor, you're looking at five of medical school. And that's assuming you've already finished college!

That's an intimidating thought, isn't it? It's no wonder people stay trapped in jobs they hate.

To become a cash flow specialist, you don't have to go to graduate school. You don't even have to get a college degree. You can use the skills and experience you've already acquired to begin a successful new career—no matter what field you're in right now.

How is that possible? As I've mentioned before, more than fifty debt instruments can be transacted in the secondary marketplace. Each one of them represents a distinct area of cash flow in which you can specialize.

Take royalty payments, for example. Anything that can be licensed produces a royalty payment. Musicians, writers, and artists all receive royalty payments; however, engineers who patent inventions, professors who develop course curricula, and individuals who register trademarks receive them as well.

The formula that makes these debt instruments "transact-able" is simple: An individual or company is owed a stream of income in the future. The individual or company wants to get all or a part of that future income in cash today. The cash flow specialist brokers or buys the stream of income for cash.

Below is a list of specific debt instruments. As you read the descriptions, consider your own personal interests, skills, and past experience. Look for connections you have that could lead you into a niche of your own.

Accounts Receivable (Invoices). An invoice is generated when a business has provided products or services to a business customer. Rather than waiting from 30 to 90 days for payment, the business can get cash immediately by selling the invoice to a funding source. When the customer pays the invoice, the funding source earns a profit. Almost any business that produces invoices can use this cash flow service.

Aerospace Notes and Leases. This income stream is generated when airplanes, helicopters, blimps, or other aircraft—anything from a single-engine Cessna to a Boeing 747—are financed or leased by private owners. A cash flow specialist can buy, sell, and broker these notes, or provide cash in exchange for future lease payments.

Annuities. An annuity is a contract sold by life insurance companies that guarantees a fixed or variable payment at some future time. Recipients of certain types of annuity payments can get access to cash sooner rather than later by selling payments through a cash flow specialist.

Automobile Notes. Automobile notes are created when car dealers offer on-the-spot financing or leasing to their customers. Through the services of a cash flow specialist, dealers can get cash for these notes rather than collecting payments over time. They can then use that cash to buy more inventory. Private individuals selling their cars with owner financing also have the opportunity to sell their IOUs for cash today.

Automobile Leases. Future automobile lease payments may be sold just like automobile notes. The lessor would get cash immediately rather than waiting for lease payments to arrive each month.

Bankruptcy Receivables. Whenever a company submits a successful reorganization plan, the bankruptcy judge approves the creation of repayment categories. Those categories produce whole classes of businesses that have to wait extended periods of time to collect on those obligations. With the help of a cash flow specialist, businesses can cash out future payments in one lump sum.

Business Notes. A business note is created when a business owner sells a business and receives a promissory note from the buyer. In the cash flow industry, a business owner can sell the note for immediate cash rather than collecting monthly payments over several years.

Cemetery Pre-Need Contracts. Consumers often pre-purchase cemetery lots and funeral services, paying for them in installments over time. The income stream generated by this arrangement can be sold for cash through a cash flow specialist.

Charitable Contributions. Charitable contributions are often pledged in advance to non-profit organizations by corporations, then delivered over a period of time. Through a cash flow transaction, an organization can sell its future charitable pledges for cash it can use today. The amount of cash the organization receives depends on past collection rates.

Club Memberships. Health clubs and country clubs receive monthly dues and annual membership fees from members. These payments can be brokered or sold through a cash flow specialist. Club owners can receive a lump sum of cash today, which they can use to pay bills, buy equipment, make improvements, or market for new members.

Collectibles Notes. A collectibles note is similar to an automobile note. It results from the sale of such big-ticket collectible items as antiques, knives, guns, artwork, coins, stamps, and so forth. A collectibles dealer may decide to sell the note for cash up-front rather than receiving payments over time from the buyer.

Commercial Deficiency Portfolios. Every year businesses write off billions of dollars of uncollected debt from other businesses. Often creditors are willing to accept nickels on the dollar for the debt, since it has been charged off anyway. A cash flow specialist can locate commercial debt portfolios and place them with investors, who then collect on them.

Commercial Judgments. A commercial judgment results from a lawsuit involving a business. When in place, a commercial judgment takes priority over all other claims. For the judgment creditor, who may or may not collect, guaranteed cash today is better than uncertain cash tomorrow.

Commercial Leases. Leases on commercial property range in length from several months to several years. Commercial property owners can sell future lease payments for cash they can use today—to improve the property, construct new buildings, or pay outstanding debts.

Commissions. Professionals who work on a commission basis (in sales, real estate, etc.) can get an advance on future commissions through a cash flow specialist.

Condominium Assessments. In order to secure the collection of condominium fees, dues, charges, etc., condominium boards have the right to assess the charge and file an assessment (lien) against condominium units. A condominium board can sell the future right of payment to an investor through a cash flow specialist.

Consumer Deficiency Portfolios. Consumer deficiency portfolios involve bad debt owed by consumers rather than businesses. Consumer debts charged off by retail stores, hospitals, utility and telephone companies, and other businesses can be sold to cash flow investors.

Contracts. A contract is similar to an invoice, but it most often involves an ongoing service rather than a product. (Commercial cleaning, pest control, computer services, and maintenance businesses all use contracts.) Businesses that provide services on a contract basis can get cash sooner rather than later by selling future contract payments.

Credit Card Debt/Chargeoffs. Institutions that have charged off bad credit card debt often sell their debt at a very discounted price. A cash flow specialist can buy credit card chargeoffs or broker them to other investors, who collect a percentage of the debt they recover from credit card holders.

Equipment Notes and Leases. Promissory notes and leases secured by equipment create yet another cash flow opportunity. Farm machinery, office equipment, and heavy construction equipment are all examples of items that are usually leased or paid for over a long period of time. The owner or lessor of the equipment can sell the income stream generated by the payments.

Farm Production Flexibility Contracts. Farm Production Flexibility Contracts are part of a federal program that provides seven years of fixed, declining annual payments to farmers and agricultural businesses. Cash flow specialists can provide farmers with an advance on all or some of the future payments they are expecting.

Franchise Fees. A franchisor with a track record of collecting on franchise fees can sell a portion of future fees for cash today in order to satisfy current capital requirements for expansion, marketing, and so forth.

Funeral Purchase Assignments. A funeral purchase assignment is created when families use the services of a funeral home, but have no money to pay the bill—only an insurance policy on the deceased. The funeral home can accept an insurance policy in lieu of cash, but insurance companies often take weeks or months to issue payment. A cash flow specialist can deliver immediate operating cash to the funeral home.

Inheritances. It takes a beneficiary anywhere from nine months to two years to collect an inheritance. An individual expecting an inheritance can go to a cash flow specialist to sell all or part of the inheritance he or she is expecting.

Letters of Credit. A letter of credit is similar to an invoice. Payment is expected—it's just a question of *when.* A cash flow specialist can answer that question.

License Fees. License fees are similar to royalties, but are paid to copyright holders or trademark owners and tend to be distributed in fixed increments. License holders may be owed payments due some time in the future, but have an immediate need or want for cash. A cash flow specialist can get the license holder cash *now.*

Lottery Winnings. Lottery winnings are usually paid out in installments over ten to twenty-six years depending on the state. A lottery winner can sell all or a portion of his or her future lottery payments and receive a lump sum payment immediately.

Marine Notes and Leases. Marine notes originate when yachts, ski boats, and fishing boats are privately financed. Individuals and businesses can sell marine notes or lease payments and get cash now rather than collecting payments over time. Marine lease payments can be sold for cash in the same way.

Mobile Home Notes. Mobile home notes are similar to automobile notes, except that they are secured by mobile homes. A cash flow specialist can create them, broker them, or buy them for a profit.

Partnership Agreements. Partnership interests often provide for an income stream from income-producing assets. If a business partner needs access to cash, he or she can sell part of the payments, instead of selling out his or her partnership interest.

Privately Held Mortgage Notes. This income stream results from an owner-financed real estate sale. An individual collecting income from a private mortgage note can sell all or a portion of the future payments through a cash flow broker. The mortgage note buyer then collects the mortgage payments over time for a long-term yield.

Prizes and Awards. Lotteries are only one of the types of future income created by the gaming industry. Prizes, awards, and sweepstakes winnings can be transacted in exactly the same way.

Purchase Orders. Companies issue a purchase order as a formal agreement that a product is going to be bought at a specific price. When a business receives a purchase order, the business often needs money in advance in order to manufacture the product that has been ordered. A cash flow specialist can advance the business cash for the purchase order, allowing the business to fulfill the order and deliver the products.

Recreational Vehicle and Business Vehicle Notes. Companies and individuals that lease or sell such high-priced vehicles as RVs, motor homes, delivery trucks, and business vans sometimes finance the lease or sale themselves. A cash flow specialist can advance a seller cash in exchange for this future payment stream.

Retail Installment Contracts. These contracts are to consumers what invoices are to businesses. A retail installment contract is an agreement between a retailer and a customer to pay for goods over time. Many furniture stores, electronics stores, and other retailers allow their customers to buy more purchases in installments. A cash flow specialist is able to get the business cash for those contracts.

Royalty Payments. Royalty payments are monies forwarded to artists, inventors, and owners from publishers, TV networks, record companies, manufacturers, and distributors for the use and sale of materials or products. There is generally a gap of 30 to 180 days between the time royalty payments are calculated and the time they are paid. A cash flow specialist can assist by purchasing or brokering a percentage of the royalties due.

Secured Non-Performing or Delinquent Debt. Just because a debt is delinquent doesn't mean it can't be collected. This especially holds true if the debt is collateralized. Secured non-performing or delinquent debt is uncollected debt that is secured by collateral.

Sports Contracts. Athletes who receive salary payments or retirement payments based on a contract can get a lump sum of cash today for some or all of their future income.

Structured Settlements. A personal injury settlement requiring payments from an insurance company to an individual creates an opportunity for a cash flow specialist. Through the services of a cash flow specialist, an individual can sell future settlement payments for a lump sum of cash.

Student Loans. Vocational, technical, and trade institutes such as cosmetology, truck driving, and bartending schools finance student tuition payments. Those schools can sell the stream of tuition payments through a cash flow specialist. The buyer then collects the tuition payments and earns a yield.

Tax Liens. When a real estate owner neglects to pay property taxes, the local government can auction off a tax lien on the property. A cash flow specialist can purchase the lien for his or her own portfolio, resell the lien, or broker it to funding sources.

Tax Refunds. Instead of waiting for a check from the IRS, an individual can receive his or her refund early by selling it to a cash flow specialist. When the refund arrives, the cash flow specialist earns a profit.

Timeshare Memberships. Timeshare memberships can be sold in the same way that club memberships can be sold. Timeshare owners and developers can sell payments they expect in the future for immediate cash.

Viatical Settlements. An individual with a terminal illness or elderly person with a chronic illness can sell his or her life insurance benefits to a funding source in order to pay current medical bills or other expenses.

Warehouse Inventory Lines. This is an arrangement in which a funding source buys inventory from a business for cash and sells it back to the business at a predetermined price, allowing the business to satisfy its cash requirements for manufacturing and distribution.

Workers' Compensation Awards. If a person is owed payments from an insurance company for workers' compensation, he or she can receive the money more quickly by selling the award for a lump sum of cash today.

In describing these debt instruments, I'm not suggesting that the list is exhaustive. The truth is, new instruments are being discovered all the time. Nor have I described them in enough detail for you to transact them. For now, I simply wanted to give you a general sense of what these debt instruments are and what they share with each other.

In Chapter Five, I'll describe the basic steps that apply to any cash flow transaction, regardless of the instrument involved. For now, suffice it to say that whatever type of cash flow you choose to transact, the same dynamic is at work. Cash flow is cash flow. It doesn't matter what type of debt created it or who is holding it.

SIX CATEGORIES OF INCOME STREAMS

In the cash flow industry, we group debt instruments into six income stream categories based on characteristics they share in common. There is no magic that separates income streams into these six groups. However, as the list of income streams has continued to grow, these categories have allowed us to understand the similarities among them:

- **Business-based income streams.** The business-based income-stream category includes payments that are owed to a business from another business or government. Invoices, commercial leases, and commercial debt are examples of business-based income streams.

- **Collateral-based income streams.** The collateral-based income-stream category includes cash flows that are secured by collateral. Private mortgage notes, mobile home notes, and automobile notes are examples of collateral-based income streams.
- **Consumer-based income streams.** The consumer-based category is comprised of income streams in which the party that owes payments is a consumer—a private individual. The party receiving payments can be either a business or another individual. Credit card charge-offs, retail installment contracts, and timeshare memberships are consumer-based income streams.
- **Contingency-based income streams.** The contingency-based category includes income streams in which the recipient is not necessarily *legally* entitled to receive payments, or in which the amount of the payment is uncertain or contingent upon outside factors. Several examples of contingency-based income streams are charitable contributions, royalty payments, and sales commissions.
- **Government-based income streams.** This category includes all income streams paid by a government, usually a state government, either directly or through an insurance company. The party receiving payments is typically an individual. Lottery payments, farm production contracts, and tax refunds are government-based income streams.
- **Insurance-based income streams.** The insurance-based category includes cash flow income streams stemming from insurance companies and paid to individuals or businesses. Annuities, funeral purchase assignments, and viatical settlements are insurance-based income streams.

THE EXPLOSION OF INVENTORY IN THE CASH FLOW INDUSTRY

For the past several years, I have been monitoring the growth of inventory within each of the six income stream categories. By *inventory*, I mean the dollar amounts of income streams available in the market waiting to be transacted. The following table shows each of the six income stream categories, along with an estimate of the amount of inventory available today within each group.

DEBT INSTRUMENTS BY CATEGORY AND ESTIMATED INVENTORY

Business-Based Income Streams

$2.4 Trillion Estimated Inventory

Accounts receivable (invoices)
Chapter 11 reorganization plans
Bankruptcy receivables
Commercial judgments
Equipment leases
Commercial leases
Purchase orders
Equipment timeshares
Partnership agreements
Letters of credit
Contracts
Aerospace leases
Commissions
Commercial deficiency portfolios
Sports contracts
Automobile leases

Collateral-Based Income Streams

$950 Billion Estimated Inventory

Privately held mortgage notes
Condominium assessments
Equipment notes
Collectibles notes
Mobile home notes
RV and business vehicle notes
Warehouse inventory lines
Business notes
Aerospace notes
Marine notes
Automobile notes
Tax liens/certificates
Private instrument securitizations

Consumer-Based Income Streams

$175 Billion Estimated Inventory

Health/country club memberships
Retail installment contracts
Credit card debt/charge-offs
Consumer deficiency portfolios
Cemetery pre-need contracts
Unsecured non-performing or delinquent debt
Time-share memberships
Prizes and awards
License impounds
Student loans
Inheritances, trust advances, and probates

Contingency-Based Income Streams

$25 Billion Estimated Inventory

License fees	Royalty payments
Corporate charitable contributions	Franchise fees
Consumer judgments	Commercial judgments

Government-Based Income Streams

$75 Billion Estimated Inventory

Tax refunds	Farm production flexibility contracts
Lottery winnings	

Insurance-Based Income Streams

$165 Billion Estimated Inventory

Annuities	Structured settlements
Funeral purchase assignments	Viatical settlements
Workers' compensation awards	

The Payor and the Payee

In reviewing the six categories of income streams, you may have noted that the common denominator among some of them is the source of the payments or the recipient of the payments. In the business, we refer to the party that owes future payments as the **payor** and the party receiving the payments as the **payee.**

If you get involved in the industry as a cash flow broker, most of your contract will be with payees, since they are the ones who are receiving the payments and, accordingly, are the ones who need or want cash for their income streams. However, cash flow buyers are more concerned with the payor of an income stream. Buyers want to know whose credit they need to investigate to make sure they will get paid on the income stream.

In order to transact an income stream for profit, you have to be able to identify the payor and the payee. In other words, you have to understand who owes the payments and who is expecting them.

The following table lists the income streams I described earlier. The column in the center shows who typically receives the payments for that type of income stream. The column on the right shows who typically owes them.

INCOME STREAMS—PAYEE AND PAYOR

Income Stream	Payee (Receives Payments)	Payor (Owes Payments)
Accounts Receivable/ Invoices	Any businesses	Any businesses
Aerospace Notes and Leases	Aircraft dealers	Individuals, businesses
Annuities	Individuals	Insurance companies
Automobile Notes and Leases	Car dealers, individuals	Individuals
Bankruptcy Receivables	Businesses	Businesses
Business Notes	Former business owners	New business owners
Cemetery Pre-Need Contracts	Funeral directors	Individuals
Charitable Contributions	Non-profit organizations	Corporations
Club Memberships	Health clubs, country clubs	Individuals
Collectibles Notes	Businesses, individuals, collectibles dealers	Individuals
Commercial Deficiency Portfolios	Businesses	Businesses
Commercial Judgments	Businesses	Businesses
Commercial Leases	Commercial property owners	Commercial tenants
Commissions	Salespeople	Businesses
Condominium Assessments	Condominium management associations	Condominium owners
Consumer Deficiency Portfolios	Retailers, banks, institutions	Consumers
Consumer Judgments	Individuals	Businesses
Contracts	Individuals or businesses that provide a service	Businesses

Credit Card Debt/ Charge-offs	Banks, gasoline retailers, department stores	Individuals
Equipment Notes and Leases	Equipment dealers	Businesses, individuals
Farm Production Contracts	Farmers	U.S. Federal Government
Franchise Fees	Franchisors	Franchisees
Funeral Purchase Assignments	Funeral directors	Individuals
Inheritances	Individuals	Insurance companies, trusts
Letters of Credit	Businesses	Businesses
License Fees	Patent and trademark holders	Businesses
Lottery Winnings	Individuals	State lottery commissions
Marine Notes and Leases	Boat dealers	Individuals
Mobile Home Notes	Individuals, mobile home dealers	Individuals
Partnership Agreements	Individuals	Businesses
Privately Held Mortgage Notes	Individuals	Individuals
Prizes and Awards	Individuals	Businesses
Purchase Orders	Businesses	Businesses
RV/Business Vehicle Notes	RV/Business vehicle dealers	Businesses, individuals
Retail Installment Contracts	Retail businesses	Consumers
Royalty Payments	Artists, writers, musicians	Businesses or individuals
Secured Non-Performing or Delinquent Debt	Businesses, banks, institutions	Businesses or individuals

Sports Contracts	Athletes	Sports teams
Structured Settlements	Plaintiffs in personal injury, malpractice, and other tort cases	Insurance companies
Student Loans	Technical and vocational schools or academies	Students
Tax Liens	Individuals	Individuals
Tax Refunds	Individuals	Federal, state, and local governments
Timeshare Memberships	Timeshare owners	Timeshare buyers
Viatical Settlements	Terminally ill or elderly individuals	Life insurance companies
Warehouse Inventory Lines	Businesses	Businesses
Workers' Compensation Awards	Individuals	Insurance companies

HERE'S WHERE THE REAL MONEY IS

So far, we've discussed how more than fifty different debt instruments can be transacted in the secondary marketplace. Now let's talk about where the *real* money is.

Ten debt instruments have surfaced as the most profitable niches in the cash flow industry at this particular time: private mortgage notes, business notes, mobile home notes, tax liens, invoices, commercial leases, bad debt, lottery winnings, viatical settlements, and annuities. Below is a brief explanation of why these income streams show the most promise in today's marketplace.

Private Mortgage Notes

Private mortgage notes continue to dominate the cash flow industry as a money-making income stream. Why? Everybody is familiar with real estate. After all, you drive around it every day. You see it on every street in every county in every state of this country. People have a certain comfort level with real estate.

Making money on a mortgage note is just a step away from making money in real estate. Hence, private mortgage notes represent a starting point for many people who get involved in the cash flow industry, even if they move on to other more profitable areas later.

If you took a survey of the most successful cash flow brokers who have ventured into more progressive income streams, such as business notes, car notes, annuities, and the like, you would find that many of them were trained in the private mortgage note arena. However, once they got their foundation, they got into other areas that boasted fewer practitioners.

For example, my former student Ed Lisogar and his wife, Sheba, were trained in private mortgage notes, but later gravitated to business notes, and now work with mobile home notes, as well. Dow Stanley started out transacting private mortgage notes and later focused most of his time on mobile home notes.

Business Notes

Business promissory notes are a profitable component of the cash flow industry for two reasons. First, the market for business note sellers is vast. Business buyers do not have many financing options—banks do not finance the purchase of most businesses, leaving most sellers financing all or part of the deal themselves.

It is currently estimated that 85 percent of business sales result in the seller carrying back a promissory note. That means that out of every 100 businesses that change hands, 85 of the sellers end up with a note. Many former business owners are holding on to promissory notes they would prefer to trade for cash.

Second, few cash flow professionals specialize in transacting business notes. There is an enormous amount of inventory and very few participants getting in the game.

Mobile Home Notes

Why do mobile home notes represent one of the most profitable areas of the cash flow industry? Simply because mobile homes now account for *one-fourth* of the total U.S. housing market. Nearly one in three new homes sold today is a mobile home.

Mobile homes are growing increasingly popular among both first-time home buyers seeking affordability and senior citizens trying to downsize their residential requirements. Mobile homes are a practical alternative for both groups.

It is difficult for most mobile home buyers to get a loan through traditional channels. Sellers often provide financing themselves. This creates unlimited profit opportunities for cash flow specialists.

Tax Lien Certificates

Tax lien certificates are another lucrative niche of the cash flow industry. For one thing, tax liens offer the same benefits as a mortgage, with even more safety. A tax lien takes a priority over any other lien on a piece of property. When you buy or broker tax lien certificates, you get the total security of the real estate on which the tax lien has been placed, as well as being in the senior position on any other liens that might exist.

Second, investing in tax lien certificates requires a minimal cost of capital. Capital providers who specialize in buying the certificates often purchase them at a very low yield, giving brokers the opportunity to earn a larger fee on these transactions than they could on other debt instruments.

Finally, tax liens offer the opportunity to purchase real estate at a substantial discount from market value, which tends to attract experienced real estate investors to these instruments.

Invoices

Invoices (accounts receivable) will continue to provide a strong market as a debt instrument for four fundamental reasons. First, when you broker or factor invoices, you deal with businesses. And businesses—by definition—always need cash flow. There is hardly a situation in which a business has all of the cash it requires.

Second, banks and lending institutions can't compete with the cash flow industry when it comes to accounts receivable financing. With their tight regulations and high collateral requirements, they "factored" themselves (pardon the pun) out of business finance a long time ago.

Third, the income you earn as a cash flow broker specializing in invoices is residual income. If you set up a client, and that client continues to factor month after month, you will continue to earn fees month after month. In other words, you work once but get paid again and again and again.

Finally, very few companies provide accounts receivable purchasing in relation to the huge volume of inventory. In 1996, for example, *less than 5 percent* of the total available accounts receivable inventory was factored.

Commercial Leases

Commercial leases represent a potential gold mine in the cash flow industry. Real estate investors all across the country own income-producing commercial properties. Many try to solve their cash flow needs by borrowing from the bank. That process is cumbersome, extremely expensive, and rarely provides a flexible solution to a short-term cash flow problem.

The market for transacting commercial leases is enormous, and property owners are easily identifiable. In addition, vast networking opportunities in the real estate community provide easy access to commercial property owners. Yet to date, few cash flow specialists have discovered commercial leases as a cash flow niche.

Bad Debt

The primary reason bad debt is a lucrative area of cash flow lies in the nature of the debt. Whether you're talking about bad commercial or consumer debt, the owners of the debt have written it off as uncollectible. Therefore, any money a cash flow specialist can offer for the debt is "found money."

The second reason bad debt is a promising area of cash flow is that debt collection falls outside most businesses' area of expertise. T-shirt manufacturers, for example, specialize in producing T-shirts, not in collecting bad debt. By selling off bad debt, business owners can get money for debt they've written off, and turn it over to someone who is skilled at collecting it.

The third reason is that a ready marketplace of funding sources specialize in buying bad debt. These companies and investors buy major portfolios of bad debt that cash flow brokers present to them.

Lottery Winnings

Lottery winnings continue to be a lucrative cash flow opportunity for two reasons. First, consider the psychographic profile of the lottery winner. Lottery winners, simply by playing, show a willingness to gamble. And any money they win in the lottery is "found" money, not earned money. In addition, lottery winners rarely have expertise at handling money. The combination of those characteristics makes lottery winners ideal candidates for cash flow services.

Within a few years, lottery winners tend to outspend the annual payment they are receiving on their lottery prize. As a result, they often seek a way to cash in some of their payments for a lump sum. A cash flow specialist can provide lottery winners cash, along with a second chance to convert their prize into a long-term investment vehicle.

The second reason lottery winnings represent a lucrative cash flow niche is the fact that at least 38 states now hold lotteries. America's lotteries have created more than 15,000 new millionaires (and tens of thousands of sub-millionaires) since the first lottery in 1964. Judging by lottery sales, lottery payouts will continue to escalate.

Viatical Settlements

The viatical segment of the cash flow industry has made incredible strides in the last several years. Once used mainly by terminally ill patients, recent breakthroughs have made viatical settlements a financial option for the elderly and their families. With the cost of living far exceeding the average senior's income, viaticals can bridge the gap between what the elderly need and what they have by allowing them to cash in all or a part of their life insurance benefits.

In addition, viatical settlements in general are now receiving increased exposure through corporate employee benefits programs. Considering that hundreds of thousands of baby boomers are now caring for their elderly parents, viatical settlements may well rise to the forefront of the cash flow industry.

Annuities

The enormous rise in the popularity of annuities in this country stems from their flexibility as investment contracts. Annuities can be fixed or tied to a variable rate. They can be used to save for retirement, structure a personal injury settlement, or provide an inheritance for heirs. In addition, annuity payments are backed by insurance companies, which makes them a relatively safe income stream.

Because annuities are being issued in so many creative ways, the available inventory of annuities has exploded from $1.7 billion to $107 billion in the past twenty-five years. In addition, because of the relative security attached to annuities, many funding sources already set up to buy other income streams can readily buy annuities. Annuities offer an immense amount of capital and few practitioners—a ready recipe for opportunity.

At this point, I've described more than fifty known cash flow instruments and which of those instruments show the most promise in today's marketplace. In Chapter Five, we'll look at the elements that *all* of these cash flow instruments share—and how you can transact any of them using the same basic steps.

REMEMBER THESE HIGHLIGHTS

- We group debt instruments into six different income stream categories: business-based income streams, collateral-based income streams, consumer-based income streams, contingency-based income streams, government-based income streams, and insurance-based income streams.
- The party that owes income stream payments is called the *payor.* The party receiving the payments is called the *payee.* Knowing the payor and payee for each income stream will help you locate sellers and buyers when you start transacting those income streams.
- Ten debt instruments in particular are the most profitable in today's market. They include private mortgage notes, business notes, mobile home notes, tax liens, invoices, commercial leases, bad debt, lottery winnings, viatical settlements, and annuities.

CHAPTER FIVE

THE BASICS OF EVERY CASH FLOW TRANSACTION

IN THE CASH FLOW BUSINESS, all profits resolve around one thing: the **cash flow transaction.** A transaction occurs any time a person or business sells future payments for cash.

For example, when you sold your "boat note" for cash, that was a transaction. Every cash flow transaction, regardless of the income stream, involves the same components and the same basic steps. In this chapter, we'll look at how a cash flow transaction works. Then I'll show you several ways you can earn money by participating in the transaction.

THE PLAYERS

In order to have a cash flow transaction, you've got to have an income stream. Someone must owe someone else a future payment or payment stream. As I mentioned in Chapter Four, we call the person or entity that owes the payment the payor. The payor doesn't play an active role in the cash flow transaction, but is important to consider because the payor creates the income stream itself.

Now, let's look at the players involved in a cash flow transaction.

First, every transaction requires a seller. The **seller** is a payee—a person or business receiving one or more future payments. The seller is expecting a future income stream but is interested in selling that expectation for cash today. The seller, in other words, is the person who needs cash.

The seller is also called the **client** because he or she is the person or business whose needs are being met in the transaction. The cash flow industry centers on the seller because the seller has the need that the buyer and the broker fill.

Second, every transaction involves a **buyer.** The buyer is the person or company that supplies the money in the transaction. The buyer, in other words, is the person who has cash. In the cash flow business, we often refer to the buyer as an investor or **funding source.**

Any person or company who has cash to invest can be a funding source. Some funding sources are large, institutional investment companies that specialize in buying income streams to generate profit. Others are private investors who buy income streams for their own investment portfolios. Either way, the funding source is usually an expert who specializes in buying a particular type of income stream.

Every cash flow transaction requires—at a minimum—those two players: a payee/seller (someone with payments for sale) and a buyer (someone to buy them).

Most cash flow transactions (but not all) involve a third player. That player is the **broker.** The broker acts as a referral source for cash flow transactions. The broker, in other words, stands between the people who *need* cash and the people who *have* cash. The broker provides for the sale, or *assignment,* of all or part of the income stream from the payor to the funding source. In exchange for his or her efforts, the broker earns a fee, profit, or commission.

Every cash flow transaction operates according to the same basic structure and incorporates those players—the payee/seller, the funding source, and the broker (see the following figure). Whether we are dealing with a lottery award, mortgage note, or invoice, the transaction structure remains the same.

PLAYERS IN EVERY CASH FLOW TRANSACTION

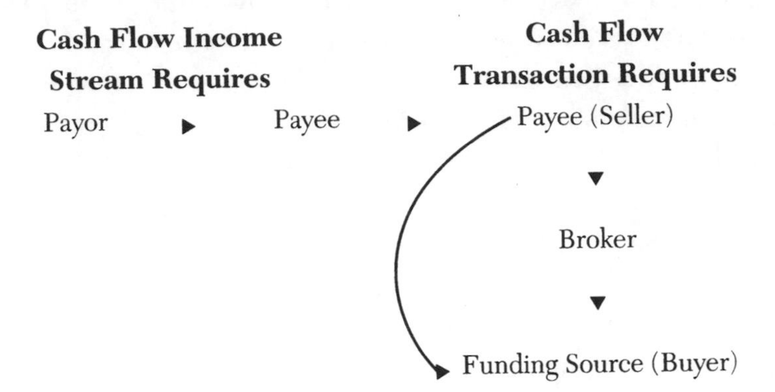

EVERYBODY WINS

The wonderful thing about a cash flow transaction is that everybody wins. Each of the players involved in the transaction benefits.

First, *the seller wins.* The seller receives a lump sum of cash immediately instead of staggered payments over time. This allows the seller to have access to the cash he or she needs without having to secure bank financing. Second, *the funding source wins.* As the income stream is collected, the funding source earns a profit or yield on its investment. Finally, *the broker wins.* He or she earns a fee on each transaction.

THREE WAYS TO BUILD WEALTH AS A CASH FLOW SPECIALIST

In the cash flow business, there are basically three paths that lead toward the generation of wealth. The route you choose will depend on your level of expertise, the amount of capital (if any) you have available to invest, your personal objectives, and your tolerance for risk.

The first way is to broker income streams and earn a fee or commission. The second is to invest in income streams and make a profit or yield over the long term. The third is to do both—broker income streams or buy income streams, depending on the transaction. Nearly every debt instrument you can transact in the cash flow business presents these three money-making opportunities.

Strategy 1: Profit as a Cash Flow Broker

If you are new to the cash flow business—and don't have a lot of money stashed away to invest—you can start out as a broker. In fact, even if you *do* have capital to invest, you should start by brokering a few transactions in order to gain experience.

Brokering simply means connecting people who have an income stream to sell with funding sources that buy them. Brokering doesn't involve significant start-up costs, collections, or a lot of paperwork. Financial risks are practically non-existent, because funding sources assume the responsibility for collecting on the income stream and the risk of non-payment.

As a broker, you risk no capital in the transaction, yet you earn an immediate profit. And even though we refer to the seller as a "client," you actually represent no one in the transaction—only yourself.

When you broker income streams, you spend most of your time locating and screening prospective clients. Once you have identified a good prospect with an income stream for sale, you select a funding source to buy the income stream. If everything checks out, and the transaction closes, you earn a fee or commission.

Commissions for brokers vary depending on the type of income stream, the dollar amount of the transaction, and the funding source buying it. In some cases, you determine your own fee and build it into the transaction. In other instances, you earn a commission based on the funding source's fee. As we review the ten most profitable debt instruments, I will discuss the income opportunity for each in more detail.

Strategy 2: Profit as a Cash Flow Investor

One you become familiar with the cash flow business and accumulate some capital, you can progress from brokering income streams to investing in them.

When you invest in income streams, you play the role of the funding source. Rather than brokering an income stream to a funding source, you buy the income stream yourself using your own capital. After you buy the income stream, you can either (1) hold on to it and earn interest or yield over time, or (2) resell it to another investor for a profit.

In some ways, investing in income streams is more complex than brokering them. By acting as the funding source, you take on the financial responsibility involved with collecting the income stream. However, through investing you can generate substantial long-term yields.

As an investor, you use your own capital in the transaction, but you also reap the long-term rewards of your investment.

Strategy 3: Profit as a Cash Flow Broker and a Cash Flow Investor

Through brokering, you can gain knowledge and experience without having to put up your own money. After you accumulate money through brokering, you can begin funding transactions with your own capital. Once you've become familiar with both the brokering process and the investing process, you can use each to your advantage.

At that point, you can act as a cash flow broker or a cash flow investor, depending on the transaction. Whenever you locate an income stream for sale, you can choose your role. If you don't have enough capital available to buy the income stream, or if you're uncomfortable with certain risk factors, you can broker it to a funding source. If you do have enough capital, you can buy it as an investment for your own portfolio, reaping the rewards over time. Either way, you profit.

THE BROKERING PROCESS

If you decide to set up a cash flow business, you will probably start out as a broker. That's an appropriate place to begin. Brokering transactions allows you to learn about the industry, look for a niche, and earn income without risking your own capital. You can broker cash flows right from your own home, over the telephone. You can broker part-time for an additional source of income, or you can make it your full-time career. Since brokering is the way to get your foot in the door, let's look at the process from a broker's perspective.

Nearly all cash flow transactions involve three basic steps: (1) identifying a seller; (2) explaining services and gathering information; and

(3) working with a funding source. Learn these three steps, and you'll be on your way to brokering any of the fifty-plus income streams in the cash flow industry.

Identifying a Seller

Your first task as a broker is to identify a seller—an individual or business with an income stream to sell. Identifying a seller could involve marketing, advertising, networking, researching, and just plain educating people about the cash flow services you provide.

Strategies for identifying sellers vary depending on the type of income stream. Brokers who specialize in private mortgage notes, for example, network with real estate agents to find sellers. Brokers who specialize in lottery winnings seek referrals from accountants or financial planners. I'll go into much more detail about how to find sellers when I discuss individual income streams in Chapters Six through Ten.

Explaining Services and Gathering Information

Once you've identified a potential seller, the next step is to introduce the appropriate cash flow service.

It amazes me how few people even know that they can sell their income streams for cash. Some real estate sellers are aware of owner financing and know that mortgage notes can be sold, but most aren't aware that car notes, boat notes, business notes, personal injury settlements, and other income streams can be transacted exactly the same way.

Often, when people learn they can sell future payments for cash, it's a genuine revelation. They had no idea it was even possible. In a sense, by simply explaining your service, you provide real value to the seller.

After educating the seller about your service, the next part of the process is to gather some basic information about the seller's income stream. The information you compile will fall into the following five categories:

1. **Specifics on the income stream.** These include questions such as: What type of income stream is the seller holding? What is the amount of the income stream? How many more payments is the seller expecting?

2. **Specifics on the collateral.** This category includes information about the type of collateral (if any) securing the income stream. Is the income stream collateralized by real estate, heavy equipment, a boat, or some other hard asset? What is the resale value of the collateral? What is the condition of the collateral?
3. **Information on the payor on the income stream.** This involves information about the party responsible for paying the income stream. Obviously, the creditworthiness and reliability of the payor is a significant factor in the transaction. Is the payor a neighbor, or the State of Florida? Is it a struggling business, or a highly rated insurance company?
4. **Documentation on the income stream.** This includes any supporting documents for the income stream or the collateral (if applicable). Is there legal documentation for the income stream? Is it a real estate promissory note? A State Notification of Award? A life insurance policy? Documentation is important to the funding source, because it validates the income stream and the collateral.
5. **Motivation of the seller.** This involves information about the seller's individual needs. What is the seller trying to accomplish? How much cash does he or she really need or want? When does the seller need the cash, and why does he or she need it? This information helps you and the funding source determine how to structure the transaction in the best possible way for the seller.

In the cash flow business, it has become standard protocol to organize the answers to these questions on a one-page worksheet, which the broker forwards to the funding sources along with a cover page. The worksheet allows funding sources to determine at a glance whether or not they can fund the transaction. If a funding source decides to move ahead with the transaction, they may request additional information later on.

Working with a Funding Source

When you've identified a seller and gathered information about his or her needs, the next step is to work with a funding source to structure and close the deal.

A funding source can be either an individual investor or an investment company. Hundreds of funding sources nationwide buy an assortment of income streams. Some specialize in funding business notes; others specialize in funding insurance benefits. Likewise, some funding sources purchase only the safest income streams, such as lottery payments, mortgage notes, and annuities. Others, however, look specifically for high-risk income streams, such as delinquent consumer debt. Certain funding sources only buy income streams in a particular part of the country; others will fund transactions all across the U.S. or overseas.

The point is, every funding source has unique funding parameters. As the broker, your job is to determine which funding source can best accomplish the seller's goals and make the seller the best offer. The process may involve presenting various offers to the seller to determine which one best satisfies the seller's objectives.

Experienced brokers maintain a profile of each funding source they work with and its particular funding requirements. They also consult detailed *funding source directories,* which are available to certified brokers through the American Cash Flow Association. In any case, the funding source gathers exhaustive information before funding a transaction. Why? Because unless the income stream is secured by collateral, the funding source rarely has recourse if the payor stops paying.

That last point is worth noting. The reason funding sources can earn higher-than-average yields is because they take on a certain amount of risk. A cash flow transaction involves the *purchase* of an income stream, not a loan. If the payor of an income stream stops making payments, the funding source generally cannot go back to the seller and recover the investment.

Before the transaction is complete, you and the funding source decide how you'll be compensated. In addition, you discuss the degree of your involvement in the transaction. The two go hand in hand. As a broker, you can stay involved in the transaction from start to finish, and possibly earn a higher fee. Or, you can step out of the way in the beginning, let the funding source take care of the rest—and earn a slightly lower fee. The choice of how involved you want to be in the transaction is *yours.* The funding source will do whatever is most appropriate to get the transaction funded. The process is summarized in the following way:

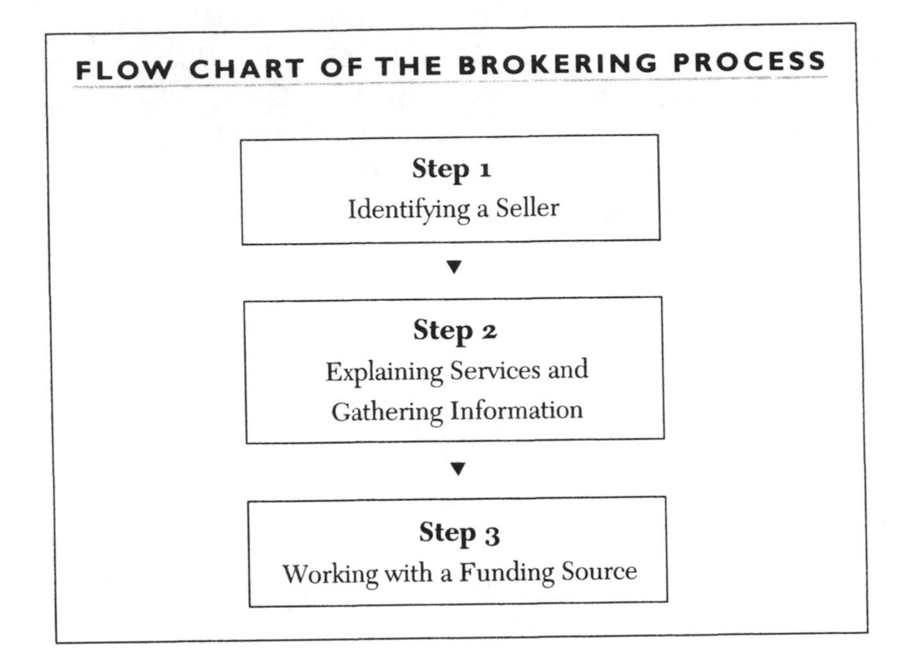

For Every Income Stream, the Process Is the Same

Whether it's a private mortgage note, an automobile note, a lottery award, royalty payment, or any another income stream, the steps you follow to broker a transaction are essentially the same. First, you identify a seller. Next, you explain your services and gather information. Then, you work with a funding source to complete the transaction.

While you are completing one transaction, you will be simultaneously looking for others. Then, you'll go through the process all over again—as often as you can.

Three Considerations That Affect Every Cash Flow Income Stream

Three simple considerations influence every cash flow transaction: (1) collectibility, (2) assignability, and (3) the time value of money. These variables determine whether an income stream is "transactable," and if so, the price a funding source will pay for it. Funding sources consider these factors *every time* they evaluate an income stream presented to them.

Collectibility

The first factor concerns the **collectibility** of an income stream. Collectibility refers to the ability to collect future income stream payments once they are purchased.

When funding sources buy income streams, they want the greatest possible assurance that they can actually collect those payments after they buy them. Collectibility is critical to funding sources, because if they can't collect payments, they can't recover their investment and earn their yield.

In essence, collectibility is a measure of the risk the funding source is taking by purchasing an income stream. Funding sources measure collectibility by evaluating two criteria.

First, they determine the creditworthiness of the payor. If an income stream is coming from a government institution, such as a state lottery commission, chances are high the funding source will receive its payments on time and as expected. If a payment stream is coming from a bankrupt business, however, chances are high it will not.

Second, they consider the value of any collateral securing the income stream. Collateral improves the collectibility of an income stream. The person making payments knows that the funding source can repossess the collateral if the payments stop.

In short, collectibility simply addresses the issue of whether the funding source will get its money back, as well as receive its expected profit, or have any recourse in the event it doesn't.

Assignability

The second factor that affects every cash flow transaction relates to **assignability.** Assignability is the ability to assign (or sell) an income stream to another individual or business.

Certain income streams, such as military retirement pensions, do not currently offer a profit opportunity, because legally they cannot be assigned to another person. In the past, lottery winnings and structured settlements presented challenges, because they were not assignable. Recently, however, funding sources have discovered ways to assign them.

In any event, a funding source has to determine whether an income stream is assignable and then decide *how* to assign it in order to complete a transaction. (All of the income streams mentioned in this book are assignable in most states.)

Time Value of Money

The third factor involves the **time value of money.** The time value of money addresses the way the value of money changes over a period of time. In short, it determines how much a future payment is worth in today's dollars.

Many different factors, including inflation, interest rates, legislation, and political unrest influence the time value of money. Inflation, for example, eats away at the future "buying power" of money. The rise and fall of interest rates also affect the time value of money. When you invest money today at a particular interest rate, you can turn it into an even larger amount of money next year or several years from now.

In some countries, legislation and political unrest affect the time value of money. We watched the value of the ruble tumble with the collapse of the Soviet Union, and saw a similar decline in the value of the Mexican peso as a result of legislation.

The time value of money concept affects the amount of cash a funding source can reasonably offer today for payments it is going to receive in the future. When funding sources buy income streams, they are giving up cash today in exchange for more cash tomorrow. For that reason, they have to consider the likelihood that the value of an income stream will decrease as it is collected over time.

With the myriad of income streams in our economy, and the trillions of dollars of inventory available to be transacted, the considerations are always the same: collectibility, assignability, and the time value of money. Understand those three concepts, and you'll understand the way every cash flow transaction works.

Four Models for Getting Paid as a Broker

Now we come to the critical question: How do you earn your fee as a broker? As a cash flow broker, you will earn your fees one of four ways, depending on the type of income stream you're transacting.

Model 1: Determine Your Own Fee

The first way is to determine your own fee. This model applies when you broker income streams that involve collateral, such as private mortgage notes, business notes, and mobile home notes. (Experienced brokers for other income streams, such as lottery winnings and insurance payments, often use this model to collect their fees.)

Let me give you a general sense of how this fee structure works. Once you get basic information from a note seller, you forward that information to the funding source. The funding source quotes you a price for all or part of the income stream, and often several variations on that offer. You select the best offer, then present a price *less than that* to the seller. The difference between what the buyer is willing to pay and what the seller is willing to accept is your profit. The table below shows sample fees determined using this model.

MODEL 1: DETERMINE YOUR OWN FEE

If Funding Source Offers	And You Offer the Seller	Your Fee Is
$50,000	$48,500	$1,500
$75,000	$73,000	$2,000
$100,000	$97,500	$2,500
$500,000	$490,000	$10,000

Model 2: Collect a Percentage of the Funding Source's Fee

The second model involves collecting a percentage of the funding source's fee. This model usually applies to income stream transactions that involve accounts receivable and other business-based income streams.

If you identify a business with invoices for sale, for example, and you place the account with a funding source, you receive a percentage of the fee funding source makes on the transaction. That percentage varies from a low of 10 percent to a high of 20 percent, depending on the type and size of the transaction and your relationship with the funding source.

The following table shows sample fees determined using this model.

MODEL 2: COLLECT A PERCENTAGE OF THE FUNDING SOURCE'S FEE

If Funding Source's Fee Is	Your Fee Is
$10,000	$1,000 to $2,000
$20,000	$2,000 to $4,000
$50,000	$5,000 to $10,000

Model 3: Earn a Percentage of the Purchase Price

The third model is based on receiving a percentage of the price the funding source pays for an income stream. This model applies mainly to transactions that involve a high purchase price, such as structured settlements, lottery winnings, and large debt portfolios.

The amount you earn is typically between 4 percent and 7 percent of the purchase price. For example, if a funding sources pays $70,000 for a series of settlement payments, your fee would fall in the range of $2,800 to $4,900.

The table below shows sample fees determined using this model.

MODEL 3: COLLECT A PERCENTAGE OF THE PURCHASE PRICE

If Funding Source Offers	Your Fee Is
$50,000	$2,000 to $3,500
$150,000	$6,000 to $10,500
$300,000	$12,000 to $21,000

Model 4: Earn a Percentage of the Face Value of the Income Stream

This model is sometimes used in factoring transactions and for portfolios of retail installment contracts. The amount you earn using this model ranges from 0.5 percent to 1.5 percent of the face value of the income stream. For example, if you brokered a $600,000 portfolio of retail installment contracts, your fee could range from $3,000 to $9,000.

The table below shows sample fees determined using this model.

MODEL 4: COLLECT A PERCENTAGE OF THE PURCHASE PRICE

If Funding Source Offers	Your Fee Is
$50,000	$250 to $750
$150,000	$750 to $2,250
$300,000	$1,500 to $4,500

From time to time, you may find the opportunity to negotiate a higher fee. For example, you might be able to negotiate a special rate on a commercial delinquency portfolio, or a hefty percentage on a lottery transaction. However, the four ways I just described are the most common ways to structure your fee on cash flow transactions.

In this chapter, you have learned the basics of every cash flow transaction. We've discussed the key players involved with any transaction, the steps involved with brokering any transaction, factors that influence every transaction, and ways to structure your fee on any transactions. Granted, that's a lot of information to absorb in one chapter.

But here's the good news. Once you learn the basics of the cash flow system, you can duplicate the transaction process over again with almost *any income stream in the secondary market.* They all operate according to the same basic principles.

And here's even better news. While I could go into more depth about each one of the subjects I discussed in this chapter, what's here is all there is. These are the basics of *any* cash flow transaction. The incredible power of the cash flow industry lies in how fundamental the system is. I have heard so many people say that once they understood the basic principles, everything from that point on was icing on the cake. The business just *makes sense.*

REMEMBER THESE HIGHLIGHTS

- Every transaction involves at least two players: a seller and a buyer (or "funding source"). Most transactions also involve a broker.
- Every transaction involves three steps: (1) identifying a seller; (2) explaining services and gathering information; and (3) working with a funding source.
- Three factors influence every cash flow transaction: collectibility, assignability, and the time value of money.
- You can make money in the cash flow industry by (1) brokering cash flow transactions, (2) investing in cash flow transactions, or (3) brokering *and* investing. Your choice will depend on level of expertise, amount of available capital, personal objectives, and tolerance for risk.
- The cash flow industry offers four basic models for structuring your fee as a broker: (1) determine your own fee; (2) collect a percentage of the funding source's profit; (3) earn a percentage of the purchase price; (4) earn a percentage of the face value of the income stream. The way you structure your fee depends primarily on the type of income stream you're transacting.

CHAPTER SIX

Use Collateral to Create Your Fortune

COLLATERAL IS AN ASSET that secures payment.

If you've ever taken out a loan to finance your car, your car was **collateral.** The bank could repossess your car at any time if you stopped making payments. Collateral increases the safety of an income stream, because if the person who owes the debt stops making payments on it, the collateral can be repossessed.

In the cash flow industry, a number of different income streams are secured by some type of collateral. In this chapter, we'll examine the four most profitable debt instruments that involve collateral: private mortgage notes, business notes, mobile home notes, and tax lien certificates. I'll show you how you can transact these income streams—as a broker or buyer—*and set your own fee.*

Privately Held Mortgage Notes

When people first hear about the "private mortgage business," they often confuse it with the concept of buying real estate with no money down. Back in the 1980s, we were bombarded with books, infomercials, and seminars proclaiming that you could make a killing buying real estate with "no money down." It was a good idea, but it crumbled under the weight of its own PR.

I can tell you from firsthand experience that the "no money down" strategy didn't work for one simple reason: *It created negative cash flow.*

As I discussed in Part I, the inevitable result of buying property with no money down was a high monthly mortgage payment. The more money real estate investors financed to purchase their property, the higher their monthly payments. Investors discovered it was practically impossible to charge enough rent on a property to cover the mortgage payment, let alone make a profit. Rather than earning money each month, they were losing money. And investors who owned more than one property were losing *a lot of money.*

Two factors, however, helped "no money down" investors offset their negative cash flow—appreciation and tax benefits.

Because inflation during the early 1980s was so high, real estate was appreciating rapidly. Many investors hung in the game, even if their properties were losing money. Their rationale was that they could recover their losses and still make a nice profit by holding on to their properties and reselling them later. At the same time, those investors were enjoying generous tax benefits by owning numerous properties.

Then, inflation went down. Appreciation slammed to a halt. And the bottom fell out of real estate values nationwise.

At about the same time, the 1986 Tax Reform Act stripped away many tax benefits for real estate owners. Real estate investors were left with *no* appreciation and *no* tax benefits—*just negative cash flow.* Consequently, a lot of sincere people took a terrible financial beating after buying real estate.

By the end of this decade, it's likely that the low-interest rate, low-appreciation cycle will come to a close, and interest rates will begin to climb. In addition, the economy will have absorbed the existing real estate; increased demand will apply upward pressure on real estate values. If that happens, real estate may once again be an appropriate and profitable investment. At the same time, however, direct real estate investing doesn't represent the investment opportunity that the cash flow industry represents.

The private mortgage business is not about buying real estate with no money down. In fact, it's not about *buying* real estate at all. It's about brokering and buying notes on real estate. And it's a unique way to cash in on the U.S. real estate market.

What is a private mortgage note?

A privately held mortgage note (or "private mortgage note") is a debt instrument created when a property seller, not a bank, finances the sale of real estate. To put it more simply, it's a promissory note a buyer gives a seller in exchange for a piece of property.

A private mortgage note serves as the legal and negotiable evidence of a debt and the buyer's written promise to repay the seller over time. It states the rate of interest for the sale, the repayment schedule, and other terms that are associated with the debt and its repayment.

THE HISTORY OF THE PRIVATE MORTGAGE INDUSTRY

People have been buying and selling private mortgage notes since the beginning of the century; the practice has become common only in the last twenty years. We can trace the boom of the private mortgage business directly to the emergence of **seller-backed** or **owner financing.**

Before the 1970s, most real estate buyers had only one way of obtaining a mortgage loan: apply at the local bank or savings and loan institution. During the 1970s and 1980s, however, interest rates topped out at 22 percent. Institutional financing for real estate was too expensive for many buyers, and real estate sales plummeted.

Individuals with real estate on the market grew aggressive enough to devise innovative methods to attract buyers. One of those ways was owner financing. The seller would hold on to the mortgage note, allowing the buyer to pay him or her directly over a period of time. Simple and straightforward, this financing option appealed to both parties. On the one hand, it allowed real estate buyers to circumvent traditional financing and beat high interest rates. On the other hand, it gave sellers a way to sell their real estate in a high interest rate market.

The development of owner financing resulted in hundreds of thousands of individuals holding private mortgage notes. Many of those individuals needed a way to sell them for cash. Investors saw these notes as a new investment opportunity.

Naturally, the first mortgage note buyers were primarily real estate professionals. At that time, the prevailing theory of buying real estate was the 10-10-10 Rule: Buy with 10 percent down, a 10 percent interest rate, at 10 percent below market value. When real estate professionals started buying notes, the notion of the "discount" stuck. They were buying mortgage notes *at a discount* in exchange for the right to receive payments over time. These "discount" transactions grew more and more common, and the "discount mortgage business" was born.

More recently, serious private mortgage professionals have shifted the focus of the discount mortgage business away from *discounting note balances* to *valuing future payments* based on a calculated rate of return. Investors now employ more flexible, creative techniques for structuring transactions, so that all parties benefit. Reflecting this shift in focus, the name of the industry has evolved from the "discount mortgage business" into the "private mortgage business."

THE ADVANTAGES OF OWNER FINANCING

Today, owner financing has become an established and accepted practice in real estate. In fact, owner financing offers significant advantages to both buyers and sellers. In an owner-financed sale:

- Financing is less complicated than institutional mortgage financing
- Sales and closings are faster
- Origination fees are nonexistent
- Mortgagee title insurance is optional
- Surveys and appraisals are rare
- Credit reports are not customary
- Loan commitments are not required

Buyers and sellers may agree to owner financing for a number of reasons. First, sellers sometimes agree to owner financing because they have no other option at the time. Many home buyers cannot obtain traditional institutional loans. Statistically, about half of all applicants for home loans do not qualify for the full amount of the loan they seek. The reasons they are turned down vary. They may be self-employed or new to the area, for example, or may have recently gone through a divorce. Many of these people are good credit risks, even though they do not meet the bank's strict lending guidelines. Second, buyers and sellers sometimes agree to owner financing in order to save money. By using owner financing, they avoid closing costs, origination fees, and appraisals. Finally, sellers sometimes agree to owner financing as an investment opportunity. By holding on to a promissory note, they can earn a higher rate of interest than they could by putting their money in a savings account or an investment vehicle.

Thanks to the private mortgage industry, owner financing is even more attractive as a financial option than it once was. Note holders now have some assurance of liquidity, and the old notions of "making a killing" or "deep discounting" have given way to strategies that benefit *everyone* in the transaction.

Why do individuals sell private mortgage notes?

A private mortgage note creates a payment stream of principal and interest over many years. So why would a note holder want to sell a note? People sell private mortgage notes for the same reasons they sell other income streams. They want or need their cash immediately, not dispensed over five, ten, or twenty years.

In many cases, the real estate seller was reluctant to accept the note in the first place, but it was the only way he or she could make the sale. Later, the seller may get tired of servicing the monthly payments or desire a lump sum of cash for some other purpose. Circumstances vary, but may include paying off debts, settling a divorce, paying back taxes to the IRS, taking a vacation, buying a new car, boat, or RV, or investing the money in a new business.

Why do investors buy private mortgage notes?

Investors or "funding sources" buy private mortgage notes for high yields and security. First, the returns on private mortgage notes can be incredibly high relative to other investment vehicles. Over the long term, they can earn yields of 12 percent, 15 percent, 25 percent, or even more. Second, private mortgage notes offer tremendous safety, because they are secured by a mortgage on real estate. When investors take ownership of a mortgage note, one of two things could happen. One, the payments will come in regularly and as scheduled. Or two, the payments will stop. If that happens, the investor can foreclose on the real estate, and possibly make even more money by selling the property. Investors and funding sources know that if they pick good mortgage notes and research the properties thoroughly, their investments will be very safe.

MAKING MONEY IN THE PRIVATE MORTGAGE INDUSTRY

The private mortgage industry does not involve buying and selling *real estate.* It involves transacting the *pieces of paper* that contain a real estate buyer's written promise to pay a real estate seller.

According to HUD statistics, about 5 percent to 6 percent of one-to-four family residences are financed privately. Private research indicates that number may be as high as 7 percent to 11 percent in some parts of the country. Yet less than 1 percent of the available inventory of mortgage notes are transacted each year.

Despite the volume of inventory, few individuals actually specialize in brokering and investing in private mortgage notes. Of about 20,000 participants in the cash flow business nationwide, about 9,000 transact private mortgage notes. Consider that number compared to the one million real estate agents operating across the U.S.! Obviously, there is a tremendous opportunity for you to share in the profits, provided you learn the system—and apply it.

As with other income streams, there are three ways you can generate wealth by participating in private mortgage transactions. First, you can make money as a private mortgage broker. Second, you can make money as a private mortgage investor. And third, you can make money as both a broker and an investor.

Let's look at how those strategies apply to private mortgages notes.

PROFIT AS A BROKER

To make money as a private mortgage broker, you find private notes for sale and place them with funding sources. *None of your own capital is at risk.*

When you broker notes, you will not purchase real estate or foreclosed properties, nor will you originate loans used to purchase real estate. Instead, you will locate motivated mortgage note sellers who need or want cash, placing their notes with investors (funding sources) looking for long-term yields, and charging a fee for your services.

Suppose Judy decides to sell her home and move to a neighboring city. She has lived in her home for a number of years, so by now she owns it free and clear. Judy is asking $80,000 for the home. Bob, an acquaintance of hers, discovers the home is for sale and expresses an interest in buying it.

For whatever reason, Bob is unable or unwilling to finance the purchase through a bank. Judy, however, is eager to make the sale. Since she already owns the home outright, she agrees to finance the sale herself.

Bob gives Judy a cash downpayment of $20,000, in addition to a *promissory note* for the remaining $60,000. He will pay the $60,000, at 10 percent interest, over the next fifteen years in monthly installments of $644.76. Bob will write his monthly mortgage check directly to Judy until the balance is paid off.

In this scenario, Judy holds a *private mortgage note.* Judy receives the payments, so she is the *mortgagee.* Bob, on the other hand, makes the payments, so he is the *mortgagor.*

Now, suppose five years pass, and Judy needs cash to pay for her daughter's college tuition for the next four years. She doesn't want to receive monthly payments from Bob anymore—she would rather obtain a lump sum of cash for the amount Bob still owes her. By this time, that's $48,789.97.

At this point, can Judy take the mortgage note to the bank and exchange it for cash? Certainly not. However, she can get cash for it in the secondary market.

Fortunately, Judy hears about Sue, a cash flow specialist who brokers and buys private mortgage notes. Judy discusses her situation with Sue.

Sue doesn't have enough capital to buy the note herself. However, she *can* broker it. She knows of several funding sources that would be eager to buy Judy's note for cash. One of those funding sources is ABC Capital.

Sue calls up ABC Capital and tells them about Judy's mortgage note. ABC Capital calculates the present value of Judy's future payments and offers to buy the note for $46,329 in cash.

At this point, Sue calls back Judy and offers to give her *$45,129* in cash for the note.

You caught that, I'm sure.

ABC offered to buy the note for $46,329, but Sue offered Judy $45,129. The difference of $1,200 is Sue's fee.

In the end, Judy decides to accept $45,129 in cash now for her note rather than waiting for her money to trickle in over the next ten years.

In this scenario, Judy wins, because she can pay for her daughter's tuition without going in debt. The funding source wins, because it earns a yield as Bob pays off the note. And finally, Sue wins, because she earns a $1,200 fee simply by matching up a willing seller with a willing buyer.

In the transaction I just described, Sue functioned as a *broker*, connecting Judy, the note seller, with ABC Capital, a funding source willing to buy the note as an investment. In exchange for her time, effort, and expertise, Sue earned a $1,200 fee.

What Sue did in that simple example, you can do, too.

UNDERSTANDING THE DISCOUNT

At this point, you might wonder why ABC would offer $46,329 instead of the full amount remaining on her note ($48,789). When investors purchase a mortgage note in full, they generally offer the seller less than the remaining balance on the note, for several reasons.

First, they have to allow for the possibility that the note could be paid off early. If ABC had bought the note for $48,789, and the remaining $48,789 balance was paid off the next day, ABC would earn absolutely nothing for its time and administrative costs. For that reason, ABC must purchase the note for an amount less than the remaining balance.

Second, ABC is giving up access to cash so that Judy can have cash. The money ABC uses to purchase the note is worth more *today* than the future payments will be worth in several years, because of inflation. It's only fair, then, for ABC to pay less today for the cash it will receive years from now.

Finally, by buying the note, ABC takes on the risk that Bob might stop paying the mortgage. Judy, on the other hand, is freed of the risk of nonpayment.

Another way to think of it is that ABC is offering Judy a second chance to make a cash sale on her home.

Suppose, for instance, that at the time of sale, Bob had offered Judy $76,340 in cash for her home instead of the $20,000 in cash and a $60,000 promissory note. Undoubtedly, Judy would have accepted the $76,340 cash sale. (Any warm-blooded mammal in the universe would have!) There's no question she would have given up $3,660 of an $80,000 sale in order to get immediate cash. In fact, she might have accepted an even bigger discount.

Selling her note to ABC Capital gave Judy another chance to do exactly the same thing. She agreed to a $3,660 discount on the $48,789 balance of her note in order to get immediate cash. Selling a note for less than the balance in order to get cash is really no different from discounting real estate in an all-cash sale.

The Transaction Process

In Chapter Five, I described the three-step process for brokering a cash flow transaction: (1) identifying a seller; (2) explaining services and gathering information; and (3) working with a funding source. That's exactly how the process works for brokering private mortgage notes.

IDENTIFYING A SELLER

To broker a private mortgage note, you first have to identify a potential note seller—someone, like Judy, who is holding a note but needs or wants cash. The majority of people who are holding private mortgage notes were pressured into it—softly, of course—for economic reasons. They needed to sell their property, and the only way they could do that was to handle the financing themselves. Many of these note holders would much rather have cash today than receive payments for the next ten or twenty years. The only trouble is, they either don't know getting cash is an option, or they have been presented with offers of cash that weren't competitive.

The key, then, is to locate possible sellers and get the word out: *Notes, like other assets, can be bought and sold,* through referral sources, networking, advertising, and research.

Referral Sources

Your most profitable leads on private mortgage notes most likely will come from *referral sources.* In fact, when it comes to any aspect of cash flow, your most profitable leads will *always* come from referral sources. Why? Referral sources are by far the most productive.

First, referral sources are easy to identify; they are specific to every cash flow income stream.

Second, referral sources are accessible. It's not always easy to access private mortgage holders. (People holding private mortgage notes don't hang out at a particular restaurant, bar, or club!) The only way you can reach them is by contacting them at their homes, either in person or through the telephone. But you can't exactly invite yourself over to dinner, can you?

On the other hand, referral sources are very accessible. You know where they are—they are in their offices, or at board meetings, or in networking organizations, and so forth.

Third, not only are they accessible, it's inexpensive to contact them. If private mortgage holders are hiding in their homes, it's expensive to mail to them and time-consuming to call them. But when referral sources are available in their offices, it takes virtually no money and far less time to communicate with them.

Referral sources also leverage results. One referral sources produces multiple referrals.

As a lawyer, I handled a closing about fifteen years ago for a business broker. He liked the way I worked and introduced me to five of the roughly 45 or 50 business brokers in the Central Florida area. Over the next four years, I kept two paralegals busy full time just on business closings referred by those brokers. I ended up closing over 800 business transactions from those five brokers alone.

Once in place, a referral source keeps on referring.

Finally, referral sources prequalify your contacts. When you are working with a referral source, the prospects that are referred to you are already prequalified for your services. They know what you do and are contacting you because of it.

In short, referral sources are professionals and acquaintances who know about your services and can refer potential clients to you. And when it comes right down to it, there is probably no other greater source of productivity, effectiveness, and profitability for the cash flow broker in general than a referral source.

Any of the following individuals are excellent referral sources for private mortgage notes:

Real estate agents. These people may be your most valuable source of leads. They, more than any other professional, know about existing privately held notes. In addition, they can work with you to educate their clients about the potential benefits of owner financing.

Steve Mitchell, a cash flow specialist in Vail, Colorado, has perfected a strategy in which he works right alongside real estate agents. When a real estate agent finds a buyer for a piece of property, Steve works with the seller to structure a promissory note. Immediately after the real estate closing, Steve steps in and brokers the note.

Every month Steve sends a flyer to every real estate office and broker in his region (there are 4,000 real estate offices in the area!). In the flyer, Steve describes how his services have helped real estate professionals make the sale.

Mortgage brokers. They know about existing private mortgage notes and look for opportunities to structure new private notes for their clients.

Long before I was involved in educating brokers for the private mortgage industry, the bulk of my private mortgage note transactions came from mortgage brokers, who have one primary interest—brokering originated notes. They are not involved in private notes to a large extent, and more often than not, they simply want to get a fee for brokering an originated note.

Mortgage brokers used to refer transactions to me in the 1980s because it gave them the opportunity to earn a referral fee from me. Once the transaction was done, they had the opportunity to refinance the payor, earning themselves a fee and increasing my yield.

Title and escrow officers. These professionals close numerous real estate transactions, many of which are seller-financed. In addition, their companies sometimes act as servicing agents for collecting payments on private notes.

Scott and Joyce Joosten, who founded JJ Capital Ventures, depend heavily on these professionals for referrals. The Joostens started their cash flow business by seeking referrals from real estate agents. However, they got to know a number of title and escrow officers during the closing process, and have cultivated a steady stream of referrals. Today, they provide their title and escrow contacts with booklets on "How to Sell Mortgage Payments," which they can then pass along to their clients.

Lawyers and financial planners. They know if their clients are holding on to mortgage notes. Specifically, estate and probate attorneys know when a mortgage note has been left to heirs in a will, and whether those heirs want to liquidate it.

I have used lawyers as a referral source for notes myself. I remember one transaction in particular I bought in the mid-1980s, a note involved in an estate we referred to as the "King Estate." The note came to my attention through another attorney who was handling the personal representative of the estate.

I kept trying to purchase the note from the attorney, but he wasn't very responsive to my phone calls. I decided to send a simple letter to the beneficiaries of the estate indicating that I was interested in buying the note. One week later, one of the beneficiaries showed up at my doorstep. He had flown cross-country some 2,500 miles to find out what it would take to get the transaction closed! Needless to say, the personal representative's attorney became much more responsive after that meeting.

Oftentimes, attorneys have to deal with multiple functions connected with liquidating an estate that involves a note. However, the *heirs* have a very strong incentive to liquidate the note. After all, when you have six heirs scattered across the country, splitting a $500 a month payment, each of them would just as soon have a lump sum of cash in his or her pocket.

Former clients. In every transaction you close, your client, as well as each person involved in the transaction, is a potential referral source. If you work out a transaction that satisfies everyone, they will undoubtedly mention your name to friends and associates who might need your service, especially if you ask.

Networking

How do you initially develop referral sources? One way is networking. The great thing about networking is that it's inexpensive. In fact, more often than not, it doesn't cost anything! When you network, you simply look for ways to tell people what you do.

In the private mortgage business, you can meet and network with good referral sources by attending Chamber of Commerce functions, real estate association meetings, Board of Realtors® functions, private real estate office sales meetings, and so on. You can also network by giving a presentation or seminar to possible referral sources, in which you discuss the services you provide and the options people have for selling their notes.

Advertising

Another way to locate prospective note sellers is to advertise. Typically, when note sellers need cash, they will look in the telephone directory or newspaper for someone to buy their notes. You can generate leads by placing ads in the Yellow Pages that read: "We pay cash for mortgage notes." You may not get an overwhelming number of responses, but the people who do contact you will be solid prospects.

Rick Jowers, who started his private mortgage business in Atlanta about twenty years ago, uses this strategy with great success. Rick takes advantage of Atlanta's vast calling area—the largest toll-free calling area in the country—and places dollar-bill-sized ads in the Yellow Pages. His ads generate a steady stream of phone calls from interested note sellers.

Judy Miller of American Note Investments used classified advertising heavily when she first started marketing for private mortgage notes and other income streams. However, she believes that because of increased competition, classified advertising has become "overworked and overworn" as a method of targeting note holders. Today, her company relies on direct marketing to niche groups using advertising mainly to target the brokerage network.

Some private mortgage brokers have discovered that offbeat, creative advertising strategies can generate leads. Rich Adams, of Elkhart, Indiana, for example, uses T-shirts, jackets, and a sign on his truck to advertise his private mortgage business.

Research

The names and addresses of virtually every mortgage note holder in your county are on file at the local County Recorder's Office, available to you for free. On each recorded mortgage, the name of the lienholder (note holder) is listed. If the lienholder listed is a bank or other financial institution, the mortgage is not privately held. However, if the lienholder listed is an individual, the note *is* privately held. When you have compiled a list of individuals holding private notes, you can contact them by telephone or by mail.

Neil and Jessica Rothman, private mortgage brokers in Coral Springs, Florida, discovered an ingenious way to research the names of note holders. The Rothmans used their PC to connect on-line with the Dade County Recorder's Office, so they could monitor in real time every single owner-financed real estate sale. Whenever a private mortgage note was recorded, the Rothmans would contact the real estate seller immediately after the closing to offer their services.

EXPLAINING SERVICES AND GATHERING INFORMATION

When you have located a prospective mortgage note seller, the next step is to educate him or her about what you do—locate sources of cash for mortgage notes. This step doesn't have to be intimidating. When you broker or buy mortgage notes, you're in a magical position. You're not asking for a check—you're offering to give someone a check! You simply explain that you have access to capital providers that buy notes as a long-term investment. Those providers can make the seller a competitive offer of cash for all or part of the mortgage note.

In order to structure the transaction and get the seller a quote, you have to gather information to submit to funding sources. That information includes the following:

- **Specifics on the note.** What is the balance on the note? How many more payments is the seller expecting? What is the amount of the periodic payment? What is the interest rate?
- **Specifics on the property collateralizing the note.** What is the value of the property? What is the condition of the property? When was the property built? How saleable is the property? What is the overall appearance of the neighborhood?
- **Information on the payor on the income stream.** How creditworthy and reliable is the individual making the mortgage payments? How long has he or she been making payments? Has the payor always made payments on the mortgage on time? What is the payor's source of income?
- **Documentation on the income stream.** Is there legal documentation for the income stream? What about the collateral? Can the seller produce all necessary documents?
- **Motivation of the seller.** Is the seller motivated to sell, or is he or she "shopping around"? What is the seller trying to accomplish? Does the seller want to sell all payments (the remaining balance on the note) or just a portion of the payments? How much cash does he or she really need or want? When does the seller need the cash?

You compile the answers to those questions on a one-page informational worksheet, which you will send to your funding sources with a cover letter. The more information you can provide to your funding sources up front, the faster they can respond with a bid.

WORKING WITH A FUNDING SOURCE

For virtually every private mortgage note in the market, there is someone willing to buy it. Private individuals and institutional funding sources all over the U.S. invest in private mortgage notes. *And nearly all have far more capital to invest than they have transactions to fund.*

Most funding sources rely on independent brokers to bring them a large percentage—if not all—of the transactions they fund. Each funding source maintains its own parameters for buying notes, from the best of the best to the worst of the worst, and everything in between. Over time, you will learn more about the notes particular funding sources prefer to buy.

When you work with funding sources, follow industry protocol and work with only one funding source on a particular transaction. Don't "shotgun" your transaction to every buyer in town. After all, funding sources do not make money by spending time quoting, analyzing, and structuring transactions. They make a profit only when a deal closes. Funding sources know that you may not be able deliver a "yes" on every transaction, but they at least want assurance that if you do, they will be the ones to benefit. By shopping your transaction to several buyers, you end up creating loyalty from none of them, and none of them will want to work with you again. If you are dissatisfied with your relationship with a particular funding source, feel free to change funding sources next time, but be "monogamous" with any given transaction.

After you send an information summary about the transaction to the funding source, it will determine if the note conforms to its buying parameters. If so, it will attempt to structure the purchase in a way that satisfies the seller's needs or desires. That's called *structuring*, and it makes all the difference in the world to a private mortgage broker interested in closing transactions and earning fees.

In the early days of the private mortgage business, when "discounting" was the name of the game, "offers" tended to be the norm—get the information from the seller, get a quote from the buyer, subtract the broker fee, and negotiate the lowest possible price for the seller. That method produced closings from time to time, but only in the most desperate circumstances. In most cases, sellers walked away from the offer because they were not prepared to take such a heavy discount and take-it-or-leave-it option.

But as the industry has matured, funding sources have become more creative and flexible in establishing structures that satisfy sellers' needs and wants. Brokers now have an arsenal of additional options to offer to sellers, including the ability to split payments, buy a portion of payments, and even fund a portion of payments today, allowing the seller to continue receiving money.

One particular funding source—Metropolitan Mortgage and Securities Company, located in Spokane, Washington—has developed the strongest structured product offerings for the purchase of mortgages. These new options permit brokers to be much more precise in satisfying sellers' needs than the early industry could. And the more precise the opportunity to satisfy the seller's needs and wants, the more closings take place, and the more money everyone makes.

Today, the industry is much less focused on "making offers" and much more committed to structuring transactions according to a win-win-win formula.

If the seller finds your offer or structure agreeable and decides to move forward with the transaction, the funding source will research the credit history of the payor, verify the property appraises at its stated value, and confirm the title on the property.

To close the transaction, you will have to collect a few more documents from the seller, including the following:

- A copy of the mortgage deed
- A copy of the promissory note
- A copy of the original real estate closing statement (verifies the total purchase price of the house and cash payments and shows the existence of any superior mortgages)
- A signed purchase agreement (indicates the terms of the purchase)

By the time the closing takes place, the funding source will have collected additional documents, such as copies of insurance policies, a payment record, existing title commitment, and other relevant documents it requires. Sometimes, funding sources will request your assistance in obtaining those documents; other times they won't.

When the transaction closes, the funding source gives the seller a check for the agreed-upon amount of cash, less the amount you determined as your fee. Then the funding source gives you a check for the amount of your fee.

RECAP OF BROKERING PROCESS

Let's summarize the steps involved with brokering a private mortgage note.

- First, you identify a seller. A seller is an individual holding a private mortgage note who is interested in selling all or a portion of the payments.
- Next, you explain your services and gather information. You explain that you have access to capital providers who can make the seller a competitive offer of cash for the note. Then you gather pertinent information about the note and needs of the seller.
- Finally, you work with a funding source to close the transaction. You compile the information on the note on a worksheet and forward it to a funding source for its review. The funding source submits structures for the purchase. You and the seller choose the most appropriate structure. You build in a realistic fee for yourself, and present the accepted offer to the funding source.

PROFIT AS AN INVESTOR

So far in this chapter, I've given you a very broad and somewhat simplistic overview of the brokering process for private mortgage notes. The important thing is not that you comprehend every detail involved, but that you understand the concept.

As a broker, you act as a matchmaker between mortgage note sellers and mortgage note buyers. In exchange for the time, effort, and research that you put into the transaction, you earn a fee.

Even if you broker only two or three mortgage notes per month, working part-time you can earn a substantial source of income. However, the key to building long-term wealth in the private mortgage business is to *progress from brokering notes to investing in them.*

When you invest in a note, it simply means you are the buyer. In other words, you serve as the "funding source" for the transaction.

Let's go back to our previous example. Judy accepts a promissory note for $60,000. Every month, Bob makes payments directly to Judy. Five years after the sale, Judy decides she wants to cash in the note. At this point, the balance on the note is $48,789.

However, Judy tells Sue, the cash flow specialist, that she needs only $15,000 cash. In this case, Judy doesn't have to sell her full note. Instead, she can sell only the number of payments that will allow her to obtain $15,000. This is called selling or buying a **partial.**

Sue has saved a certain amount of capital, so she decides to buy the partial herself rather than brokering it to a funding source. Sue offers to buy 30 payments from Judy in exchange for $15,000 cash. Judy happily agrees to the transaction.

In this scenario, Sue does not receive an immediate fee, because she's an investor, not a broker. Instead, Sue earns a yield of 20.7 percent over time as Bob pays off the note.

Even though Sue makes a whopping yield on a very safe investment, it is a winning situation for Judy, too. After all, Judy receives $15,000 in cash now, and thirty months from now she will start collecting payments from Bob again.

Are you ready for the best news? *The remaining balance on Judy's note 30 months from now will be $40,710.06.*

Not bad considering the note had a balance of $48,789 when Judy and Sue started talking. In other words, Judy obtains $15,000 in cash now. Two and a half years later, she gets her note back, which by that point will only have been reduced by $8,079. She's effectively given up $8,079 in principal for the right to collect $15,000 in cash. Truly, it's a win-win for everyone involved.

The most successful people in the private mortgage business are those who make the transition from broker to investor. When they don't have enough capital to buy a note, they broker it. When they do, they buy it.

Take Dee Jones, for example. Dee took one of my training programs on private mortgages a number of years ago. The first time I remember speaking to Dee after class was in 1994. She told me she was out marketing—sending brochures out everywhere—and developing a strong brokerage business. The following year, I spoke to Dee at the 1995 Cash Flow Convention. She was very proud to tell me that she had just bought her first note.

When I saw Dee again at the 1996 Cash Flow Convention, she told me 40 percent of her business involved buying notes, and 60 percent involved brokering. Today, virtually all of Dee's business is in buying. The only time she brokers a note is when the size of the note is too large to buy for herself. Dee is a classic example of someone who began as a broker and made the progression to buyer.

THE BENEFITS OF INVESTING IN MORTGAGE NOTES

As Dee knows, private mortgage notes are a lucrative investment for a number of reasons.

First, they yield high returns. Few other investments in the financial marketplace come close when adjusted for risk and safety considerations. Second, private mortgage notes are backed by real estate. Compare that to stocks, which hold value only if the institution remains solvent over the life of the investment and the market is bullish. A mortgage note is a promise by the mortgagor of a property to pay a certain sum over a period of time. If the mortgagor doesn't pay, you can foreclose on the property. And if you take back the property, you can sell it, rent it, lease it, or perhaps move into it.

STRATEGIES FOR INVESTING IN MORTGAGE NOTES

Entire books have been written about the technicalities of buying private mortgage notes. My goal in *this book* is not to cover the subject in every detail. I simply want to introduce you to the concept because it's a thriving cash flow investment opportunity.

If you decide to make money as a mortgage note investor, you can approach it several ways. Below are some of the more common methods buyers use:

- **Buy a note, then quickly resell it to another investor.** You keep the difference between what you paid for the note and what you receive for it. This scenario requires that you use your own capital, but you can recover your money immediately and earn a significant profit.
- **Buy a full or partial note and hold on to it as a long-term investment.** You keep the note in your own personal portfolio and earn the long-term yield on it. This method also requires you to use your own capital. However, it also produces substantial long-term returns.
- **Create a note by financing a real estate sale yourself.** In other words, sell a property with owner financing. Then hold on to the resulting note over the long term and collect the yield as the buyer pays the mortgage.

Factors to Consider as an Investor

If you make the transition from broker to investor, two significant variables will help you determine whether or not a note is a good investment.

The first variable is **seasoning.** Seasoning is the length of time the mortgagor has been making payments on the mortgage. That length of time is a measure of the commitment the mortgagor has displayed in the past and a good indicator of his or her ability or willingness to pay in the future.

If a mortgagor has been making payments on the mortgage for the past three years, and on a timely basis, obviously the chances are strong the mortgagor will continue to make payments in the future. (On the other hand, if the note is new, and the mortgagor just began to make payments on the note two months ago, the seasoning is an inadequate reflection of the security of the note, the track record insufficient to determine whether the mortgagor will continue to make payments in the future.)

The second variable is the **loan-to-value ratio (LTV).** LTV is a simple formula used to express the amount of the original down payment and mortgage reduction relative to the value of the property.

LTV equals the total amount owing on all senior liens, plus the current balance of the note, divided by the current market value.

The math is simple. Suppose a person wants to sell a $15,000 second mortgage on a home with a value of $100,000 and a first mortgage of $60,000. $60,000 plus $15,000 is $75,000, and $75,000 divided by $100,000 equal 0.75, or 75 percent. So the LTV equals 75 percent.

The LTV on the notes you buy should not exceed 75 percent on single-family owner-occupied homes, 70 percent on residential rental property, and 60 percent on commercial property.

If calculations are new to you, they may seem tricky, but actually, they are quite simple. And they become child's play if you buy a good business calculator that's set up for these transactions. Then, it's just a matter of entering a few numbers. In seconds, you get perfectly accurate financial information that allows you to make an evaluation and decision.

(While my intention in this book is not to introduce business calculators, I might suggest the Hewlett Packard 10B. It's user-friendly and can handle all of the transactions you will ever do in the cash flow industry. In addition, a number of computer programs on the market can help you with private mortgage calculations. I recommend John Moren's *NoteSmith,* John Richard's *Note Quoter Pro,* and Metropolitan Mortgage's *Broker Net.* Call the American Cash Flow Association for more information on these products.)

In a sense, as an investor you must evaluate two considerations. First, is it likely that you will continue to receive the payments once you purchase the note? Second, what happens if you don't get paid and have to foreclose?

Seasoning and LTV help you answer the first of those two questions, because they deal with the issue of whether or not you will have to be concerned about a default on the transaction. Calculations aside, once you understand how to determine seasoning, LTV, your yield, and so forth, it's still a matter of judgment as to whether you feel comfortable with purchasing a note.

Several years ago, I purchased a promissory note secured by real estate which, on the basis of LTV, would not have met most investors' criteria. The home had been purchased for $55,000, with $3,000 down, and the buyers of the property had closed on it just three months before I bought the note. In other words, it had little to no seasoning, and an LTV well in excess of 75 percent. Nonetheless, I bought the note.

Several important considerations swayed my decision. For one thing, the buyers were first-time home buyers in their late twenties. The couple had been renting the home from the seller for the previous five years. Therefore, even though the seasoning after the purchase was only three months, their actual track record was more than five years. In addition, they had been renting the property for $585 a month in rent, but their mortgage payment was only $525. Finally, the buyers had lived in the town in which the real estate was located their entire lives and had lived in that particular neighborhood for the past ten years.

Even though seasoning and LTV would not have supported the purchase of the note, I bought it based on "soft" considerations that addressed the central issue: Did all of the available information, taken as a whole, support the conclusion that I was likely to get paid after I purchased the note? My guess was that the buyers would continue to pay—which they did.

Lucrative Investment Strategies

As I noted earlier, this book is not meant to serve as a textbook on buying private mortgage notes. However, I do want to make you aware of the *principles* behind some of the most lucrative note investment strategies: (1) buying a partial; (2) structuring a tail; (3) buying delinquent notes; and (4) creating notes.

As you review these strategies, a key concept to grasp is that you can use *some of the same techniques* to buy many other income strategies secured by collateral—including business notes, automobile notes, RV notes, and others.

Strategy 1: Buying Partial Notes

Real estate itself is very rigid. You can't, for example, buy only the second floor of a conventional house when you only have a limited amount of money to spend. But buying a mortgage note is different. A mortgage is a series of payments—a payment stream. And as such, it can be broken up into increments. If a seller needs only a particular sum of money, you can buy a portion of the payment stream, just as Sue bought a portion of Judy's payments in the earlier example.

The majority of private mortgage transactions are structured as partials. *Partials are an incredibly flexible, simple, and secure way to obtain a high investor's yield on a limited amount of cash.*

When you buy a partial, you buy only a part of a note. If an individual is receiving payments on a note for 30 years (360 months), and he or she needs an amount of cash less than the remaining balance on the note, you might offer to buy just five years' (60 months') worth of payments. In that case, you would give the seller a lump sum of cash today in exchange for the next 60 months of payments. At the end of the 60-month period, the remaining payments would revert to the seller.

Let's look at another example.

Suppose Mary is holding a $60,000 mortgage note. The note pays her an interest rate of 8 percent; she will receive monthly payments of $501.86 for the next 20 years. Mary would love to get her hands on $10,000 to take a dream vacation to Europe. She's holding this $60,000 note, but has access to only $501.86 a month.

Suppose you are a cash flow specialist who brokers private mortgages. You hear about Mary's predicament from a friend and give her a call. After considering the present value of the future payments, as well as a profit for yourself in the form of a nice yield, you tell Mary she can get $10,452 (and small change) in cash today—and keep her note—simply by selling the next 24 months of payments to you.

For Mary, there's good and even better news. The good news is she gets $10,000 cash and only has to give up 24 months of her $60,000 note. The better news is that when she gets her note back, the balance will be $57,357.87. *In other words, she gives up just $2,642.12 of her mortgage balance in exchange for $10,000 in cash now.* It is definitely a super-win for Mary.

From your standpoint, it's also a win. You receive 24 payments of $501.86 for a total of $12,044 (and small change), representing a 14 percent yield on a very secure investment!

That is the power of the partial. The seller gets the cash he or she needs today. And when the mortgage reverts back, the reduction in the mortgage balance is relatively minor.

Remember Steve Mitchell? He knows all about the power of the partial. Steve has negotiated a number of large deals, including a $280,000 note on a ranch in Colorado and a million-dollar deal on multiple condominium units. One of his most memorable transactions, however, involved a small partial.

A woman called Steve one day and told him she had a note she needed to sell. The note was four and a half years old and worth $78,000. Steve arranged to meet with her.

When he met with her face to face, Steve asked her how much money she really needed. She hesitated, then answered, "Why do you ask?" (She believed Steve was going to make her an offer based on what she needed, not on what the note was worth.) Steve quickly calmed her fears. "I ask," he said, "because you don't have to sell your entire note if you don't need all that money."

She thought about that, then told him, "Well, I really only need about $8,000." She had never dreamt she could sell just part of her note. When she found out she could get the income back after Steve had collected a certain number of payments, she was thrilled.

Steve ended up buying an $8,000 partial on her $78,000 note. And after closing that transaction, Steve got two referrals from the same woman.

Strategy 2: Structuring a "Tail"

Structuring a "tail" is a creative way to earn a fee now plus a bonus later. When you structure a tail, you simply negotiate to receive the final payments of the mortgage yourself.

Suppose you broker a note with 140 remaining payments. You select a funding resource to buy the note for cash. Then, you indicate to the funding source that the last 20 mortgage payments will come to you. Those last 20 payments are your "tail." (Why would the funding source agree to that? Because the present value of those 20 payments ten years from now is negligible to them, and in any event, the funding source can price only the first 120 payments, if that is what you are requesting.)

When the deal closes, you still earn your usual brokerage spread. But ten years down the road, you start receiving those last 20 mortgage payments. It's an ongoing savings plan that doesn't cost you a dime.

You can use the "tail" strategy whether you're brokering a whole note or a partial. If the funding source buys only 24 payments of a note, for example, you can negotiate to receive the last four payments yourself.

Rick Jowers is a big proponent of the tail strategy. Like Dee Jones, Rick brokers some notes and buys others. However, Rick often negotiates to receive a tail of payments at the end for himself. When a deal closes, Rick earns his fee from the transaction as usual. However, five or ten years down the road, guess what happens? Rick starts receiving those "bonus" payments he structured. Rick has been brokering notes for more than fifteen years now, so the tails he has been structuring all this time are now coming due.

Strategy 3: Buying Delinquent Notes

A delinquent note is simply a mortgage note on which the payor is delinquent on payments. And the longer he or she has been delinquent, the better for you. Let me explain why.

When you buy a delinquent note, you earn the right to collect the delinquent mortgage payments plus the accrued interest. And if the payor continues to neglect paying on the note, you can foreclose on the property.

For example, let's say you find a 15 percent interest-only mortgage note with a $28,000 balance that has been in default for two years. The note seller is tired of fighting the legal battle necessary to collect the payments in default, or he or she doesn't want the headache of foreclosing on the property. That note holder would be delighted just to get back the balance remaining on the note: $28,000.

Suppose you intervene at this point and buy that note for $28,000, making sure all rights of the mortgagee are assigned to you. That same day, you begin a foreclosure proceeding, which takes between three and six months to complete.

In the foreclosure settlement, you, as the holder of the mortgage, are entitled to receive the original principal ($28,000) plus any payments in default with interest. Typically, you receive this in cash at the time of the foreclosure auction.

Remember that when you originally bought the mortgage, the payments were already two years delinquent. After an additional three to six months of foreclosure proceedings, how much does that mortgagor owe you now? $40,645.17!

Why so much? Well, when payments are in default, interest accrues on the payments at a prescribed rate. In the example above, the defaulted payments have been earning interest at an annualized rate of 15 percent.

That means six months after you paid $28,000 for the mortgage, you are entitled to receive $40,645.17 in cash at the foreclosure auction. And the annual return you achieved? An unbelievable 76.89 percent! And that's assuming you bought the note at full face value. In reality, most delinquent notes are bought at a substantial discount. Few investments offer a rate of return like that.

Unless you buy delinquent notes, your goal should *not* be to foreclose on property. The foreclosure process will slow you down. And even if you *do* buy delinquent notes, you still may not want the real estate. After all, in the example above, your annualized return of more than 70 percent was based on dealing strictly with the note, not dealing with the real estate. On the other hand, if you decide to go after the real estate, you can use other applied strategies to double and even triple your money.

Strategy 4: Creating Notes

With private mortgages (and virtually any other income stream that involves collateral), you can earn a significant yield by *creating* notes. Creating a note simply means that you sell your piece of property and finance the sale yourself.

Suppose, for example, you have recently retired and own your home outright. You put your home up for sale, and when you locate an interested buyer, you offer to finance the purchase. The buyer gives you a downpayment for the property and a promissory note with a predetermined interest rated for the balance due. Then the buyer makes payments directly to you, getting the property without bank hassles; you earn a more competitive interest rate on your money than you would by putting a lump sum of cash in a savings account, CD, or other conservative investment vehicle.

I have employed exactly this strategy for the purchase and sale of dozens of residential and commercial properties, nine retail sporting goods stores, and countless other small businesses that I have been involved with, either by myself or with partners.

As I mentioned earlier, I bought and sold a great deal of real estate in the early 1980s. My strategy for purchasing the real estate was always the same—make a small downpayment and allow the seller to finance the rest of the mortgage. At a certain point, when I had decided against investing in residential real estate, I began to buy real estate for the specific purpose of reselling it. I would finance the sale myself, accepting a small downpayment and a note that carried a higher interest rate than the rate for the mortgage on which I was making payments.

I used the same process to sell my sporting goods stores. After I had sold a few of the stores we were operating, I began opening small retail stores specifically for the purpose of reselling them. I required a downpayment that would cover most of the cost of the inventory in the stores, and would take back a note secured by the entire store.

Graduates of my training programs have used this strategy with mobile homes, cars, boats, businesses, and many other assets. Regardless of the collateral, the process is the same:

- Buy the item with favorable terms of payment.
- Resell the item to another buyer with the maximum amount of downpayment you can obtain. Finance the remainder of the sale at the market interest rate.
- Hold a promissory note on the sale and collect the payments over time.
- In the event of a default, unless you want to repossess or foreclose on the item, renegotiate or restructure the payment terms, permitting a repayment schedule that your buyer can live with.

The end result is always the same—an income stream secured by the underlying collateral.

RECAP

At this point, you should clearly have a handle on the concept of transacting a collateral-based promissory note. Let's quickly review the principle.

An individual is holding a note that promises him or her future payments. This individual would rather have cash today for all or a portion of the future payments. As a cash flow specialist, you have access to cash. If you don't have your own capital to invest, you can broker the note to a funding source. If you do have capital, you can buy the note yourself.

Everybody wins. The individual gets cash, and you earn an up-front fee (as a broker) or a long-term yield (as a buyer).

Brokering or buying future payments for cash—that's the concept behind transacting a private mortgage note. But a private mortgage note is just one of many income streams you can transact in the cash flow industry. In the remainder of this chapter, I'll show you how to use the same system to make money with other income streams secured by collateral: business notes, mobile home notes, and tax liens.

Business Notes

A **business note** is another type of promissory note you can broker or buy just like a private mortgage note. A business note is similar to a private mortgage note in that it's a promissory note backed by collateral. *The difference is that a business note is collateralized by a business rather than a piece of real estate.* You'll recall that a private mortgage note is created when an individual sells a piece of property and finances the sale himself. The note is collateralized by the real estate.

Similarly, a business note is created when an individual sells a business and finances the sale himself. A business note is collateralized by the business.

The primary way a business note differs from a private mortgage note is the length of time for which the note is structured. As you may recall, private mortgage notes are often structured for up to twenty years. Most business sellers, however, are unwilling to take the risk of financing the sale twenty years into the future. A business's current success doesn't guarantee that it will be successful fifteen or twenty years from now. Too many variables—trends, location, competition, the economy—can affect a business's profitability. Business notes, therefore, are typically structured for no more than five to ten years.

THE MAJORITY OF BUSINESS SALES INVOLVE OWNER FINANCING

Did you know that about 85 percent of all business sales involve owner financing? About 85 percent of the time, a business owner takes back a promissory note from the buyer. Why is that the case? *Because a person who wants to buy a business has virtually no other source of capital.*

It's much more difficult to get a bank loan for a small business than it is to get a loan for a home. First of all, small businesses have a historically high failure rate. Many fail within the first two years of operation. Second, many businesses do not own enough collateral to secure a bank loan. Often, the name and reputation of the business are worth significantly more than its actual assets.

Not long ago I heard about the sale of a general contracting company. The business had one employee, a rented office, no furniture, no equipment, no real estate, no contracts pending, and no receivables. The company's tangible assets totaled only about $20,000. *And yet the business sold for $400,000.*

Why would a buyer pay that high a price for a business with minimal assets? In this particular case, the contracting business had been operating for twenty years and had established a solid customer base. The name and reputation of the business were worth that high a price to the buyer.

Do you think the buyer could have obtained a bank loan for $400,000 to buy that business? Not likely. How would the buyer have convinced a bank officer that "the potential for success" was worth *$380,000*? Most likely, a bank would have financed only a portion of $20,000—the amount that could be collateralized with the company's hard assets.

Banks simply aren't realistic sources of capital when it comes to buying a business. Business sellers, then, usually have no choice but to finance the sale themselves. They accept a cash downpayment for part of the sale and a promissory note for the rest. The business itself—its property, inventory, equipment, name, and reputation—then serves as collateral for the note. Now that can be both bad and good for the business seller, as I know firsthand.

My father and I used to own an institutional athletic distribution business, which we ran out of a rented warehouse. We operated the business by getting on bid lists for the State of Florida. School boards, recreation departments, prisons, and other institutions would request a bid for athletic equipment, and we would put together an offer. Then, we would be sent a purchase order for whatever we were awarded. When we got the purchase order, we would ship the goods either from our warehouse or straight from the manufacturer.

What were our hard assets? Aside from inventory, we owned little more than some wooden shelves and a computer. Our hard assets totaled less than $5,000.

When my father decided to retire in December of 1994, we sold the business. I accepted a business promissory note equal to about two and a half times the value of our inventory. Today, I still receive monthly payments from the buyer.

As long as the business continues to prosper, I can rest assured the note payments will keep arriving every month. But what if the business doesn't do well? What can I get back?

First, I can repossess any remaining inventory. However, after several months of default on the note, it is doubtful the business would have any inventory left worth selling.

Second, I can reclaim the business name and the right to operate in the State of Florida using that name. That's a dubious right for a business that presumably has been run into the ground after it was sold!

Consider the situation from my perspective as the business seller. If I am holding a business note, and the payments stop, my only recourse is to get my business back. That is worth something to me only if: (1) the business name and reputation are still valuable; and (2) I am *willing* to get back into the sporting goods business again.

Suppose that, like my dad, I had sold my business in order to retire. If a business note was providing a great deal of my retirement income, a default would be disastrous. Can you see why I would want to exchange my business note for cash?

With cash, I could start a new venture or pay off debts. With cash, I would no longer wonder each month if I would get my monthly payments. With cash, I wouldn't have to lie awake at night thinking about the possible alternative—taking the business back.

Fortunately for me, my former business is thriving to this day, and my payments do come in according to schedule.

Business owners all over the country are holding notes following the sale of their businesses. They would jump at the chance to sell their notes for cash—if they only knew it was possible.

On the other side of the coin, funding sources across the country are seeking business notes to buy as an investment. Business notes are attractive to investors for many of the same reasons private mortgage notes are: they offer high yields and are secured by collateral.

What does the gap between business sellers and note buyers mean to you? It means nearly every business sale creates an opportunity for you to profit as a cash flow broker, investor, or both.

THE BUSINESS NOTE TRANSACTION

The system for brokering a business note is based on the same process involved with brokering a private mortgage note. As a business note broker, you simply identify a note seller and broker the note to a funding source. In return, you earn a fee. *And you decide what that fee is.*

Here's how it works. Suppose Amy owns a laundromat with hard assets of about $60,000. Amy decides to sell her business in order to open a bookstore. She prices the business at $70,000, then locates a buyer, Paul. But Paul is able to secure only a $30,000 loan from the bank. Paul gives Amy a $30,000 downpayment for the business, along with a $40,000 promissory note. The note is payable over five years in monthly installments of $850 per month. The laundromat itself is the collateral that secures the note. If Paul stops making his payments, Amy can take it back.

You, a business note broker, have read about the laundromat sale in the Finance section of your local newspaper. You approach Amy and ask her if she would like to get cash for her $40,000 promissory note.

Amy is interested. If she had cash, she could pursue another dream—to open a bookstore. If she had cash, she wouldn't have to worry that Paul might go broke, forcing her to foreclose on the business. You take down some information on the note and submit it to a funding source. The funding source examines the transaction and offers to pay $33,000 for the remaining payments on the note. You then go back to Amy and offer her $31,000 for the note.

The funding source offered $33,000 for the note, but you offer Amy $31,000. That's a difference of $2,000. That $2,000 is your fee.

Amy happily accepts the guaranteed $31,000 you offer. But isn't Amy losing $9,000 of the $40,000 note? Not really. Remember, she originally priced the business at $10,000 more than its *actual asset value*. For Amy, the convenience of having cash now rather than five years from now is well worth the cost.

When the transaction closes, everybody wins. Amy gets the cash she needs to buy inventory for her bookstore. The funding source earns an 18 percent yield collecting the note over time. And you end up with a $2,000 fee for connecting Amy with a source of capital.

Make Money as a Broker

As is the case with most income streams, brokering is the most immediate opportunity open to you in business notes. The basic steps you would follow to broker a business note are the same as those you would take to broker any other collateral-based income stream. First, you identify a seller. Next, you explain your services and gather information. Then, you work with a funding source to finalize the transaction.

Identifying a Seller

The most valuable sources for leads on business notes are referrals from professionals involved with business sales, such as business brokers, bankers, and mortgage brokers.

Business brokers. When a business is sold, chances are it was listed with a business broker. A business broker performs the same function in a business sale that a real estate broker performs in a property sale. A business broker earns a fee whenever he or she sells a business. You can locate business brokers in the Yellow Pages or the classified section of the newspaper.

Business brokers are the key referral source for business notes. They know which businesses are for sale, which businesses have already sold, and whether or not the seller took back a promissory note in the sale. Therefore, they can give you the names and telephone numbers of business sellers who are holding notes.

In many cases, business brokers actually can get you involved in a transaction before the sale is finalized. The business broker can explain the owner financing option to the business seller. You can then offer to liquidate the promissory note once the sale takes place. After you get acquainted with a business broker, you have the opportunity to work on future deals together.

Business brokers have three reasons to help you. First, they can list more businesses for sale if they can make owner financing more appealing to the business seller. Second, they can sell their businesses faster if buyers have owner financing as an option. And third, they can earn a referral fee from you (if you choose to pay one) when transactions close.

Small loan officers and business loan officers. Bank officers are another great source of referrals for business notes. It's common for a previous business owner to want to launch a new business. The former business owner usually turns first to their bank for a small business loan to get the new venture off the ground. If the loan officer has to turn the individual down, he or she can recommend you as an alternative source of capital.

Small loan and business loan officers also routinely reject applications for *business acquisition loans.* Referrals from loan officers can give you the opportunity to work with a seller to structure an owner-financing program that will allow you to liquidate the note later.

Mortgage brokers. Mortgage brokers handle real estate sales, not business sales. However, commercial mortgage brokers often know who sold which businesses along with commercial properties. They can give you the names and phone numbers of business sellers who might be holding a promissory note.

Other than referral sources, another source of leads for business notes is the newspaper classifieds. Most newspapers or other business publications have classified sections devoted to financing. By reading the classifieds periodically, you can keep an eye out for local businesses in need of cash. Very often they have business note assets or other cash flow assets available to liquidate.

In the classifieds under "Businesses for Sale," you will find business owners who are attempting to sell their businesses directly as opposed to through a business broker. If you communicate to business owners that you can work with them in structuring a promissory note, then they have the opportunity to provide more attractive financing options to prospective buyers.

Finally, you can always use the classifieds to place a simple ad that says, "We pay top dollar for business notes."

Explaining Your Services and Gathering Information

When you've located a prospective seller of a business note, the next step is to present your services and gather information. The process is similar to explaining private mortgage services, because the benefits are essentially the same: liquidity, a lump sum of capital, no collection hassles, and so forth.

The information you gather, however, is a little different from that which you collect in a private mortgage transaction, because a business note transaction involves a business rather than a piece of property. Issues you have to address with the seller include:

- **Specifics on the note.** What is the balance on the note? What is the interest rate on the note? How many more payments is the seller expecting? What is the payment amount? What were the terms of the business sale?
- **Specifics on the collateral.** Is the note secured by the business? What is the value of the business? How saleable is the business? Is it a franchise? Is it in a good location? What is the relationship between the business and its location—owned or leased? How long has the business been in existence (including the time when the original seller owned it)? Does the business have inventory? What is the condition and value of the inventory? Does the business own any collateral in the form of equipment?
- **Information on the payor on the income stream.** How creditworthy and reliable is the individual paying on the business note? How long has the payor been making payments?

- **Documentation on the income stream.** Is there legal documentation for the income stream? Can the note seller produce all necessary documents? What about the documents creating the collateral interest?
- **Motivation of the seller.** What is the seller trying to accomplish? Does he or she want to sell all of the payments, or just a portion? How much cash does he or she really need or want, and how soon?

Once again, you organize the answers to these questions on a worksheet to provide easy reference for the funding source.

Next, you need to explain to the seller that investing in business notes is riskier than investing in other cash flows. Because of the added risk, funding sources usually expect a higher yield when they buy business notes. Your seller needs to understand this up front so he or she will have realistic expectations about the amount of cash you can get for the note.

Working with a Funding Source

If the seller is interested in pursuing the deal, the funding source will begin researching the business. Most likely, they will ask you to provide a copy of the business note, a UCC-1 financing statement, and the security agreement. The funding source will then obtain other required documents needed to complete the transaction directly from the seller, or from you, if you prefer.

Fees on business note transactions work basically the same way as for private mortgage transactions. The broker builds his or her fee into the funding source's offer. The size of the fee is up to the broker.

How high are typical fees? It depends on the size of the transaction. Recently, a California-based funding source purchased a business note for $1.3 million. The broker who located the deal received a $39,000 referral fee.

On the other hand, the transaction need not be that large in order for you to receive a substantial broker fee. I recently bought, for my brother-in-law's account, a note secured by a restaurant and liquor license. Even though the purchase price was only $38,000 plus change, the broker made a fee of $8,500 on that one transaction.

That is not unusual, considering the fact that with business notes, the investor generally receives a higher yield, and the broker generally earns a higher fee than in real estate transactions.

Make Money as an Investor

When I discussed opportunities in the private mortgage business, I explained that the key to building long-term wealth is to progress from brokering notes to investing in them. The same holds true for business notes.

When you invest in a business note, you buy the note yourself instead of brokering it to a funding source. Rather than earning an immediate profit in the form of a fee, you earn a long-term yield by collecting payments on the note. You can employ some of the same techniques for buying business notes that you use to buy private mortgage notes, such as: (1) buying a partial; (2) structuring a tail; and (3) creating notes.

What to Look for in Business Notes

If you decide to transition from brokering business notes to buying them for your own portfolio, you'll want to research more of the technical aspects of the process than I discuss in this book. However, let me offer a few brief suggestions on the types of notes you should buy.

First, seek out notes on businesses secured by substantial assets—equipment, machinery, and so on. Laundromats, dry cleaners, printers, and small manufacturing companies, for example, tend to own a high value of collateral. In the event you have to foreclose on the business, you can sell off the hard assets to recover your investment, or resell the business far more easily.

Second, look for notes on businesses in good locations, such as convenience stores. Businesses in high-traffic areas are less likely to go bankrupt, which lessens the likelihood of foreclosure. In addition, they are easily resaleable in the event you do have to foreclose.

A few years ago, I had the opportunity to obtain a business note on a laundromat in Charlotte, North Carolina, for my own portfolio. One of the cash flow brokers I had trained, Winston Head, had presented the note to me.

Why did I consider a note on a laundromat an attractive investment? First, laundromats are secured by a great deal of collateral. I knew that if for some reason I had to take over the business, I would have a lot of valuable assets (mainly equipment) available to me to resell. Second, laundromats and dry cleaners are very saleable businesses. They are usually located in busy shopping centers. I knew that if the note went into default, I could probably sell the business quickly. Fortunately, I never had to do this.

Resaleability is an important consideration with business notes. The more resaleable the business, the more likely you are to recoup your investment, and sometimes even a higher profit, simply by reselling the business.

For example, I tend to like notes secured by restaurants, even though that flies in the face of conventional wisdom. Conventional wisdom indicates that restaurant notes are very risky investments, because restaurants often fail. That may be true, but I've found that a restaurant, once foreclosed on, is easy to resell.

First, the business is virtually intact, except for a few minor provisions. The kitchen equipment, tables and serviceware, and furnishings are all there. A person wanting to open a business could start up almost immediately with a restaurant simply by purchasing enough food and beverages to last a few days.

Second, an existing restaurant is an attractive target for prior restaurateurs and other former business owners. Hence, the resale value is substantial, especially if the restaurant is attractive cosmetically.

While I have owned business notes secured by restaurants throughout my cash flow career, I have never lost money when I was forced to take them back. Most often, I made a significant profit after I resold them.

BUSINESS NOTES TO AVOID

Whether you are brokering notes or buying them for your own portfolio, you probably should steer clear of certain types of businesses.

First, avoid notes on franchises. The problem with a franchise is that in the event of default, the franchiser usually will not allow the owner of the note to continue operating the business under the franchise name. Think about it. What good is a Häagen-Dazs, Baskin Robbins, or Ben & Jerry's ice cream shop if you can't call it by its franchise name?

Second, use caution in buying notes on service-based businesses, like photography studios or florists. The primary value of service-based businesses is the service provided. Hence, those businesses typically do not own enough collateral to secure the note. Therefore, as an investor, you would have to find security in something else—and oftentimes, there *is* nothing else.

And finally, be very careful when buying a note on a business that has potential environmental concerns. An ex-gas station, transmission, or tire store, for example, often has underground tanks or other environmental hazards. In the event of default, those businesses could have little value because of the clean-up costs required to resell them.

Recap

You should recognize obvious similarities between transacting a business note and transacting a private mortgage note by now. Both transactions revolve around the same principle.

In a business note transaction, a former business owner is holding a note that promises future payments. The individual would rather have cash today for all or a portion of the future payments. As a cash flow specialist, you have access to cash. If you don't have capital of your own to invest, you can broker the note to a funding source and earn a fee. If you do have capital, you can buy the note yourself and earn a long-term yield.

Mobile Home Notes

Do you realize that mobile homes make up 25 percent of the current U.S. housing market? It's true—more than 18 million people (7 percent of the U.S. population) live in mobile homes nationwide. Ever since the recession of the 1980s, more and more Americans have come to view mobile homes as an affordable alternative to traditional residential housing.

The rapid growth of the mobile home market has created a booming opportunity for cash flow specialists. If you live in an area that has a large number of mobile home parks, you can bring in big profits with little capital in this segment of the cash flow industry.

What Is a Mobile Home Note?

A **mobile home note** is similar to a private mortgage note, except that the collateral securing the note is a mobile home rather than a site-built home. People who buy mobile homes often have a difficult time obtaining financing. Like cars, mobile homes depreciate over time, so banks do not consider older mobile homes adequate collateral for a loan. They typically will not finance a mobile home that is more than five years old.

Because of the lack of financing for buyers, mobile home sellers often have to finance the sale themselves. The seller accepts a downpayment and agrees to receive monthly installments from the buyer. This transaction results in a mobile home note.

Only in the past ten years have mobile home notes become a brokerable debt instrument. Until recently, an individual holding a note didn't have much choice but to collect the payments over time. Today, several funding sources have expanded their real estate note-buying business to include mobile home notes, which can be bought and sold on the secondary market almost as easily as mortgage notes.

Cash flow specialists have discovered a variety of creative strategies for making money in mobile home notes. I'm going to devote less space to describing these strategies than I did discussing mortgage note strategies, because I assume that by now you've caught on to the concept of buying future payments.

MAKE MONEY AS A BROKER

If you don't have capital to buy or create mobile home notes yourself, you can broker existing notes. You earn your fee the same way you do brokering private mortgage notes or business notes.

Let's say Ron is holding a mobile home note with 27 remaining payments of $300 each. Ron sees an advertisement for your cash flow services and calls you. He says he wants to sell the note for cash in order to make improvements on his new house.

After discussing Ron's situation, you contact a funding source that offers to pay $6,500 for the note. You then offer Ron $6,000 for the note. You collect the $500 difference as your fee.

The step-by-step process for brokering a mobile home note is basically the same as for brokering a private mortgage note: (1) identifying a seller; (2) explaining your services and gathering information; and (3) working with a funding source.

Identifying a Seller

Naturally, you would go about finding a mobile home note holder a little differently than you would a private mortgage note or business note holder. Instead of contacting real estate agents or business brokers, you would contact professionals who work in the mobile home industry.

One good source of leads on mobile home notes is mobile home dealers. Most mobile home dealers offer in-house financing to their buyers. The dealers then hold on to the promissory notes themselves. At some point, these dealers may want to sell some or all of their notes for cash in order to buy more inventory. You can give them the opportunity to sell some or all of the payments they are receiving.

Another good source of leads on mobile home notes is mobile home park managers. They usually know which mobile homes in their parks have sold recently or are currently for sale, and may offer to give you the name and telephone number of the sellers. Get to know park managers and explain that you provide an alternative method of financing for home owners in their parks. Since park managers need to maintain high occupancy rates, anything you can do to facilitate the sale of a home in their parks will help them.

Moreover, it is perfectly appropriate to pay mobile home park managers a referral fee for each referral that brings you profitable transactions. Even paying a fee as low as 10 percent of what you earn would, by and large, guarantee a continuity of referrals from mobile home park managers.

Another way you can track down notes is to create flyers or business cards with the message, "We pay cash for mobile home notes." Post them in locations where mobile home owners would be likely to see them, such as park offices, park laundromats, or nearby convenience stores.

Explaining Services and Gathering Information

When you've located a potential note seller, the next step is to explain the benefits of your cash flow service. Once again, this is the easy part. You are offering your prospect the chance to get cash *now* instead of waiting on monthly installments to arrive over the next several years. Who wouldn't want to know about that opportunity?

If your seller decides to pursue the deal, you will gather basic information about the mobile home note and the collateral that secures it—the actual mobile home. In addition to the standard income stream information, you will want to know:

- How old is the mobile home? What is its current value?
- Where is the mobile home located? Is it in a park or on a private piece of property?
- Is the mobile home attached to the property or detached?
- Does the payor own the pad or rent it?

Working with a Funding Source

The final step is to work with an investor or funding source to close the transaction. Several funding sources in the U.S. specialize in buying mobile home notes. Each has different requirements for the notes they buy. Some, for example, buy notes only in a particular part of the country. Others limit their buying according to the size of the mobile home or mobile home note.

You have to find out from each funding source what type of notes they specialize in buying. Then you send the details of the transaction to the funding source you decide to work with. At that point, the funding source gives you an offer. You subtract your fee and present that offer to the note seller. If the deal closes, you earn your predetermined fee.

If you use the brokering strategy, look for notes on newer mobile homes. You can earn a higher fee on them, because the principal balance on those notes is likely to be high. On the other hand, notes with a low balance (less than $5,000) will earn you only a minimal brokerage fee.

MAKE MONEY AS AN INVESTOR

Experienced investors will tell you that the largest windfall profits are in *investing* in mobile home notes. You can invest in mobile home notes even if you have very little of your own capital. The process is similar to brokering, except that *you* act as the funding source.

There are basically two strategies for investing in mobile home notes: (1) buying existing notes; and (2) creating new ones.

Strategy 1: Buy Existing Mobile Home Notes

The process for buying a mobile home note is basically the same as for brokering a note. First, you locate a seller using referral sources or advertising. Then, you explain the benefits to the seller. However, instead of working with a funding source, you use your own capital to buy the note.

As the payments come in over time, you earn the difference between the total note payments and the amount you paid for the note. It can add up to a substantial yield on your investment.

Suppose, for example, you locate an individual holding a mobile home note with 20 remaining payments of $250 each. The seller is willing to accept $3,500 in cash for the note. When you collect the last payment, you will have received a total of $5,000—a profit of $1,500 in just 20 months. That's a total yield of 44 percent—and virtually no risk!

Strategy 2: Create Mobile Home Notes

To create a note, you buy a mobile home at a low price, provide for a few cosmetic fix-ups, and resell it at the market price, handling the financing yourself. You can invest as little as $2,500 to $5,000 and still get yields of 70 percent or more this way.

Let's say you buy a used mobile home for $2,000 and make $500 worth of minor cosmetic repairs to it. Then you immediately put it up for sale at $6,000. You locate an interested buyer, but he or she cannot afford to pay you $6,000 up front. *That's to your benefit.*

You then ask for a $1,000 cash downpayment and accept a promissory note for the remaining $5,000. You agree to accept $200 a month for 28 months.

When the buyer finally pays off the loan, he or she will have paid you $5,600 in addition to the $1,000 downpayment, for a total of $6,600. Remember, your investment in the mobile home was only $2,500. Not only have you helped a person get affordable housing, you have more than doubled your initial investment, earning a total yield of 80 percent per year.

Moreover, if you decide to sell the note rather than collecting the payments, you only have to get $1,500 cash for it to cover your entire investment in the mobile home.

Lonnie Scruggs, founder of DOW Enterprises, popularized this strategy for the public. Lonnie would buy a few used mobile homes, fix them up, and resell them for more than he paid for them, retaining the financing.

You can apply this strategy to virtually any income stream that involves collateral. Jeff Akers and Frank Blankemeyer, for example, use this strategy with automobile notes. Jeff and Frank operate Mr. Car Man, a used car business in Roanoke, Virginia. When they make a sale, they finance the deal themselves, creating an automobile promissory note. Then they either hold on to the note and collect income from it over the long term, or they sell the note for cash in order to buy more inventory.

Other cash flow specialists apply the same strategy to marine notes. Some purchase existing notes on ski boats, fishing boats, and yachts. Others create notes by selling watercraft and financing the sale themselves.

RECAP

The system for brokering and investing in mobile home notes is consistent with the process involved with transacting other collateral-based income streams. In a mobile home note transaction, a mobile home seller receives monthly payments from a buyer. The mobile home seller would rather have cash today instead of waiting to receive his or her payments in the future. As a cash flow specialist, you can broker the note to a funding source and earn a fee, or buy the note yourself and earn a long-term yield.

TAX LIEN CERTIFICATES

Tax lien certificates are one of America's most lucrative low-risk investment opportunities, yet few people know anything about them. Like other income streams, tax lien certificates are a win-win-win transaction for the parties involved.

First, they provide local governments with the cash flow they need to continue running their budget. Second, they offer investors a safe way to get a high rate of return. And third, they give property owners an opportunity for government-sponsored and promoted financing for the payment of the annual real estate property tax bill.

Most states have their own unique systems for selling tax lien certificates, so I won't try to address every aspect of transacting them here. However, I do want to make you aware of this low-risk vehicle for building wealth.

What Is a Tax Lien Certificate?

When a property owner neglects or refuses to pay property taxes, the government places a tax lien on the property. The lien stays in place until the taxes are paid. If the taxes aren't paid after a certain amount of time, the State has the right to step in and take possession of that owner's property.

Why would people neglect to pay taxes on their property and risk losing it? The reasons vary. Some people move away and forget to pay their taxes. Others go broke and simply can't afford to pay them. Sometimes a property owner dies, and his or her heirs don't even know about the property. Finally, some people neglect to pay their taxes *on purpose* as a short-term method of financing. These people realize that eventually they will have to pay the taxes, but in the meantime they use their tax money as a private loan.

Thirty states have laws allowing county governments to issue tax lien certificates on all properties on which taxes are overdue. These **tax lien certificates** are first made available at public auctions, then at the county Tax Collector's Office. Private investors can buy the certificates by paying off the back taxes and any late penalties.

If a property owner wants to redeem the certificate, he or she must pay the back taxes due, plus the penalties that have accrued, plus a *guaranteed* rate of interest that the State has mandated. In many states, that's an exceptionally high rate of return.

In Iowa, for example, interest accrues on certificates at a rate of 24 percent; in Florida, at 18 percent; and in Arizona, at 16 percent. Other states charge even higher penalties. Michigan, for instance, charges a 15 percent penalty the first year taxes are overdue and a 50 percent penalty the second year.

Whatever the taxes, penalties, and interest amount to, the property owner is responsible for paying that money to the county tax collector's office. The county tax collector's office then informs the investor that the certificate has been fully redeemed. The investor delivers the certificate to the county tax collector and receives a check for the principal invested, plus the mandated interest and any other penalty fees accrued to which the investor is entitled. In other words, the county tax collector actually becomes the collection agent for your investment!

What happens if a property owner doesn't answer the county's call to pay up and redeem the property? That depends on the state. In Arizona, for example, the investor can get the title to the property if the taxes haven't been paid for three years. In the majority of these cases, property acquired this way is purchased for just pennies on the dollar. In Florida, the property is sold at an auction. The certificate owner can bid for the property, but he or she competes against other bidders. In Maryland, the investor is *required* to foreclose on the property if the taxes have not been paid after two years.

Buying tax lien certificates is, in most cases, a no-lose situation. If the owner pays the taxes, you get a high yield on your investment. If the owner doesn't, you could end up with valuable property for pennies on the dollar.

MAKING MONEY WITH TAX LIEN CERTIFICATES

Tax lien certificates differ from many other cash flow income streams in that there isn't yet an established market for brokering them. In recent years, however, several funding sources with major capital budgets have sprung up to purchase volumes of tax lien certificates. Some of these funding sources hire "researchers" to go from one county to another on their behalf and bid for as many certificates as they can buy. The researchers charge a fee for their time, reflected as a percentage of the total amount of tax lien certificates purchased for the funding source.

Out of these activities a secondary market is emerging for tax lien certificates. In this market, cash flow brokers can operate ostensibly as "researchers," but under a structure compatible with the way other debt instruments are brokered. For now, however, the real opportunity in tax lien certificates lies in buying them for your own investment portfolio. The good news is you can purchase them for as little as several hundred dollars.

The Benefits

What are the benefits of investing in tax lien certificates?

First, tax liens are safe. The interest is mandated by the State Legislature and assured by the county government.

Second, they provide good leverage. When you buy a certificate, you automatically become the senior lien-holder on the property. That means you are in control of thousands of dollars' worth of property simply by paying the back taxes that are due.

Third, they offer a high yield. You can earn up to 50 percent interest plus any penalties that have accumulated, depending on the state in which the property is located.

Fourth, there are no negotiations involved. You and the property owner never come face-to-face to negotiate. The state and county take charge of the transaction, and they do it by the book.

Finally, you can enjoy tax benefits by investing in tax lien certificates. The money you earn could be tax-exempt or tax-deferred if you buy the certificates through a retirement fund or an IRA. Also, if you buy tax lien certificates as a business, you may be able to deduct expenses for travel, telephone, and postage on your income tax return.

The Risks

Is it possible to lose money on a tax lien certificate?

Yes, it's possible—but not likely. In many cases, the owner of the property comes forth and pays the taxes and interest he or she owes. In that case, the only risk is that your county's office is inefficient. Since you're entitled to interest only during the time the money is actually invested in certificates, any delay on their part in turning over a redeemed certificate means a slight loss of revenue to you.

In the event that the owner never pays the taxes, you could become the owner of the property. That means you might owe taxes on the property and possibly some attorney fees. So what happens if you don't pay the taxes? The County simply issues another certificate to be auctioned off. If someone else comes along and buys it, you still receive all of your principal plus the State-mandated rate of interest.

The very worst that could happen if the owner doesn't redeem the certificate is that the property is unsaleable. If the property is underwater or near a toxic waste dump, for example, the chances of selling it are slim. But you can avoid that scenario by researching properties before you buy the tax certificates on them.

THE PROS AND CONS OF INVESTING IN TAX LIENS

In addition to benefits and risks, there are several factors I consider the "pros and cons" of investing in tax lien certificates, strictly from the vantage point of an investor.

I began to invest in tax liens for myself in the early 1980s, a few years before I purchased my first private real estate note. A client of mine, a retired air force colonel, and several of his buddies, including a retired brigadier general, used to make an annual trek down to the county courthouse to invest in tax liens. Those retired air force officers were investing virtually all of their retirement portfolios in tax lien certificates.

They turned me on to the investment in 1981, and I began to make trips down there as well. Shortly afterward, Dad got enthused about it, and both Dad and I—either personally or through representatives—started buying as many tax liens as we possibly could. We were investing every spare dollar we had in tax liens at 18 percent yields. I was happy enough; Dad was ecstatic. We continued buying them through the 1980s.

It's hard to say how many tax lien certificates we bought—so many of them were bought for family members, clients, and various companies. However, I can tell you I discovered one major advantage to buying tax liens.

For a small investor with a very limited amount of money to invest, tax liens are the best game in town. They can be purchased for as little as $150 or $200 or as much as $500,000—and everything in between. Therefore, for a small investor who wants leveraged yields at the highest rates available anywhere, tax liens are perfect. Tax liens offer an excellent and very flexible way to get extremely high yields with very limited investment dollars.

The disadvantage of tax certificates, however, is that there is no reliability as to when they will be redeemed.

At any one time, we had anywhere from $50,000 to $100,000 invested in tax liens, and no idea when they would be redeemed. We would go three months without having any redeemed, and then all of a sudden, $15,000 or $20,000 would get redeemed. It was perfectly all right for Dad and me, but for a retiree on a budget, the uncertainty of the redemption made tax certificates a little less than reliable. (Of course, once you invest enough money in tax liens, on a random basis alone, you can expect redemptions to occur regularly.)

At any rate, the pro of tax liens is that you can get very high returns for very few investment dollars. The con is that you never really know when they are going to be redeemed. When they are, you make money. But when they aren't, you simply can't count on having that money in your bank account to pay bills.

That is one of the reasons I moved away from tax liens toward private mortgages. As a private mortgage investor, I got fairly equivalent yields. In addition, I had the reliability of monthly payments and knew at any time what the payment schedule on the mortgage was. I could count on mortgage notes for my monthly cash flow.

The disadvantages of private mortgages, however, were the advantages of tax liens. While I could buy tax liens for a few hundred dollars, the smallest private mortgage note I could buy was about $20,000 to $25,000. (Once I discovered how to invest in partials, I could invest as little as $5,000 to $10,000. But that's about as low as I could go.) Private mortgages also were less accessible than tax liens and more difficult to locate. To buy private mortgage notes, I had to track down private mortgage holders; to buy tax liens, I simply drove to the courthouse.

All things considered, tax liens are an excellent investment program, especially for someone who is just beginning to invest and has limited investment dollars to use. Tax liens offer high returns and security, require limited investment dollars, and are easy to access.

WHAT YOU NEED TO KNOW TO BUY TAX LIEN CERTIFICATES

Depending on the state, tax lien certificates are also called "certificates of purchase," "tax certificates," or "certified lists of liens purchase." Every tax lien is unique and must be individually selected and purchased.

The first step in buying tax liens is to determine where to buy them. The state in which you buy them will depend on your objective. Is your goal to acquire property? In that case, you buy in states like Texas, where they are seldom redeemed. Is your goal to earn a high rate of interest? Then buy certificates in Florida, where you can earn an interest rate of 18 percent, but don't have to acquire the property.

When you've determined where you want to buy certificates, contact the county Tax Collector's office and learn as much as you can about the local process. If possible, build a rapport with the people who work there. You will find their knowledge of local conditions invaluable.

You will want to ask the Tax Collector what rate of interest certificates earn and how much the potential penalties are. Are there public auctions? What are the bidding procedures? Are most certificates purchased by companies or individuals? How long does the owner have to redeem his or her property? What happens when an owner doesn't redeem? How can you pay for the certificates? Can you buy certificates over the phone, or only in person?

In addition, you'll need to get a list of actual properties that will be auctioned. If and when you choose several particular certificates, visit the county Assessor's office and research the duration of delinquency on the property and the amount of taxes owed. (The lower the taxes, the less a property is worth.) Try to look at the Assessor's Parcel Book to find assessed values and other information about the property.

After you research specific properties, decide which ones you want. Consider factors such as potential appreciation of the property, likelihood of redemption, and whether your objective is to earn interest or acquire the property for yourself. Then, revisit the Tax Collector's Office and indicate that you have made a selection. They can then tell you how much is owed for taxes and penalties.

One of my graduates, Herb Spencer of Woodland Hills, California, specializes in buying and researching tax liens. According to Herb, the majority of tax liens are redeemed in less than a year. Fewer than 3 percent of them are never redeemed.

There isn't really any way to predict whether or not a certificate will be redeemed by a taxpayer. However, if you choose a property on which taxes haven't been paid for, say, four years, then it's likely that peculiar circumstances are involved, such as a death or bankruptcy. If you want to own the property, that's a positive. But if you don't want to own it, that's a red flag. If someone hasn't bought the certificate after four years, it's possible the property isn't attractive to investors.

You can go about buying tax liens a number of ways, depending on your state's particular rules. The first way is to attend an auction, where they are first offered to the public. Some states hold auctions once a year; others hold them every month. Contact the county Tax Collector's Office for information and dates.

The bidding procedure also varies depending on the state. Sometimes the process is to bid the *price* up. Other times it's to bid the *interest* down. If you bid up the price, you pay more for the property, but earn a lower interest rate. In some states, bidding is a round-robin process. In others, bidding is handled through a random lottery.

If you do attend an auction, get a feel for what's going on at first. Wait until you really feel confident about the ins and outs of the process before you bid. Don't get caught up in the excitement of the auction. Instead, prepare for the auction and know precisely what property you want to bid on and what price you want to pay. If you are approaching the process as an opportunity for lucrative cash flow, your goal is to find a high-yield investment. Proceed accordingly.

The second way to buy tax liens is to wait until after an auction has been held and visit the appropriate county office to inquire about certificates that were not sold (you can do this on any working day). If you decide to buy a certificate, the county Tax Collector simply hands it to you, and you keep it in your possession, just as you would any other receipt.

The third way to buy certificates is to purchase them from another investor. Buying tax liens ties up an investor's money for at least two years. If the investor changes his or her mind and needs cash right away, you can negotiate to buy those certificates at a discount.

One thing to remember is that you probably will not be notified when you have to pay the next year's taxes on a certificate. That's because the county sends tax bills (usually twice a year) only to the owner on record for a particular property, not to tax lien holders.

Therefore, as the senior lien holder, but not the owner of record on the actual property, it is your responsibility to take the initiative and pay the taxes when they are due. Accordingly, when you acquire your certificate, ask about when the taxes are due, then follow up later to determine how much is owed. Remember, if the certificate is redeemed, you get all your money back plus interest.

THREE WAYS TO BUILD WEALTH WITH TAX LIENS

Strategy 1: Buy Certificates and Resell Them

With this strategy, you buy tax liens and then assign them to individual investors or funding sources for a fee. Or, you act as a "researcher," locating quality tax liens for your investor to buy. In exchange for your time, you earn a fee.

Strategy 2: Use Tax Liens to Acquire Properties

With this strategy, you seek to acquire attractive properties whenever possible, hold them awhile, then sell them for a tidy profit. You can carry the financing yourself, so you continue to receive income every month. By carefully selecting tax liens that are expected to go into foreclosure, you can make as much as one hundred times your original investment this way.

Strategy 3: Use Tax Certificates as Leverage

With this strategy, you use your tax liens as collateral for obtaining a loan from a lending institution. Then, you use the loan to purchase more certificates. Or, you can assign the certificates to someone else as a downpayment for other property or real estate that you want to purchase.

Tax liens are creative, flexible, lucrative, and relatively safe as long as you understand what you're doing and you go about it in a professional way. Keep in mind that there is a great deal of variation among individual states and even among various counties in each state. That requires some research on your part. (For a list of states in the U.S. that sell tax lien certificates, see the Resources section.)

Remember These Highlights

- Collateral is an asset that guarantees payment.
- Many types of income streams are secured by collateral, including private mortgage notes, business notes, mobile home notes, and tax liens.
- Private mortgage notes, business notes, and mobile home notes all originate from owner financing. You can profit at least three ways with these income streams: (1) brokering them; (2) investing in them; or (3) creating them.
- With tax liens, opportunities lie mainly in researching them for other investors and buying them for your own portfolio.

CHAPTER SEVEN

TARGET BUSINESSES AND "FACTOR" YOUR WAY TO PROFITS

IN CHAPTER SIX, I DISCUSSED HOW TO MAKE MONEY transacting four debt instruments secured by collateral—private mortgage notes, business notes, mobile home notes, and tax liens. I pointed out how you can broker those instruments and earn immediate fees, or buy them and earn significant long-term yields. However, there are dozens of ways to make money in the cash flow business, even when no collateral is involved.

In this chapter, I'll introduce you to two debt instruments that do not involve collateral, but *do* involve big returns: business invoices and commercial leases. What do these instruments have in common? Both result when one business owes another business money. For that reason, we refer to invoices and leases as business-based income streams.

BUSINESS INVOICES (ACCOUNTS RECEIVABLE)

Most businesses deal with two types of transactions: retail transactions and commercial transactions. When a business sells its product to a consumer, that's a retail transaction. The buyer (usually the end-user) pays for the product on a cash-and-carry basis, gets a receipt, then takes the product home.

When a business sells its product to another *business,* that's a commercial transaction. The buyer usually doesn't have to pay for the product immediately, but may wait 30 days or even 60 days to pay for it. Instead of getting a receipt, the buyer gets an invoice. The invoice spells out how many goods were ordered, how many were shipped, how much they cost, and how many days the buyer can take to pay for them. *In nearly every type of commercial transaction, an invoice is the basis for payment.*

The term **accounts receivable** is often used interchangeably with invoices. Accounts receivable simply refers to a list of all invoices that have been sent to a business's customers but have not yet been paid. In short, an invoice is a bill; accounts receivable is a collection of bills.

After a business invoices its customer, the business is left with two choices. First, it can wait for payment to arrive weeks or months in the future. Or second, it can collect the money *immediately* by selling its invoices to a third party.

This second option is called **factoring.** Factoring is the purchase of accounts receivable from a business for a fee. Let's look at an example.

Mailbox marketing is a business that offers printing and direct mail marketing services to companies. Mailbox Marketing recently provided one of its customers, a power company, with $100,000 worth of printing and direct mail services. The business has sent the power company an invoice for $100,000.

The invoice requests payment within 30 days—typical payment terms for a business-to-business sale. However, it's possible the power company will not pay the invoice within 30 days. In fact, it may not pay the invoice until 60 days or even more. In the meantime, Mailbox Marketing has to pay its rent, utilities, and its employees.

Anyone who has owned a business can relate to this dilemma. The business has spent money to produce a product or provide a service, but it has to wait to make a profit—or even to cover its costs. In this scenario, Mailbox Marketing could get cash for the $100,000 invoice more quickly by *factoring* it. Here's how it works.

A *factoring broker* approaches the owner of Mailbox Marketing. The broker explains that within forty-eight hours, he or she can get the owner cash, less a reasonable fee, for the $100,000 invoice. By factoring the invoice, Mailbox Marketing can cover its production expenses, pay rent, meet payroll, and still make a profit. Mailbox Marketing can even use some of that immediate cash to buy paper, ink, and postage to fill its next order.

The owner of Mailbox Marketing eagerly agrees to pursue the transaction. The factoring broker then contacts a factor—a funding source for factoring transactions—and tells the factor about the transaction. The factor offers to purchase the $100,000 invoice for $95,000. In other words, the factor buys the invoice for cash in exchange for a $5,000 factoring fee.

The whole process works like this: First, the factor sends Mailbox Marketing a cash advance of $75,000. Then, the factor waits for the power company to pay the $100,000 invoice. As soon as the power company pays, the factor gives Mailbox Marketing the remaining $25,000, less a fee of $5,000.

The factor then mails the *factoring broker* a $500 check for locating the transaction.

Let's consider the transaction graphically (see p. 135).

As you can see, all three parties win. Mailbox Marketing wins, because it gets immediate cash for its invoice. Moreover, Mailbox Marketing gets the opportunity to factor as many invoices in the future as its requires to accelerate the collection process. The factor wins, because it collects a $5,000 fee in 30 to 60 days.

Finally, the factoring broker wins, because he or she earns $500 on a single invoice from one company on one transaction.

That is how factoring works, regardless of the business, regardless of the product.

THE FACTS ON FACTORING

Historians say some form of factoring was used in commerce in civilizations as far back as the Phoenicians. The term "factoring" comes from the Latin, *factor*, meaning "doer," or "one who transacts business

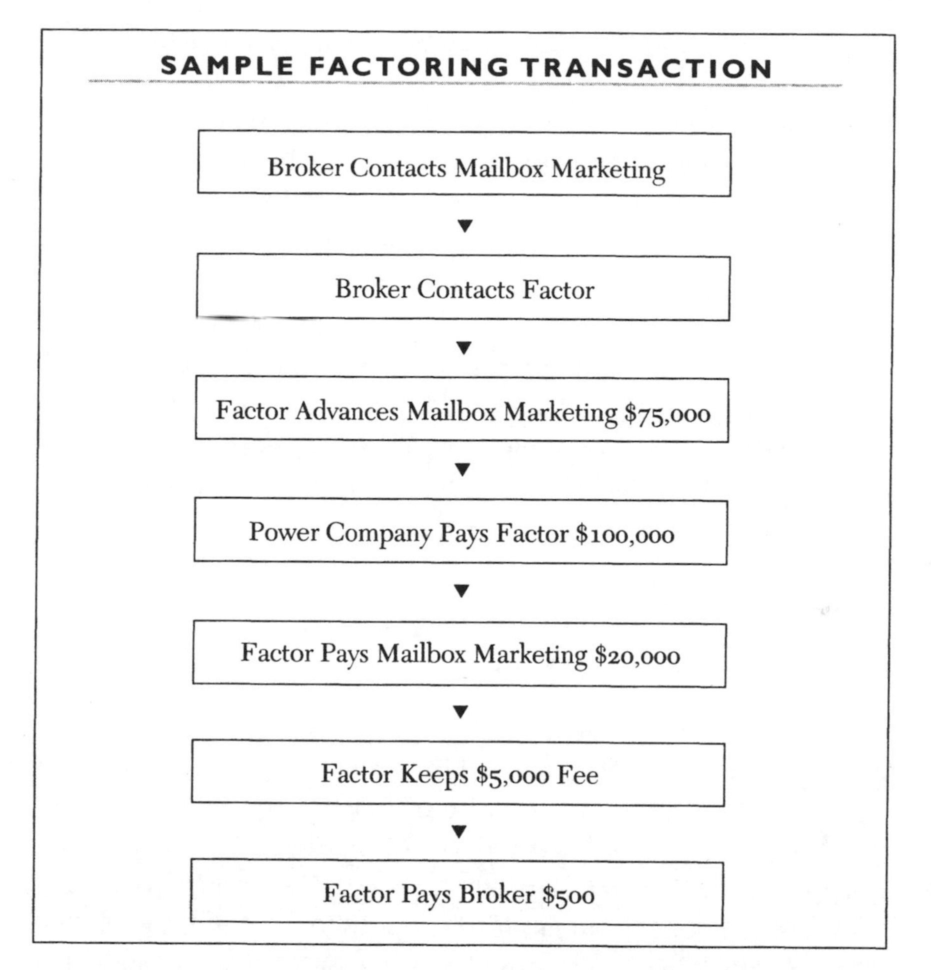

for another." Factoring dates back thousands of years, but it has evolved into a very modern financing technique.

While it may be one of the oldest forms of financing, it is also one of the least understood. Few people have even heard of factoring. Even fewer think of it as a cash flow business that can be operated out of the home. And those who have heard of it usually misunderstand it.

The main reason factoring is such a well-kept secret is that many people who participate in factoring do not come from a financial services background. Most banks do not offer factoring, because it involves *buying* accounts receivable. Banks tend to *lend* money collateralized by accounts receivable. So banks seldom have in-house factoring experts. Likewise, stockbrokers, insurance agents, and other financial services professionals may never come in contact with factoring.

So who does get involved in factoring? Frequently, it's business owners or merchants who have used factoring in the past.

My friend Peter Baronoff, for example, who operates Sun Capital in West Palm Beach Florida, learned about factoring when he was a wine importer. Early on in his business, Peter discovered how factoring can stimulate cash flow—in fact, his own company's cash flow. Without factoring, his wine company certainly would have been harder to operate. Eventually, Peter realized he could make more money factoring than he could distributing wine. Today, he gets the best of both worlds. He makes money in his factoring business, then sips wine at home—expanding his prestigious wine collection!

FACTORING TRANSACTIONS ARE MORE COMMON THAN YOU REALIZE

The truth is, *factoring is used more often than all other types of financing combined.* An amazing statement? Consider this: Every credit card transaction is, in reality, a factoring transaction.

When a business sells a product or service and accepts payment through a credit card, the merchant receives a credit card slip in lieu of cash. Then the vendor submits those slips to MasterCard, Visa, or another credit card company in exchange for cash. In other words, the credit card company advances the money that still has not been collected. In turn, the credit card company charges a fee (a discount) as compensation for providing this service to the merchant.

The service that MasterCard, Visa, and other companies offer is actually a type of factoring. If they did not offer this service, merchants would be forced to (1) stop offering credit sales; or (2) patiently wait until the credit card customer paid his bill weeks or months later. In these fast-moving times, very few businesses could afford to wait that long. That's why merchants willingly pay a 2 percent to 6 percent discount fee to credit card companies in exchange for cash up front.

When merchants convert their credit card receipts into cash, we call that **consumer factoring.** When businesses use the same principle to convert their invoices into cash, we call that **commercial factoring.** Commercial factoring offers the same benefit for a commercial business that consumer factoring offers a retail business.

The Purpose of Factoring

Factoring fulfills two basic purposes. First, it fills the money gap between the time a company makes a sale and the time the customer pays. After delivering a product or service to a customer, businesses often can't afford to wait for payment. Sometimes they need money immediately to meet payroll expenses, rent, or other operating expenses. Other times they need money to buy supplies needed to fill incoming orders. Factoring gives those businesses access to cash within a few days instead of a few months.

Second, factoring gives funding sources a good rate of return on their money. When a factor purchases a business's accounts receivable, it advances the business 70 percent to 80 percent of the face value of its invoices. The factor then collects the money due from the client's customers. When the factor receives payment, it pays the remainder of the invoice back to the client, minus a fee. If the factor can continue circulating and recirculating its money every 30 to 60 days, it can generate significant fee income and a more significant return on invested capital.

How Factoring Is Different from a Loan

While factoring qualifies as a method of financing, it is not a lending service—it is a *discounted purchase.* A factor typically does not charge interest. A factor simply buys invoices at a discount then collects its fee as "discount income."

A factoring transaction is actually very similar to a discounted sale. If a business sells something for $100, takes back an invoice, and factors the invoice for $97, in essence the business is left with a cash sale for $97.

The disadvantage is that it cost the business $3 of revenue to factor the invoice. The advantage, however, is that the business gets its cash now, without having to borrow anything. In a sense, then, factoring is a way to convert an invoiced sale into a cash-and-carry sale.

Consider the fact that most businesses routinely offer their customers a 2 percent, 10-day "prompt payment discount." If the customer pays an invoice within 10 days, the customer can take a 2 percent reduction off the invoice. *Factoring is just like a prompt-payment discount, except that the discount isn't being offered to the customer, it's being offered to the factor.*

How many businesses would be willing to offer their customers a 5 percent discount for payment in twenty-four hours? Most businesses would do that in a heartbeat. It would be well worth extending a 5 percent discount to receive payment in one day.

Any business that would offer a 5 percent discount for payment in twenty-four hours should be factoring. When businesses use factoring, that's exactly what they're doing; the only difference is the discount is being paid to the factor, not to the customer.

WHY BANKS CAN'T COMPETE WITH FACTORING

Why would businesses use factoring to generate cash flow instead of borrowing money from the bank? The truth is, most businesses owners *do* turn first to their banks when they need cash; however, they often come away disappointed. Bank financing simply can't compete with factoring as a short-term cash flow solution for a number of reasons.

First, banks must follow strict federal and state guidelines when they issue loans. They are required to maintain a certain level of capital or equity in order to lend out money. The more capital a bank has, the more money it can lend out.

Factoring is not a loan, but an outright purchase that has to be deducted from the bank's available capital. That restricts the amount of money the bank can lend out. See the problem? If the bank lends money, that's okay. But if the bank buys invoices, it limits the amount available for future loans to other customers.

Second, banks generally require a great deal of collateral to secure a loan for a business. A business may be generating $1,000,000 a year in sales—obviously a good volume of business—yet own few assets that would secure a loan.

Suppose, for example, you run a mail order office supply business out of a leased warehouse. When orders come in, you call up your suppliers and order the products. As soon as the products arrive, you turn around and ship them to your customers. Your business is generating $5 million a year in sales volume and growing by leaps and bounds—clearly a thriving operation.

Now, suppose you need cash to in order to expand the distribution of your catalog, which in turn, will increase your revenue even more. When you visit your bank, what's the first thing your loan officer will ask? He or she will want to know how much collateral you have. Since your catalog business doesn't require a lot of equipment, and you don't own your warehouse space, guess what? You probably don't have a lot of collateral. In your case, bank financing is out of the question.

Even if your bank were willing to lend against your accounts receivable, the bank would structure it as a loan, collateralized by your accounts receivable. If your mail order business had $100,000 worth of outstanding invoices, the bank would only lend you between $30,000 and $50,000.

In my athletic equipment business, I never used factoring, but the advantages would have been clear. Our sales were about $1 million a year, and as I've already mentioned, we didn't own a lot of tangible assets. Our business, after all, was based on inventory. Getting a loan from a bank based on our financial statement would have been next to impossible.

On the other hand, our financial statement wouldn't have mattered to factors. Our customers were government offices—the State of Florida, the Dade County School Board, the City of Orlando Recreation Department, and so on. Any factor would have been thrilled to buy our invoices for cash.

The third reason bank financing can't compete with factoring is that banks base their financing on the strength of the business, not on the business's accounts receivable. Even if a business's customers are solid and dependable, the bank still will not give a client a loan unless the client's business has a strong financial statement independent of the accounts receivable.

On the contrary, when a business enters a factoring arrangement, the factor bases the purchase on the credit of the business's customers, not on the credit of the business itself.

Suppose you approached a factor to buy the accounts receivable of your mail order business. The factor would be less concerned with *your* credit history and more concerned with the credit history of the customers who owe you money.

The fourth reason bank financing can't measure up to factoring is that even if a client can qualify for a loan, banks most often will lend only the amount of money that the client has *on deposit* in the form of a "compensating balance account." Now, why would a business need to borrow money in the first place if it already had the money in the bank? And if that isn't enough, the business will earn 0 percent to 4 percent interest on the money it has in the compensating balance account, but will be charged 8 percent to 12 percent interest for the line of credit. Does that make any sense?

The fact is, virtually every bank in America approaches financing in the ways I just described. *Therefore, banks have effectively eliminated themselves as competitors of factors.*

WHY FACTORING MAKES MORE SENSE

Let me point out some additional reasons why factoring makes more sense than borrowing from a bank.

First, factoring can provide more cash than may be available from any other source. There's no ceiling beyond which a factor must stop providing cash. The amount a business can factor is limited only by the business's sales.

Second, factoring can provide continuously increasing amounts of cash for growing businesses. Factoring doesn't require amortization, so businesses don't have to worry abut periodic payments or interim payoffs. Unlike traditional financing, there are usually no penalties for terminating a factoring arrangement.

Third, factoring is flexible. If a business takes a bank loan, it may not need all the money it borrowed over the entire duration of the loan. That is very inefficient. When a business factors, it can sell only enough invoices to provide the exact amount of cash it requires.

Fourth, factoring provides a dependable source of cash. As a long as a business is generating invoices, it can continue factoring. This last point is critical for growing businesses. As a growing company's total debt increases relative to equity, bank loans, as a matter of policy, do not increase proportionally. Bank financing can't accommodate rapid growth, but factoring can.

How Factoring Benefits a Business

Factoring can improve cash flow for virtually any business that produces invoices, whether the business is struggling or successful. For a struggling business, factoring provides an alternative to financing, cutbacks, and even bankruptcy. For a successful business, it provides capital for growth or aggressive expansion, increases administrative support, improves collections, and reduces accounting costs.

Below are listed some of the ways businesses can benefit from factoring:

- **Keeping pace with growth.** Failing to collect money owed slows down a company's progress. Lacking cash to purchase new supplies, a business cannot increase its production, and therefore, its sales. Factoring improves cash flow, which stimulates growth.
- **Meeting payroll.** If employees aren't paid on time, they won't come back to work the next day. And with limited employees, there is no product, let alone any morale. Factoring offers businesses quick cash they can use to cover payroll costs.
- **Paying payroll taxes.** Businesses sometimes delay paying taxes to the IRS (not wise, but common). By factoring invoices, a business can get a lump sum of cash it can use to cover payroll taxes.
- **Taking advantage of cash discounts.** Business often qualify for discounts of 2 percent to 15 percent when they pay their invoices within 10 days. Those businesses can use factoring to get cash quickly in order to earn these discounts. They can even earn a profit on that type of transaction, if the factoring fee is less than the prompt-payment discount.
- **Lowering overhead.** Factoring can decrease a business's overhead costs, by simplifying its accounting process. In fact, I've seen companies eliminate their accounts receivable departments altogether by factoring, thereby saving money and increasing profit.

- **Facilitating acquisitions.** First, factoring generates cash immediately, which is particularly desirable to a business seller. Second, factoring offers a revolving line of credit, which eliminates the concern about debt amortization. Third, factoring provides a dependable source of cash flow after the transaction. Finally, factoring can be used to restructure debt, finance a new venture or product, or fuel expansion.

IMPROVED CASH FLOW MEANS INCREASED PROFITS

The more successful a business is, the more cash it needs. Why? Because the business is selling its products or services so quickly, it can't get cash in the door fast enough to increase production, or provide more services. By improving cash flow, a company can boost its purchasing power, which allows it to increase production, multiply sales, and generate more profits.

The natural cash flow process is to convert cash into inventory or payroll expense, then inventory or payroll expense into accounts receivable, then accounts receivable back into cash. Until accounts receivable are collected, they serve only as evidence of money owned. They cannot be used to buy or produce more inventory or pay wages until they are collected. Therefore, uncollected accounts receivable holds up the entire cash flow cycle.

Consider the printing industry. Printers spend large amounts of cash to purchase supplies, such as ink, paper, and equipment, yet they tend to be one of the last vendors to get paid. Ask printers what their major cash flow complaint is, and they'll tell you that they are always pressed to deliver on time, but they seldom get paid on time. They get sent to the back of the line when it comes to receiving checks.

The lapse between delivery and payment can make it difficult for printers to purchase the supplies they need to fill their next order. That, in turn, slows down growth. By factoring its accounts receivable, a printer can get immediate cash it can use to purchase supplies, increase production, and therefore boost sales.

Not only does production involve costs, even sales involves costs. To make a sale, businesses have to pay for advertising and marketing, in addition to paying salespeople's commissions. Those sales costs can make it difficult for a business to make additional sales. Business often lack the cash necessary to generate new sales, because they are still paying the costs associated with the last sale.

If a business could eliminate that problem, it could effectively double its sales. Wouldn't that in turn double the business's profits? Actually, it would do much more than that.

Suppose on the first $100,000 worth of invoices, a business nets 3 percent profit. On the second $100,000 of invoices, the business will net much more than 3 percent. How? Because the revenue generated by first $100,000 pays for salaries, rent, insurance premiums, and so forth. The revenue generated by the second $100,000 goes directly to net income. That's not 3 percent or even 6 percent; more likely, it's 30 percent.

The bottom line is simply this: *Factoring increases profits because it increases cash flow.* And cash flow stimulates sales, which in turn increases revenues.

How You Can Make Money in Factoring

Now that you understand the diverse ways factoring benefits *businesses,* let's get to the point—how factoring can benefit *you.*

First, let's summarize what we've covered:

- The 30- to 90-day wait for customers to pay their invoices creates a serious cash flow concern for businesses. Money is owed, but it's not yet available to pay the bills.
- Factoring provides a cash flow solution for businesses. In a factoring transaction, a funding source called a factor pays cash for a business's accounts receivable.
- The factor earns a fee in the form of discount income.

So how do you fit into the factoring picture? If you make a career of the cash flow industry, *you* will be able to turn a $100,000 invoice into cash in as little as two days.

That's two days—not 90 days. The benefit is obvious, both to you and to business owners who need the money they are owed to pay bills, buy inventory, and increase sales.

But what if you don't have capital? You don't *need* capital. In the next few pages I'll show you how you can make money in factoring without using any of your own.

THE PLAYERS INVOLVED IN A FACTORING TRANSACTION

First, let's identify the players involved in most factoring transactions.

The **client** in the factoring relationship is the company that is in need of cash and wants to sell its invoices. It may be a commercial printer, a catering service, or a construction company. It doesn't matter. The bottom line is, the business has provided goods or services to another business, and now it is waiting for payment.

The **customer** is the company that bought the goods or services from the client and received the invoice. In factoring jargon, the customer is also called the **account debtor.** The customer, in other words, is the company that owes the client money. Normally the customer pays the invoice in the form of a check.

The **factor** is the funding source that buys invoices from the client. The factor, in other words, provides the capital for the transaction. Some factors are large, institutional companies owned and operated by banks. Others are smaller, independently owned companies that specialize in servicing this particular niche in the industry.

And of course, there is one more party to consider: the **broker.** Brokers are the field force that independently owned factoring companies rely on to bring in business. The broker is the person who locates business owners who need cash and introduces them to factors.

THREE WAYS TO MAKE MONEY

In Chapter Five, we learned how the cash flow industry offers three ways to make money. First, you can work as a cash flow broker. Second, you can function as a cash flow investor. And third, you can operate as both a broker and an investor, depending on the transaction.

The same three-fold money-making principle holds true for the factoring segment of the cash flow industry. In the factoring business, you can profit as: (1) a factoring broker; (2) a factor; or (3) both.

The most immediately accessible opportunity for someone just getting started in the factoring business is brokering. Funding sources all across the country specialize in buying accounts receivable. And most of those companies have more *capital* than they have transactions. They rely on independent brokers—people just like you—to bring them clients in exchange for a fee.

You can earn part-time spending money or six-figure income as a factoring broker, and you can do it *without using your own capital.* You simply act as a "middleman," introducing businesses in your area to professional factors.

What you have to do is locate a client, gather information about the business, and submit a one-page client profile to a factor for its approval. After that, the factor usually takes over. The factor handles the background check on your client and its customers and prepares all the documents for you to get signed by your client.

After the factor purchases your client's invoices, the client's customers will pay the factor instead of your client. Once the funding system is set up, you sit back, collect your brokerage checks, and call on your client occasionally.

You risk none of your own capital. And you receive a healthy and continuing commission from the factor for locating the transaction.

How big is a commission? A broker's compensation ranges from 10 to 20 percent of the factor's fee to much as 1 percent of the face value of the transaction. The table below shows average broker commissions for various factoring transactions.

FACTORING BROKERAGE COMMISSIONS

If the Factor's Fee Is	Then You Make
$5,000	$500 to $1,000
$10,000	$1,000 to $2,000
$25,000	$2,500 to $5,000
$50,000	$5,000 to $10,000
$100,000	$10,000 to $20,000

You Earn a Commission Every Time Your Client Factors

Keep in mind that a commission on one factoring transaction is probably just the beginning of a long series of commissions. A company that discovers factoring almost never factors just one invoice for just one month. The fact is, the company has cash flow needs every month of every year. And from that point on, every time that client uses your factor, you earn a commission.

When you introduce a company to factoring, you open the door for continuous use of factoring services. Next month, next year, or even next decade, you can continue to earn money every single time that client factors.

I can't emphasize this point enough: *You make money every time your client factors.*

An average factoring account lasts 14 to 24 months. But for the sake of example, let's assume your first client factors for only 12 months. If that client factors one $100,000 invoice every month for a year, it would produce approximately *$12,000 in commissions for you.* Whether it's one month or 12, one invoice or 100, one customer or 50, you earn income over the life of your accounts.

The example above holds true if you have one client that factors one invoice a month. Of course, most businesses have many customers, and those customers produce numerous invoices each month.

Let's say in your first month as a broker, you obtain one client and earn a $1,000 commission. Each month, that client continues to factor, so each month, you earn $1,000.

Now, suppose you maintain that pace. After two months, you have two clients and are earning $2,000 a month. After three months, you have three clients and are now earning $3,000 a month. For an entire year, you continue gaining one client a month for a year, and each client factors $100,000 worth of invoices each month.

If you continue at that rate, your income for your first year in operation will be $78,000. Did you get that? $78,000 for obtaining one client a month! Do you understand now the possible magnitude of the income you can earn as a factoring broker?

Whether you devote eight hours a month or 60 hours a week to your business, it takes time to locate clients and cultivate relationships. However, once that's achieved, the time you have put into locating clients will produce a stream of income to you every single time your client uses your factor. This is a classic example of *working smarter*, not harder.

When you introduce a client to factoring, you effectively create an "annuity" for yourself for as long as the factoring relationship continues. The time you put in may dwindle or stop, but checks will keep rolling in.

Brokering is all about leverage. Leverage means expending something in order to get greater returns. It's an essential element of money-making. When you are a factoring broker, you are leveraging your *time*—not your money—to accelerate your returns.

Improved Cash Flow for Your Client Equals Improved Cash Flow for You

Once you've established a factoring client, an even bigger opportunity emerges. Your client, benefitting from improved cash flow (thanks to you), can now multiply its production and sales. And more sales translates into more invoices.

Why is that significant? As sales increase, the company will need more and more cash. Your client will begin to factor more of its invoices each month, and you will continue to get a percentage of every invoice that's factored. Only then, the percentage will be calculated on a larger amount of money. *That means even larger commissions for you.*

Ron Provart, a factoring broker and former student of mine, saw firsthand how factoring increases cash flow, which in turn increases sales, which in turn increases factoring.

Ron and his partner started a brokering business, J & R Financial Group, in 1994. Their first client factored about $30,000 worth of invoices a month. Within six months, that client was factoring $80,000 worth of invoices a month. That client referred another client to Ron, and then another.

Ron's initial goal was to transact $300,000 of invoices by the end of 1994. He ended up transacting an unbelievable $2 million. And within two and a half years, he had transacted over $8 million.

Working on a part-time basis, you could work up to brokering as much as $350,000 to $1 million a month in invoices. That would earn you $3,500 to $10,000 a month in commission income. Just imagine what you could do if you made it a full-time occupation!

THE THREE STEPS OF BROKERING A TRANSACTION

So how do you get started as a factoring broker? By learning the transaction process. The process for brokering invoices is almost identical to the process for brokering any other income stream: (1) identifying a seller; (2) explaining your services and gathering information; and (3) working with a funding source.

Identifying a seller

As a factoring broker, your job is to locate clients that have invoices to sell and connect them with factors who have capital. Which businesses can benefit from factoring? Nearly every business on the planet! The truth is, almost any company you target could benefit from factoring services. However, I've found that *companies within a very particular market hold the most potential for you as clients.*

What is that market? Generally, it's not large manufacturers. They have been using factoring for a long time. Most know about factoring and are being serviced by factoring professionals with a high level of expertise. Their factors tend to be bank subsidiaries or affiliates.

On the other hand, it's not small businesses, either. Businesses that do less than $500,000 of sales each year usually do not need factoring services as badly. Besides, the small invoices they generate would not attract a factor's interest or bring you worthwhile commissions.

The most promising factoring opportunities lie in the niche that needs capital the most, yet is serviced the least. **That lucrative niche is small to mid-sized businesses that produce $500,000 to $50 million a year in sales.** Businesses in the $500,000 to $50 million category are not being serviced by traditional factors, large bank-affiliated factors, or small banks. They typically don't have access to capital because they don't have sufficient assets to secure loans. Factoring is a godsend to these businesses.

Believe it or not, the $500,000 to $50 million niche constitutes more than *one million businesses* in the U.S. alone. Combined, those business generate in excess of $1.7 trillion in annual accounts receivable. That means a million potential clients for you, and $1.7 trillion of invoices on which you could earn a commission.

Within this niche, you should target businesses that meet certain criteria.

First, focus on businesses that use invoices in their sales. Some businesses, especially retailers, do not use invoices at all. When you shop at a grocery store, for example, the store doesn't invoice you. You have to give them cash, a check, or a credit card immediately in order to walk out with your groceries. Some businesses invoice a percentage of their customers, but require immediate payment from others. Obviously, you don't want to target businesses unless their customers are predominantly other businesses, not consumers, and invoiced sales represent the bulk of their transactions.

Second, target businesses that sell relatively simple goods and services, with no after-sale services or warranties provided by the client other than those normally expected in a commercial transaction.

Third, seek out companies that are young, growth-oriented, and intent on expansion. Chances are, those companies are in need of additional working capital and are having a hard time getting adequate bank financing. Because of their growth, they may be having trouble meeting payroll, paying taxes, and producing more product.

Finally, target any company that provides goods or services under a government contract. The government tends to be reliable as a payor, so government-related factoring transactions are attractive to factors.

The following table lists companies that provide goods and services and could be ideal candidates for factoring.

PROSPECTIVE FACTORING CLIENTS

Accessories	Apparel	Business machine
Airfreight companies	Audio or video tapes	repair

Camping equipment	Furniture manufacturers	Printers
Caterers	Garden equipment firms	Remediation and abatement
Carpet manufacturers	Hazardous waste firms	Restaurant equipment
Chemicals	Independent truck driving	Sign companies
Computers	Jewelry companies	Steel
Construction materials	Lawn maintenance	Sporting equipment
Construction projects	Neon signs	Telecommunications
Cosmetics	Packaging	Temporary employment agencies
Decorating	Paint manufacturers	Textiles
Defense contractors	Paper manufacturers	Timber
Dental and medical supplies	Paving contractors	Tires
Direct mail companies	Photographic equipment	Transportation
Electrical contractors	Plastics	Valves
Electronics		Website/Internet providers
Fire equipment and service		

NARROW YOUR MARKET

There is a number of ways you can further narrow your market to find the most profitable niche for you.

First, you can narrow your market based upon the industry you want to service. You can decide, for example, to focus on paper manufacturers. You will work with any company in the United States as long as it's a paper manufacturer. The industry you choose to service could be an area in which you're already familiar or have prior experience.

Laurie Javier, one of my graduates and the founder of Advance Capital in San Francisco, limited her niche by focusing on the health care industry. She locates factoring clients by targeting physicians, independent laboratories, physical therapy providers, medical equipment companies, and other health-care-related businesses.

Second, you can narrow your market based on geography. You can opt to work with any *type* of business, as long as it's located in your city or state. Many factoring brokers limit their niche this way. By concentrating on businesses in their own areas, they can meet with business owners and referral sources face to face, which is far more effective than working over the phone or by mail.

Third, you can narrow your niche based on size. Some factoring brokers choose to work only with large companies with high sales volume. Others focus on small companies that aren't aware of factoring services.

Jeff Callender found a lucrative niche in companies with small accounts that didn't meet the typical size requirements for factoring. Today, he specializes in funding small accounts.

Mike Brennan, a former student and a personal friend, narrowed his market based on the track record of the payor. Mike located a substantial payor that was certain not to go out of business, but took a long time to pay its bills—a utility company. He obtained a directory of all the utility's approved vendors. Then, he contacted each of the vendors on the list and explained the general benefits of factoring, without referring to the utility company by name. His research paid off; he received a great deal of business from the utility company's vendors.

Of course, combining any of the factors above allows you to identify your market more specifically. If you limit your market by industry, geography, *and* size, for example, you can arrive at a manageable list of prospects (preferably less than 500).

Marketing Through Referral Sources

Your success at finding good factoring prospects will be directly related to how well you reach businesses in your niche market. And the best way by far to reach potential factoring clients is through referral sources. Listed below are a number of ways you can generate factoring referrals.

Develop Professional Relationships

The first way to is to build relationships with professionals who are in a position to know which businesses need working capital. Those include bankers, insurance agents, leasing agents, accountants, and purchasing agents. When a business is short of cash, those individuals are likely to know about the situation.

Bankers, particularly commercial loan officers, are one of the very best source of referrals for factoring transactions. When a business owner needs money, the first place he or she goes is the local bank. Few banks are involved in factoring, so bankers will not consider you a competitor. In fact, knowing about your service is to their benefit. If they have to turn down commercial clients for loans, they can refer them to you for an alternative source of funds.

Elinor Newman, a cash flow specialist in Las Vegas, Nevada, uses bankers as her primary source of factoring referrals. She began by visiting her own local bank and leaving her card with the officers in charge of commercial accounts. Then she met with banking representatives at various branches in her area to inform them about her accounts receivable financing services. Now she simply maintains those contacts for ongoing business.

Accountants are another potential source of referrals. A business's accountant knows if its clients are having cash flow problems and can determine whether factoring might be a good alternative. Likewise, purchasing and shipping agents are likely to know which companies are the most active and which ones are having difficulty managing their cash flow. If you already have existing business contacts, that's even better.

When Winston Chee began his cash flow business, Chee International, he turned to the hundreds of business contacts he had developed in the U.S. and abroad while working in the engineering industry. Over the years, many of his colleagues had worked their way into high-level positions within their organizations, and many had started their own companies. Today, he gets inquiries from CEOs and business owners all over the world who are interested in expansion funding and asset-based lending.

Giving Presentations

Another highly effective way to develop referral sources for factoring is by giving presentations to business owners and professional organizations. In your presentation, you can explain what factoring is and how it can stimulate cash flow.

Groups like the Rotary Club, Kiwanis Club, Lions Club, and the Jaycees are always looking for luncheon speakers. Most members of these organizations are business owners and professionals—the perfect audience for your message about factoring. Since your subject matter is mysterious even to many long-term businesspeople, you should have no trouble getting booked by the program chairmen of those local organizations. It's a perfect opportunity to get free advertising.

One former student of mine, Don Henk, has used the presentation strategy with great success. Don gives presentations every month at the local chapter of SCORE, a retiree business advisory organization. His presentations produce referrals both from people who have seen his presentation and from other professionals who were speaking that day.

John and Peggy Mikkelson, who broker and factor small accounts, also use the presentation method. Their most successful marketing strategy has been speaking at Chamber of Commerce meetings and small business forums.

Even ordinary daily activities can lead to factoring referrals. In a recent conversation, a former student of mine, Clifford Feldman, shared this story about his cash flow business in South Florida. When he first started his business, Cliff found the idea of "marketing" intimidating. His preconceptions about marketing changed, however, once he went to a doctor's appointment. In the waiting room, three or four other people were waiting to see the physician. When he checked in with the receptionist, she said, "I called your office to confirm your appointment. I'm just curious—what does your company do?"

Cliff wondered how he would explain factoring to her in just one sentence. So he said, "I provide companies with better cash flow."

As he turned away to sit down, one of the women in the waiting room asked Cliff the same question. She told Cliff she thought her husband would like to talk to him. So Cliff handed her one of his business cards and continued with his appointment for the day.

Three days later, the woman's husband did call. He owned a glass and mirror company in Palm Beach and wanted to meet to discuss his cash flow situation. Cliff set up a meeting and went to see him. After the meeting (which went very well), Cliff had some time to kill before his next appointment. He decided to hand out some flyers in the immediate area. His first stop was a sign company right next door. As soon as he told the owner of the sign company what he did, the man grabbed hold of his arm and said, "Come in, I need to talk to you."

One week later, Cliff closed a transaction with the glass and mirror company *and* the sign company. Now, those two clients alone continue to bring him $1,200 a month in commissions.

Finally, one of the richest sources of referrals is one that brokers often overlook—your clients themselves and your client's customers. When you solve a business's cash flow needs, that business will recommend you to other businesses who could benefit from factoring, including their customers. You can contact your client's customers and show them how factoring could benefit their businesses, too.

ADVERTISING AND PUBLIC RELATIONS

Advertising is another way to identify potential invoice sellers. You can advertise your cash flow business in the Yellow Page under "Factors" or "Commercial Finance" or "Finance/Commercial." Also, you can place an ad in business or trade journals—these allow you to target a specific audience with a specific message.

Some basic public relations also can attract interest in your services. Many cash flow specialists promote their services by writing informative news releases about factoring and faxing them to local newspapers.

One of my former students, Dan Kelso, got publicity by promoting himself as "The Money Doctor." He transitioned into his *third career* when he became a factoring broker. After retiring from the military, he had become a chiropractor. Ironically, he sustained a back injury, and found the long days on his feet troublesome. That led to his third, and he hopes, final career as a factoring broker.

Dubbing himself "The Money Doctor," Dan managed to get three large articles written about his business in his local Jacksonville, Florida, newspaper. Those articles alone provided a healthy flow of prospective clients.

COLD CALLING

If you present yourself convincingly over the phone, you can market your services by making cold calls to business owners in your area or by mailing an introductory letter and following up with a phone call. You can get lists of prospects from list brokers, the Chamber of Commerce, direct mail companies, and data companies.

Cold calling as a factoring broker is far different from cold calling in any other type of business or industry. Remember that a factoring broker doesn't ask for money, he or she *delivers* it. When you view yourself as a consultant, not a salesperson, and recognize that you have the opportunity to *give* money to businesses, your attitude alone will get you in the door more often than not.

Fred Steinberg, one of my graduates and the founder of Express Business Funding, insists that he built his business by perfecting the cold call. He would get lists of prospects from Dun & Bradstreet or other computer data firms, and then call all the names in a particular region. When he had set up several meetings in one area, he would go on the road to meet with his potential clients.

The general tendency is to believe that only "born salesmen" are good at cold calling. Fred Steinberg is a perfect illustration of why that rule simply does not hold true in factoring. None of Fred's former careers—which included restauranting, building homes, and a stint as a Buddhist monk—would have qualified him as a hard-nosed cold-calling salesperson.

"But," says Fred, "the value I had as a factoring broker came from being able to deliver the money that could solve business needs."

As you are looking for ways to market your cash flow services to potential clients, remember that the best marketing resource of all is a satisfied customer. A reputation for integrity, helpfulness, and believability is worth more than all the marketing dollars or time you can spend.

Explaining services and gathering information

Once you've identified a potential factoring client, the next step is to meet in person and gather some information from the client. When you talk with a business owner the first time, keep two objectives in mind: (1) to explain factoring; and (2) to understand the business's needs.

One way to explain factoring to a prospective client is to compare it to a credit card transaction, as I did earlier in this chapter. Just as MasterCard waits for its money, the factor waits for its money. MasterCard charges a small fee for its service; the factor also charges a small fee. Your client gets the benefit of getting paid all at once.

After you've explained the concept of factoring, you can point out the specific benefits factoring offers a company. As I've already mentioned, those include increased purchasing power, improved credit rating, increased production and sales, accounts receivable maintenance, and access to credit reports on the company's customers.

If the business owner becomes seriously interested, he or she will want to know why factoring is superior to other more conventional forms of lending. This is the most critical part of your meeting—and the crucial aspect of your message. I've summarized the advantages of factoring in the table below:

ADVANTAGES OF FACTORING	
Factoring stimulates cash flow.	•Selling accounts receivable can increase cash flow and working capital, which the owner can use to increase sales, pay bills, or buy needed inventory.
Factoring is accessible.	•Businesses that have not been operating for very long or that have insufficient hard assets have a difficult time qualifying for a loan.
Factoring gets quick results.	•Factoring can quickly raise the levels of funds available to meet the needs of an expanding business, without a lot of red tape.
Factoring allows the business owner to maintain control.	•If the owner accepts money from a venture capitalist, he gives up partial control of the company. Factoring avoids this ownership change.
Factoring is flexible.	•A business is not required to factor all of its invoices, only enough to cover the money it needs.
There are rarely penalties.	•With factoring there are rarely lump sum payments or penalties for ending the factoring relationship.

Factoring offers help with accounts receivable administration.	•The client can choose to maintain control of accounts receivable or hand them over to the factor to maintain. Often the factor can do a better job than the company's in-house personnel, at a comparable cost.

Once you have outlined the advantages of factoring, the next step is to help your prospective client evaluate whether factoring is appropriate for that company's circumstances. You do this by asking the prospect questions and compiling information into a report—a mini-profile of your prospect. Later, your funding source will use the client profile you complete to determine whether the company is a serious candidate for factoring.

Funding sources for factoring transactions tend to have their own information requirements. Generally, however, you will need to ask the following questions:

- How long has the company been in business?
- How many customers does it have?
- How long do its customers generally take to pay their invoices?
- What is the number and dollar amount of invoices the company generates?
- Does the company need working capital?
- Does it need bad debt cover?
- Does it need administrative help with accounts receivable?

With this information, you can usually determine quickly whether or not the business has a need for factoring services.

Working with a funding source

After you've gathered information on your client, the next step is to present the transaction to a funding source or "factor." If you're just starting to build a relationship with a factor, you will have to find out the following information:

- Will the factor work with an independent broker?
- How much commission is the company willing to pay?

- What type of receivables does it prefer?
- How long does the approval process take?

The answers to these questions will help you decide whether you want to work with the company on this transaction.

Remember that a factoring company has only one goal in mind: to buy receivables and put its money to work earning high returns. The factor isn't interested in a social relationship, but in working with brokers who can bring the company profitable clients.

Let's assume you have already established a working relationship with a factor that may be interested in handling this account. You already know exactly what information the factor needs and how to put the data together in a logical format. At this point, you present the transaction to the factor over the phone or by fax. Then you wait for the factor to respond.

After reviewing the transaction, the factor will tell you if it's interested in funding the transaction, what fees it will charge your client, how much of a commission (percentage) it will pay you if the transaction is completed, and what additional information, if any, is needed from you.

In a factoring transaction, the factor handles almost all of the paperwork. Factoring companies usually design their own specific applications that the prospective client must complete. They may also have a list of documents which must be submitted along with the application package directly to the prospect.

If this is the case, you have two choices. You could either offer to meet with your prospect to assist in filling out the factor's application, or you could simply leave that process to the factor to handle. Regardless of which choice you make, the decision is yours—not the factor's. The factor will do whatever is most appropriate to complete the transaction and sign on a new client.

Once the official application is complete and all forms are attached, you forward the package to the factor for processing. In most cases, the client and factor deal directly with each other in executing documents and processing the initial set of invoices. In some situations, however, the factor may ask you to assist the client in this final process. But once the initial set of invoices has been presented to the factor, the factor deals directly with the client from that point on.

Before funding a transaction, the factor performs **due diligence** on the prospective client's accounts receivable. Due diligence simply means checking out the client and the customers that owe the client money. Your client provides the factor with an aging report that contains the names of its customers. The factor uses this list to determine which customers it prefers to factor.

The factor is less concerned with the creditworthiness of the client than with the creditworthiness of the customers that owe the client money. The factor wants to know whether your client's customers have the ability to pay their invoices and will obtain a credit report on each customer whose account the client wants to factor.

If the factor decides to move forward with the prospect, then you and a factoring representative meet with your client to execute documents that solidify the relationship. While many ways can be used to commence the transaction, the factor often provides the client with stickers and stamps to apply to invoices before mailing them to the customers. The stickers (1) show the factor's name and address; (2) inform the customer that the client has assigned that invoice to the factor; and (3) indicate that the customer is now required to make payment directly to the factor. The factor also obtains deposit tickets from the client in order to deposit funds into the client's account, when requested.

When the factor finally advances cash to the client, you start receiving a monthly commission check based on the amount of invoices factored during that month. At that point, your role as a broker is finished. The only thing you need to do is touch base occasionally with your clients to make sure they are being properly serviced by the factor. You continue to receive checks on a monthly basis, usually by the 10th of the month, for any commissions earned during the prior month.

In time, you'll grow more familiar with various factors and more sensitive to your client's needs. If the existing factor is unable to respond to your client's concerns, you may find it appropriate to place your client elsewhere. If you can assist your client in this way, it will enhance your relationship with that client considerably. And, of course, that's an important goal.

Identify a seller, explain your service and gather information, and work with a funding source. That's the process.

You earn a commission whenever you place a client with a factor. And while circumstances will vary according to your own particular talent, lifestyle, and time constraints, you can expect to earn anywhere between $12,000 a year working part-time to $120,000 a year or more working full-time. The key is that your efforts must be consistent and adequate.

As a factoring broker, you can create an immediate impact by making manufacturers and distributors aware of important factoring services. Working out of your own home with very little overhead, you can satisfy national economic needs that can't be delivered by anyone else. If you are conscientious about your work, factoring brokerage is deeply fulfilling, both personally and monetarily. Once you have a client in hand, residual income comes in each month as your client continues to factor.

MAKE MONEY AS A FACTOR

As we just discussed, the first way to make money in factoring is to function as a broker. The second way is to function as a factor.

When you are a factor, you provide the capital to fund a transaction. That means your own money is at stake. You are 100 percent responsible for researching and evaluating all of the concerns related to the transaction. Obviously, that means you take certain risks. On the other hand, it also means you can earn yields as high as 60 percent to 125 percent, or more, on your capital each year.

Because it takes a large amount of capital to become a factor, most people ease into the factoring business by brokering transactions. Fred Steinberg is one of the few cash flow professionals I know who skipped brokering and immediately began factoring.

The story of his road to success is a powerful one. Fred used to manage several large restaurants for a private owner in New York City. In the mid-1970s, he moved down to Florida and started a general contracting business—building luxury homes, shopping centers, animal hospitals, and so forth. He ran that business for eighteen years and had a staff of 60 employees.

In 1993, Fred's son died tragically. Fred was unable to concentrate on his business, and in time his once-thriving contracting company went bankrupt. Within a matter of months, he lost every asset he owned—stocks, bonds, IRAs—everything.

In the spring of 1995 Fred attended one of my free workshops on cash flow. That fall, he attended a five-day comprehensive training program on factoring, and in November—over a million dollars in debt—he started a factoring business. Fred didn't have time to learn the business as a broker. Instead, he borrowed $20,000 from family members and went straight to factoring.

Just two years later, Fred's factoring business has grown into a multi-million-dollar operation. The company has four senior vice-presidents now and operates with a regular base of about 375 factoring brokers.

What You Need to Know as a Factor

Factors make their money by buying a company's invoices and collecting on them, then charging the client a fee. They usually do this by discounting the face value of the invoices. In some cases, however, factors *lend* against accounts receivable until they are collected; then, they charge daily interest on the open account, plus a one-time commission. Either way, the factor buys, pays for, and owns the receivables outright.

The factor assumes the collection process, including mailing out the invoices. To ensure that the collection process goes as expected, the factor conducts professional credit checks on all its clients' customers.

Two Forms of Factoring

In the factoring industry, there are two basic types of factoring: recourse factoring and non-recourse factoring. When a company wants you to factor its accounts, it decides whether it wants credit protection from the factor (non-recourse factoring) or no credit protection (recourse factoring).

Recourse Factoring

In recourse factoring, the factor does not give any protection to the client against a customer's failure to pay any sums outstanding. Although the invoice is assigned to the factor, the credit risk remains with the client. And if for any reason the customer doesn't pay the factor, the debt will be reassigned to the client.

If the factor has advanced monies against delinquent invoices, the factor is entitled to require that these be repaid by the client. In other words, recourse factoring eliminates any risk the factor assumes on his or her own behalf. Let's run through a case of how that works.

Suppose you find a client who wants to factor a $100,000 invoice. You advance the client $70,000 up front, then tell the client you will advance an additional $26,000 in 40 days to settle the account.

During the 40-day period, you are able to collect only $90,000 of the $100,000 worth of invoices. So, at the end of that time, $10,000 worth of invoices remain uncollected.

You don't have to go back to your client for a check. You simply deduct the $10,000 not collected out of the $26,000 you still owe your client. Instead of sending your client a check for $26,000 to settle the account, you send the client a check for $16,000, along with the uncollected invoices. From that point on, it's the client's responsibility to collect on those.

With recourse factoring, before you buy invoices from a client, you would:

1. Approve the client and the creditworthiness of the client's customers under the invoice
2. Charge the client an up-front application fee
3. Set a limit for each customer beyond which the client may not extend credit.

Non-Recourse Factoring

In non-recourse factoring, the factor assumes the risk of the debtor not being able to pay for the goods or services provided. (The factor, however, *does not* assume credit risk when the debtor doesn't pay because of defective goods or services.) If a factor is unable to collect on a particular set of invoices, the factor cannot return the invoices to the client for a refund.

If you do a very thorough job of checking out the creditworthiness of customers who have been invoiced, it can be enormously profitable working in non-recourse factoring. However, I don't recommend that strategy until you have the experience behind you and are set up with credit bureau assistance and credit insurance.

How Much to Charge

The amount of time it will take to collect the money you have advanced against the invoices you've bought directly affects the fee you charge and the yield you earn.

Let me give you two examples to illustrate what I mean. The first shows the type of fee you earn if the receivables can be collected in 40 or fewer days. The second shows the type of fee you would earn if the receivables took more than 40 days to be collected.

Suppose you are a factor buying a $100,000 invoice, and it will take less than 40 days to collect the money from the client's customer. As soon as you agree to buy the accounts receivable, you would advance, say, about 70 percent of the invoice immediately. So your client would collect $70,000 against the invoice within as little as 48 hours of the time you agreed to buy it.

You then go about the task of collecting the money from the client's customer. Because you will get your capital back relatively quickly, your fee would be relatively small. When you collect your $100,000, you send your client an additional $26,000 to settle the account. So, the client ends up with $96,000, and you earn $4,000 (4 percent) for keeping your money out on the street for less than 40 days.

However, sometimes invoices take more than 40 days to collect. The longer it takes to collect, the higher your fee is, because the more you deserve to earn on your investment. Given the same scenario as above, suppose it takes 70 days to collect the invoice. You would then send the client a check for $23,000 and keep $7,000 (7 percent) as your fee.

To be sure that the collection process goes as expected, the factor conducts professional credit checks on all the client's customers before buying the invoices from the issuer. Credit reports can be ordered from one of many credit bureaus that provide reports on businesses (not consumers or individuals).

In addition, most factors set up professional credit insurance. To evaluate a transaction, factors examine not only the client that comes to them with invoices to sell, but the strength of the receivables the client is selling as well. The factor then assumes the collection process, including mailing out the invoices.

In the final analysis, how much do you charge for factoring services? It depends. Factoring fees can range from as little as 2 percent per month to as much as a one-time fee of 18 percent off the face value of an invoice. The arrangement could be recourse or non-recourse for the client. Or, it could be recourse for some of your client's customers and non-recourse for others.

The bottom line is, you structure the arrangement and charge a fee that is appropriate in order for you to be competitive and still make a solid yield on your capital.

HOW THE "TIME VALUE OF MONEY" MULTIPLIES YOUR PROFITS IN FACTORING

The concept of the time value of money is central to understanding profitability in factoring, as it is with every other type of cash flow. The faster you collect your money, the higher your rate of return. In other words, if you borrow money at 10 percent over a one-year period of time, and pay that money back in less than one year, the rate of return to the person who gave you that loan will go up.

The following is an elementary example, but it demonstrates my point.

Suppose a guy named Pete gives a $100 loan to his friend, Cathy, but tells her, "When you pay me back, you have to pay $200."

Well, that's a rip-off for sure (the interest is 100 percent!), but at least it's easy to calculate as an example.

If Cathy decides to pay back the loan and shell out $200 after only two months, her interest will be 100 percent, or $100. However, to Pete, the person who gave her the loan, it's actually a 600 percent rate of return, because he gave up his money for only two months, not an entire year.

That simplistic example illustrates this important point: Factors earn a much higher yield than you might initially think, because of the time value of money.

For purposes of illustration, let's go back to the previous example. Your client has a $100,000 invoice to be collected within 50 to 70 days. So you advance the client $70,000 to begin with, then $23,000 when the invoice is collected. You keep 7 percent of $100,000 ($7,000) as your fee.

Now, suppose it takes you 60 days to collect the invoice. The yield you have actually earned is far greater than 7 percent. You haven't earned 7 percent in a year; you've earned 7 percent in *less than 60 days.* That's one-sixth of an entire year.

If you advance your $100,000 six times a year, and each time you earn $7,000, you'll end up generating $42,000 per year on your money. That's a 42 percent–plus rate of return!

Even 42 percent isn't entirely accurate, however. Your yield is even higher than that. As a factor, you advance only 70 percent of the full value of the invoices. To phrase it differently, you never really put up $100,000 of your own cash. You actually only advanced $70,000 of your own cash to control $100,000 worth of invoices.

So, $70,000 of your own money is earning a $7,000 fee every 60 days. That equals a 10 percent yield. If you circulate that money every 60 days, that totals a 60 percent–plus rate of return per year.

Sounds good, doesn't it? However, that's *still* not a completely accurate picture of the potential earnings. On $100,000 worth of invoices, the average length of collection in the industry is actually 50 *days,* not 60 days.

As a factor you can turn over your money over seven *or more* times per year (since 50 goes into 365 seven times). *Seven times a year at 10 percent each time is an annual return of 70-plus percent!*

One of the smallest factors I know started out a few years ago with $50,000 of his own money. Then he borrowed money from relatives and friends and obtained a bank line of credit. Now he has about $1 million a year to use for buying receivables. If he keeps 70 percent of that amount working continually, that amounts to over $350,000 in annual earnings, after expenses.

FIND YOUR UNIQUE FACTORING NICHE

Almost any type of business that has annual sales in the $500,000-to-$50-million range can benefit from factoring. That means there are vast opportunities for you to carve out your unique niche in the industry. Whether you work as a broker or a factor, you can look for niche industries and businesses in your area that are not currently being serviced by factors. Medical receivables, construction receivables, and international factoring are a few up-and-coming niches in factoring worth mentioning.

Medical Receivables

The medical receivables segment of the cash flow industry involves factoring accounts receivable specifically for health-care-related businesses. Factors that specialize in medical receivables deal with Medicare and Medicaid claims, insurance companies, workers' compensation, health management organizations (HMOs), and preferred provider organizers (PPOs).

In the medical industry, repayment can take anywhere from 60 to 120 days, whether the funds are coming from private insurance companies or government sources. Delays in receiving payment create serious cash flow problems for physicians and other health care providers. They often use up their bank lines of credit and have no other way to obtain additional financing. For that reason, medical receivables are a prime candidate for factoring. Through factoring, health care businesses can meet their expenses and even stimulate growth.

Laurie Javier, a former student of mine, recently shared a factoring success story involving a medical equipment company. The company, a dealer for durable equipment such as wheelchairs and hospital beds, sells its products to consumers, but is reimbursed by insurance companies and government agencies.

About two years ago the company began factoring $360,000 in net receivables per month. With the increased cash flow, the company was able to take advantage of significant early payment discounts as high as 25 *percent* offered by its product manufacturers. With these savings, the company increased its volume, and in turn, its sales. Soon the company was factoring $600,000 a month. Today, the company has opened two additional facilities, and each of the three facilities now factors *$2 million* in net receivables every month.

Virtually any businesses that provide services related to health care are excellent candidates for factoring. Specific health-care-related product and service providers you could target as a broker include physicians, diagnostic facilities, independent laboratories, physical therapy providers, home health care providers, or medical equipment companies.

Construction Receivables

Construction companies may seem like natural candidates for factoring. After all, when a construction company gets a new project, it has to have cash on hand to buy materials, pay contractors and subcontractors, and purchase equipment. Until recently, however, factors steered clear of funding construction receivables. It was simply too risky, because of the lien laws and the possibility of disputes with a contractor's work.

Today, factors have discovered ways to fund construction receivables. The key is for the construction project to meet the following criteria:

1. **The project must be non-residential.** Residential construction receivables are too high-risk. If the customer isn't satisfied with the contractor's work, it is likely he or she won't pay for it. Thus, factors do not want to buy the receivables for residential jobs.

The project, then, should be commercial or institutional. A large shopping center or office building would be an ideal candidate, for example. If the project has been contracted by the state or federal government, like a government building or schools, it's an even better prospect. Any scenario in which the government is the debtor is going to be safer than most, because the government always pays its debts—eventually!

2. **The contractor should be a large, national contractor with excellent credit.** Factors aren't willing to get involved if the contractor providing the work is a small general contractor.

3. **The contractor on the project must be bonded.** Factors generally will not fund projects in which the contractor is not bonded. On the other hand, any subcontractors on the job should NOT be bonded. That's because the bonding company has first position on receivables if a subcontractor is bonded.

4. **The contractor must NOT be a holding company or a limited partnership.** The contractor should listed as an individual for legal purposes.

The process of factoring construction receivables is more complicated than a conventional factoring transaction. But that's not necessarily bad news for you, since the factoring company handles the majority of the paperwork involved with the deal. If you broker construction receivables, then your main job is to scout out prospects and determine whether they are factorable.

If you pursue construction receivables as a niche, be aware that there are specific terms used in the construction industry. For example, construction jobs are billed not with an invoice but with a **progress billing.** A progress billing is a statement that lists all work that has been completed to date. Contractors bill their customers when one step of the job is completed, then bill again when the next step is completed.

In short, factoring of construction receivables has its challenges. On the other hand, it is wide-open market, with very few factoring brokers or factors specializing in the field.

International Factoring

International factoring is a third up-and-coming segment within the factoring industry. Only 4 percent of U.S. export business is being factored today. As world trade increases, and factoring becomes more widely employed, new opportunities will arise for cash flow brokers who are willing to expand internationally.

Mel Elliott, a graduate of my five-day intensive training course on factoring, recognized the potential profits in international factoring early on. Today he has established for himself a very lucrative niche in the industry, factoring domestically and globally with Alliance Capital Factoring in Boca Raton, Florida.

Factoring is an ideal solution for companies in need of a trouble-free procedure for financing export sales and collecting payment from buyers. Through factoring, exporters can maximize their cash flow, minimize their risks, and still provide flexible payment terms for their buyers.

Factoring facilitates the shipment of goods on "open account" (meaning without guarantee of payment). Importers usually prefer open account payment over a letter of credit, since a letter of credit ties up credit lines from a bank. In any event, when a bank refuses to issue a letter of credit, the open account option is the only alternative.

In an export factoring transaction, the factor (1) assumes responsibility for the customer's ability to pay; and (2) performs the necessary administrative duties associated with collecting the receivables. In most cases, export factors have developed vast business networks overseas and have extensive experience in the factoring business.

In the U.S., an exporter typically begins a factoring arrangement by contacting or being contacted by a U.S. factor that offers export services. The U.S. factor then requests a credit investigation on the importer from an affiliate (import) factor through an international correspondent factor network. Then, once the credit is approved locally, the exporter ships the goods on open account and submits the invoice to the export factor, who assumes the credit risk and the responsibility for collecting the receivables.

Like construction transactions, international factoring transactions are more complicated than domestic transactions, for obvious reasons. Language differences, political unrest, currency fluctuations, foreign laws, and local customs all influence international transactions. In addition, international transactions require more labor on the broker's end.

However, as a niche, international factoring has relatively few players in a huge and ever-expanding marketplace. Factors and factoring brokers who position themselves in international factoring today can rest assured that global economics will bolster the need for their services and the opportunity for substantial prosperity in the coming years.

RECAP

Let's quickly review the process that occurs in a factoring transaction:

- A broker locates a business with invoices for sale.
- The broker contacts a factor.
- The factor advances about 70 percent of the face value of the invoices.
- The factor collects the invoices from the business's customers.
- The factor advances the remaining 30 percent, less a fee.
- The broker earns a commission, typically a percentage of the factor's fee.

As you can see, the principle behind factoring is getting cash *today* for a payment due some time in the future. It's a recognizable principle, isn't it? It's the same dynamic at work in dozens of other cash flow transactions.

COMMERCIAL LEASES

If you've got a grip on the concepts behind transacting invoices and private mortgages, you'll recognize exactly the same principles at work in transacting commercial leases. A commercial lease is nothing more than another business-related income stream that can be sold for cash today. Transacting commercial leases applies many of the same processes you learned in Chapter Six regarding collateral-based income streams.

What is a commercial lease?

To rent an apartment or home, you have to sign a residential lease. The lease guarantees the property owner that you will pay rent on the property each month for a certain number of months, or else you will have to pay a penalty.

A **commercial lease** works the same way. The difference is that a commercial lease involves commercial property—office buildings, retail stores, and warehouses, for example—rather than residential property. Owners of commercial property establish leasing contracts with their tenants that range in length from several months to several years. The owner's tenants are then indebted to pay him or her a certain amount of rent income over the terms of the lease.

If you look at it from a cash flow perspective, a commercial lease is simply another type of debt instrument that creates an income stream flowing from the tenants to the property owner. In the secondary market, a property owner can sell off future lease payments rather than going through a bank to get capital.

Suppose a property owner needs $75,000 to replace the carpeting in a $3 million building. If the owner refinanced the mortgage through the bank, he would have to pay closing costs as high as $45,000 on top of the interest on the loan. Even if the owner simply borrowed the $75,000 with a conventional loan, he or she still would end up paying anywhere from $3,000 to $5,000 in closing costs and attorney's fees. As you can see, it makes a lot more sense for the owner to sell a portion of the future rents his tenants owe in exchange for an advance of the cash today.

Brokering Commercial Lease Payments

As a cash flow specialist, you can help commercial property owners get funding on the income generated by their leases. All you have to do is identify prospective lease sellers and connect them with buyers. As long as the owner can be trusted to hold up his or her end of the lease, and the tenants are locked into paying rent for the full term, the funding source can be assured of a steady flow of income.

Here's how a typical transaction works.

Suppose you talk to the owner of an office building. The owner is receiving a total of $10,000 each month from his tenants. In an effort to make his property more appealing to tenants, the owner has decided to make $45,000 of cosmetic enhancements.

As a cash flow broker, you locate a funding source that buys lease payments. The funding source offers to pay the property owner $45,000 in cash in exchange for half of the next 11 lease payments. For 11 months, the owner receives half of his lease payments, and the funding source receives the other half. After the 11 months are over, the property owner starts receiving his full lease payments again.

Once again, everybody wins. The owner receives $45,000 in cash, without the hassle of going to the bank. The funding source earns a $10,000 profit in just 11 months. And you receive a $1,000 fee for locating the transaction.

IDENTIFYING SELLERS

The good news about brokering commercial leases is that commercial property owners are very identifiable.

First, they have street visibility, meaning you can simply drive around your town, look for the buildings, and find out who owns the property.

Second, commercial property owners are required to hold permits. If you go to your local county or city government, you can obtain certificates of occupancy for all commercial establishments. You can choose properties based on the type of building, amount of square footage, and so forth, then write down the names and addresses of the owners of the buildings that fit your parameters.

Third, commercial leasing agents and real estate professionals specialize in commercial leases and are easy to identify as referral sources. You can locate them through the Yellow Pages or meet them personally in real estate networking groups.

Finally, miscellaneous organizations and associations of property owners, managers, and other real estate professionals have cropped up over the years. Through these forums, it is relatively easy to get the word out to the marketplace in your community that you provide services as a cash flow broker.

PROPERTIES TO TARGET

Two types of properties in particular are ideal for targeting prospective lease payments. The first type is office buildings of less than 75,000 square feet, with tenants who are professionals, such as doctors, lawyers, and accountants. The second is shopping centers with less than 150,000 square feet and tenants that are either national tenants or rateable tenants, such as retail chains, publicly traded companies, and government agencies.

Remember that with this cash flow, just as with factoring, the creditworthiness of the owner of the property is less important than the creditworthiness of the tenant. The funding source is purchasing the income stream paid by the tenant. If a tenant otherwise meets the requirements considered to be "factorable" or "rateable," a funding source would find it creditworthy for the purpose of buying its lease obligations.

Explaining Services and Gathering Information

When you locate a property owner who is interested in selling future income generated by a commercial lease, you proceed with gathering whatever information your funding source wants to know. This information could include financial or business information about the tenant, details about the property, and the terms of the lease.

A funding source would also want answers to such questions as:

- What type of property insurance does the property owner have?
- Are the tenants happy with the property owner? Is the owner accessible to them?
- What is the owner's business situation? Is the owner part of a corporation or partnership?
- Does the owner use a property management group?
- What are the owner's liabilities and cash flow needs?

As with any other income stream, you have to forward the one-page informational worksheet about the lease, the property owner, the property, and the tenant to your funding source.

Working with the Funding Source

If the funding source is interested in pursuing the transaction, the transaction will be structured in a safe way. You don't have to worry about the collection process or the risk that a tenant will stop making payments. The funding source takes care of those details. When the funding source closes the deal, you earn a one-time commission based on the size of the transaction.

THE FUTURE IN COMMERCIAL LEASES

Commercial lease payments are an attractive niche for cash flow brokers because of the availability and accessibility of prospects. In addition, they are attractive to funding sources for several reasons.

First, the commercial lease payment category offers a higher than market yield on invested capital. In some cases, that yield can be as high as 5 percentage to 10 percentage points above what could be expected on a private mortgage or other comparable income stream.

Second, the risk is relatively minimal to funding sources, because they only purchase lease payments being made by rateable, creditworthy tenants. Moreover, funding sources can lessen their exposure by:

- Limiting the payments it purchases to no more than 25 to 50 percent of the monthly cash flow.
- Purchasing no more than six to nine months of monthly payments.
- Buying lease payments only from rateable tenants.
- Ensuring that the property management is, at minimum, stable—and, preferably, longstanding in its history.
- Ensuring that a default on the part of the property owner, either in its obligations to lenders or tenants, is not likely.

And third, the fragmented marketplace for commercial lease payments makes the few players in the industry far more desirable for the services they perform.

Of all the debt instruments in the cash flow industry, commercial lease payments could prove to be one of the most profitable. Few funding sources and brokers have stepped up to the plate in this area, leaving the field wide open for new entrants. Moreover, the income stream is new and evolving. This opens the door for new entrants to have a serious impact on how this segment of the industry develops.

Funding sources appear to be showing interest and excitement in the commercial lease area. Recently, a large institutional funding source involved in private mortgages set aside $60 million just to test the commercial lease segment of the market. That type of eagerness leaves substantial opportunity for us all.

Remember These Highlights

- In nearly every type of commercial transaction, the invoice is the basis for payment. An invoice creates a payment stream from one business to another business.
- The term "accounts receivable" is often used interchangeably with invoices. Accounts receivable means a list of all the invoices that have been sent to a business's customers.
- Factoring is the purchase of accounts receivable from a business for a reduced amount. Factoring is not a loan, but an outright purchase.
- Factoring offers a number of advantages over bank financing.
- The most lucrative factoring niche is businesses that produce $500,000 to $50 million a year in sales. These businesses typically do not have access to capital through banks.
- Factoring brokers earn a fee by locating clients and placing their invoices with factors.
- Factors earn a yield by buying invoices, collecting on them, and charging a fee.
- Commercial lease payments are an income stream created when tenants pay a commercial property owner.
- Property owners can sell off future lease payments for cash instead of going to a bank to get capital, which in many cases is more costly.
- To broker lease payments, you simply identify prospective lease sellers and connect them with buyers.

CHAPTER EIGHT

When Bad Debt Is a Good Investment

Do you cringe when you hear the word "debt"? When you're in the cash flow industry, you don't have to. In the cash flow business, "debt" presents tremendous opportunities for you to *make money*. In this chapter, I'll explain why.

In the industry, we divide debt into two broad categories—**consumer debt** and **commercial debt.** The definitions are simple common sense. Consumer debt refers to debt owed by individual consumers; commercial debt describes debt owed by businesses. Both types of debt can be transacted in the cash flow industry.

When a debt is not paid on time, we refer to it as a **delinquent debt** or **bad debt.** As you might expect, the odds of collecting on delinquent debt decline significantly over time. According to statistics, the chances of collecting a bill that's overdue decline by about 25 percent after two months. The odds drop by about 40 percent after six months. And after one year, there is only a 25 percent chance of ever collecting a delinquent debt.

Obviously, bad debt means trouble for businesses—but it represents a very profitable niche of cash flow for you. By brokering and buying consumer and commercial debt, you can provide a valuable service to businesses and earn significant fees or yields for yourself.

Three Types of Debt

In the cash flow industry, we divide debt into three performance categories: performing debt, sub-performing debt, and non-performing debt.

Performing debt is debt that is no more than 30 days delinquent. These accounts are only slightly overdue.

The next level—**sub-performing debt**—is debt that is from 30 to 120 days delinquent. These accounts are labor-intensive and expensive for companies to maintain.

Finally, **non-performing debt** is debt that is more than 120 days delinquent. If delinquency extends beyond 180 days, companies can take a charge-off for the debt. The account then gets deducted as a loss. It may be placed with a collection agency, sold to an investor, or simply written off and forgotten in the company's computer archives.

In this chapter, I will be referring to this last category of debt—non-performing debt.

Consumer Debt

"No Money Down—No Interest for 12 Months!" How many times have you seen that phrase in recent advertisements? Consumer debt in America is up to $1.2 trillion today. Virtually every bank, retail store, and gas station in America offers credit to its customers. Consequently, many credit customers go into default, leaving businesses with hundreds of millions of dollars of delinquent debt.

Nearly every type of business that sells to consumers ends up with bad debt. And those businesses rarely collect on it. The bad news is, a lot of people owe money and aren't paying. The good news is, this creates a tremendous opportunity for you as a cash flow broker or investor.

As a cash flow broker, you can place large portfolios of consumer debt with funding sources that specialize in buying them. The types of non-performing consumer debt funding sources purchase include:

- Bank credit cards
- Vendor credit cards
- Student loans (non-GSL colleges, universities, trade and vocational schools)
- Retail installment contracts
- Delinquent medical receivables
- Bad checks
- Delinquent automobile loans
- Travel club and health club memberships
- Judgments

Let's take a closer look at three types of non-performing consumer debt you can broker in the secondary market: credit card charge-offs, student loans, and retail installment contracts. (Student loans and retail installment contracts in particular represent a lucrative area of cash flow, regardless of whether or not the accounts are delinquent. However, in this section we will approach these debt instruments from the point of view of delinquent debt.)

Credit Card Charge-Offs

A credit card charge-off is created when a bank decides it is no longer profitable to collect on their customers' outstanding credit card debt. Cash flow investors can buy these charge-offs for pennies on the dollar. And banks will accept these offers—because they have nothing to lose. *Any money they can get is better than none.* Funding sources who purchase credit card debt usually do so in bulk at a very high discount.

Student Loans

Everyone knows that colleges and universities—both public and private—offer student loans. But what about privately-owned truck driving schools, culinary institutes, bartending schools, and other technical or vocational schools? Nearly all of them offer some type of in-house financing to their students. And chances are, many of them have offered loans that haven't been repaid.

Retail Installment Contracts

A retail installment contract is an agreement between a retailer and a customer to pay for goods over time. They are the latest craze among retailers these days. Many retailers—especially those who sell such big-ticket items as a furniture, stereo equipment, jewelry, satellite dishes, and appliances—offer installment payment plans to their customers. Some of customers, attracted to the opportunity to buy with "no money down," are likely to default on their payments.

Make Money as a Broker

Delinquent debt provides a lucrative opportunity for investing. And any time there's an opportunity for investing, there's an opportunity for brokering.

Here's how a typical bad debt transaction works. Let's say I own a major appliance business. I have hundreds of customers who have purchased washers, dryers, stereos, and other equipment on credit, but haven't paid me. Over the course of about a year or two, I've accumulated $200,000 worth of bad debts.

Now, you're a cash flow broker. You approach me and offer to liquidate those debts for cash.

How much cash?

What difference does it make?

The fact is, those bad debts are just sitting in my file cabinet anyway. I'm not going to collect on them. I'm delighted to have the opportunity to sell any of my bad debts to somebody else. The fact of the matter is, I've already written off those debts. Any money I can get for them is better than none at all.

After gathering some specific information about the debt, you connect me with a funding source. The funding source investigates the creditors that owe my business money, and agrees to pay me $20,000 for those $200,000 worth of bad debts.

I end up with $20,000 cash (which is more than I ever expected to get in the first place). The funding source gets the right to collect $200,000 worth of debts. And you get a commission of $1,000 for locating the transaction.

Everybody walks away a winner.

Identifying a Seller

Where do you go to buy non-performing consumer debt? The accounts receivable department of virtually any business with consumer delinquencies that are at least 90 days past due. In many cases, businesses have delinquent debt that is several years old. They do not want the hassle of pursuing collection on those debts.

Your best prospects are businesses that generate consumer delinquencies on an ongoing basis, because they will produce repeat business for you. The best prospects to target include banks, private colleges and vocational schools, utility companies, hospitals, clinics, physicians' offices, retailers, and large chains of funeral homes.

Another way to locate prospects is by networking with corporate CPAs, collection agencies, and collection attorneys. They often know when a credit issuer is about to write off an account or a full portfolio of delinquent accounts.

Explaining Services and Gathering Information

When you locate a potential delinquent debt seller, the next step is to explain your service. Many business owners do not even know it's possible to *sell* their debt. They may assume you offer collection services rather than cash flow services. You have to explain that you work with institutional funding sources that *buy* bad debt portfolios for cash.

There are two primary benefits of selling delinquent debt.

First, it provides immediate cash for the business. The business no longer has to wait to collect a percentage of the accounts when—and if—they are paid.

Second, selling delinquent accounts takes the collection burden off the business's shoulders. Few businesses have expertise in collections or in-house employees to handle collections. By selling bad accounts, they no longer have to tackle the collection process.

The next step is to point out how selling delinquent accounts to a funding source differs from selling to a collection agency. First, a funding source will pay cash on every legally collectible account. Second, selling delinquent accounts removes the seller from the picture entirely. If the business subcontracts debt collections to an agency, rather than selling the debt, the business remains in an ownership and liability position on the accounts.

If your prospect decides to move forward with the transaction, you will gather information regarding:

- The type of debt (credit card, student loan, installment contract, etc.)
- The size of the portfolio (number of accounts, average size account, total size)
- Aging of the accounts (how long the debt has been delinquent)
- Previous collection efforts
- Collateral (if any collateral is involved)

Marilyn and Larry Singer, founders of Capital Funding Group in Buffalo, New York, specialize in brokering and purchasing delinquent debt. According to the Singers, the most attractive portfolios to funding sources are large portfolios (worth $200,000 or more) with numerous debtors involved, and on which collections have been attempted only once or twice. The higher the number of debtors and the fewer the collection efforts, the higher the chances that a significant portion of the debt can be collected.

Working with a Funding Source

Your primary role as a broker is to introduce your client to the funding source. However, you also may coordinate the exchange of information and documentation. The funding source will take care of negotiating the price and contract terms and will handle all of the closing procedures. In most cases, funding sources make an offer on the debt portfolio within just a few days.

Funding sources typically pay between half a cent and ten cents on the dollar for a debt portfolio, depending on the collectibility of the debt. When the seller and the funding source agree on a price, the seller legally assigns ownership of the debt to the funding source. At that point, the seller releases contact information on each debtor.

When the transaction is complete, the funding source sends you a check. Usually commissions are about 5 percent of the purchase price the funding source pays the seller for the debt. Suppose, for example, you locate a company that sells $800,000 of delinquent credit card debt for 9 cents on the dollar. The funding source pays $72,000 for the debt. They in turn pay you a referral fee of $3,600 for locating the transaction.

The table below reflects typical brokerage commissions:

DELINQUENT DEBT BROKERAGE COMMISSIONS

If Funding Source Pays	Then You Make
$20,000	$1,000
$50,000	$2,500
$100,000	$5,000

MAKE MONEY AS AN INVESTOR

The second profit opportunity in bad debt lies is in buying portfolios for your own account. Let's look at another example.

Suppose I own a business and have $500,000 worth of delinquent debt. In this scenario, you have capital to invest, so you decide to buy the debt yourself rather than brokering it to a funding source. You negotiate to pay me 5 cents on the dollar (or $25,000) for the $500,000 worth of debt.

After you purchase the debt, you can either (1) attempt to collect on it; or (2) resell it to another investor or collections agency for a profit.

Suppose you decide to collect on it yourself. If you are able to collect just 20 percent of the debt from the business's delinquent customers, you would collect $100,000, for a total profit of $75,000.

In the alternative, suppose you decide to resell the debt. You immediately locate another investor who is willing to pay $35,000 for the $500,000 worth of debt. You earn a profit of $10,000.

Either way, delinquent debt offers massive investment leverage, because of the significant discount taken on the front end.

As you might expect, there are unique challenges involved with collecting bad debt. Funding sources who buy delinquent debt must contact the individuals who owe the money and negotiate with them to pay. The risk is compounded by the fact that a bank and possibly even a collection agency already have attempted to collect the money with no success.

Because of the risk issues, funding sources who purchase delinquent debt do so only at a very high discount. However, they also earn a healthy profit. According to one cash flow professional who specializes in debt, you can earn a return as high as 200 percent to 300 percent on your investment.

The most attractive types of consumer debt to buy are credit card and charge-offs, student loans, retail installment contracts, and delinquent medical receivables. Bad checks, deficiency balances, and legal-related debts are the least desirable.

Why Buy Delinquent Debt?

When I lecture, people often ask, "Why is it that anyone would want to buy a debt that has already been written off as uncollected?"

That's a good question. Let's look at it from the consumer's standpoint.

First, people tend to believe that because somebody can't pay a debt today, he or she is not going to be able to pay tomorrow. The truth of the matter is, *most people change. Circumstances* change. A person who can't afford to pay today because of a job loss may find a new job in a matter of months. A person who can't afford to pay today because of medical bills, a disability, or a death in the family, may be able to pay three years from now. *Just because a person can't pay today doesn't mean he can never pay.*

Second, people assume that once someone is delinquent in paying debts, that's the way he or she wants it to be. That is usually not the case. The old concept of "deadbeats" doesn't hold true anymore. Most people aren't deadbeats; they are circumstantially in a bad situation. If given the opportunity, most would like to take care of their financial commitments and clean up their credit.

FOCUS ON CREDIT RESTORATION

If you pursue delinquent debt as a cash flow niche, don't focus on "collections." Focus on helping people clean up their financial situation in a way that restores their credit. Just because people can't afford to pay a debt today, that doesn't mean they don't have an interest in getting their credit restored.

When you buy a debt for half a cent to five cents on a dollar, you are in a position to restore someone's credit for a whole lot less than face value and still make an enormous profit. Suppose, for example, you buy a $5,000 debt for $250. You contact the individual who owes the debt and say, "You owe $5,000. Tell you what—I'll give you a clean bill of health if you'll write me a check for $1,000."

From the debtor's standpoint, you have provided an incredible offer. For just 20 percent of his initial $5,000 debt, he can have it paid off in full, reported as "satisfied" on his credit report, and leave it behind forever. From your standpoint, you have turned a $250 investment into a $1,000 return with just a few phone calls or letters.

That same principle holds true even if the statute of limitations on the debt has already run out. The statute of limitations is the length of time the owner of a debt has to file a lawsuit for collection of a debt. (See the Resources section for the statute of limitations in each state.) Even if the statute of limitations is up, and the debt holder cannot sue the debtor, that doesn't mean the debtor doesn't want to restore his or her credit. After all, the debt can still be reported as unpaid to credit reporting agencies. By paying off the debt, the debtor can get that negative mark taken off of his or her credit report.

In short, when you focus on credit restoration, you are turning lemons into lemonade. You provide cash for a business that has already taken a write-off for its bad debt, you help a debtor restore his or her credit, and you earn a substantial yield for yourself. Bad debt, like other cash flow instruments, is a win-win-win for everyone.

COMMERCIAL DEBT

Commercial debt transactions operate the same way as consumer debt transactions. The main difference is that commercial debt involves money owed by businesses, usually to other businesses. Commercial debt portfolios are significantly larger than consumer debt portfolios, so unless you have quite a bit of money to invest, your primary profit opportunity is in brokering them.

Let's look at a sample commercial debt transaction. Suppose that instead of an appliance store, I own a printing business. I have several business customers who have ordered printing, but haven't paid their invoices. Over the course of about a year or two, I've accumulated $100,000 worth of bad debts from those customers.

As a cash flow broker, you offer to find a funding source willing to purchase my bad debt. Once again, I've already written off those debts, so any cash I can get for them is better than none at all.

You locate a funding source that buys my $100,000 worth of bad debt for $8,000. When the transaction closes, the funding source sends you a referral fee of $400. The funding source then takes on the responsibility of collecting on the debts from my customers.

The same considerations apply to transacting commercial debt as consumer debt. The main distinction is that credit restoration is only a motivator if the debtor is still in business or still has assets.

As long as a company that owes the debt is still in business, there's value to credit restoration. The business owner has a desire to pay off old debts in order to maintain or restore the business's good credit. However, if a company goes out of business, the owner may not see a need to repay that debt.

On the other hand, even when a debtor company goes out of business, there could very well be a profit opportunity obtaining assets through the bankruptcy courts or legal process. However, those strategies are sophisticated, and the techniques that govern them are best learned after you have been in this business for several years.

REMEMBER THESE HIGHLIGHTS

- There are two broad categories of delinquent debt—consumer debt and commercial debt. Both types of can be brokered and bought in the secondary marketplace.
- There are three subcategories of delinquent debt: performing debt (no more than 30 days delinquent), sub-performing debt (30 to 120 days delinquent), and non-performing debt (more than 120 days delinquent).
- Businesses often sell their delinquent debt portfolios for pennies on the dollar. As a cash flow broker, you can broker these debt portfolios to funding sources and earn a fee. As a cash flow investor, you can buy these portfolios and either resell them or attempt to collect on them.
- If you pursue delinquent debt as an investor, approach it from the standpoint of credit restoration. By buying bad debt for a fraction of the amount owed, you can restore consumers' credit and make a profit, too.
- Commercial debt transactions operate the same way as consumer debt transactions. The main difference is that commercial debt involves money owed by businesses to other businesses.

CHAPTER NINE

WIN A SHARE OF THE LOTTERY WITHOUT EVEN PLAYING

HAVE YOU OR SOMEONE YOU KNOW ever won the lottery?

Would you like to?

You can!

When people win a lottery, the events that follow typically play out something like this. First, you see them on the news holding one of those enormous five-foot checks, surrounded by spotlights and cameras.

"This is great," they say into a microphone, "but I'm still going to work tomorrow morning, and I'm still going to live in the same neighborhood."

Sure enough, they show up at work the following day, just as usual. They tell their friends and colleagues that they're going to buy Mom a nice new Cadillac, but nothing else is going to change.

Several weeks go by, and they show up every day.

Then, they get their first check.

The next day, they don't show. They don't even call!

I recall seeing in the newspaper a photo of a New York City sanitation worker who had won $10 million in the New York lottery. In the photo, the man was tossing a bag of trash into a garbage truck. The caption underneath read, "Still plans to haul trash for two years until his pension kicks in." I don't know about you, but I have a hard time believing that guy tossed another bag of trash after he got his first lottery check!

What would *you* do if you won a million-dollar jackpot? Quit your job? Build a house on a small island in the Pacific? Buy a private jet?

Sorry to burst your bubble, but if you won $1 million in the lottery, chances are you couldn't do any of those things. You couldn't even buy a $500,000 new home. At least not right away.

Why not?

Because in most states, lottery payments aren't paid out all at once—they are paid in yearly installments over 10 to 26 years. If you won one million dollars, paid out over 26 years, your prize would work out to just over $36,000 a year. A mere $36,000 a year—and that's before taxes! Considering that, would you still quit your job?

If you won $1 million, I'm sure you'd be pleased. But face it: Getting $36,000 a year for the next 26 years *is not the same* as getting $1 million in cash today.

For one thing, you wouldn't have access to all of your million-dollar prize. The first year, you would have access to only $36,000 of it. Meanwhile, the purchasing power of payments you would receive in the future would decrease with each passing year. While prices would continue to go up, your annual payment would stay the same. By the time you received your last $36,000 payment, it would be worth about one-third of what it would be worth today.

It's really no wonder that even multimillion-dollar lottery winners end up going broke. First of all, a typical lottery winner is a bit of a gambler. He or she obviously must have *played* the lottery in the first place in order to win it. Second of all, lottery winners typically do not have a lot of experience managing money—large or small.

The first year, they have to struggle to spend their prize. It's more money than they've ever had before. By the second year, they start getting pretty good at it. By the third year, they've got it down cold. In fact, by May of the third year, they often find themselves with no money for the rest of the year, and no job.

Eventually, their annual payments stop all together, of course. If they haven't done some top-notch financial planning, they are left with nothing.

When you weigh the facts, it's easy to see why lottery winners often seek a way to cash in their promised payment stream for a lump sum of cash. With one large sum, they can pay off debts, get an education, start a business, buy their dream home, hire a good financial planner and prepare ahead for the day when the payments stop.

This need to "cash in" lottery winnings creates a promising opportunity for people like you to broker those winnings. Brokering the winnings on just one lottery prize could bring you an entire year's worth of income. It's *the way* to get a slice of the lottery pie without having to buy a ticket.

The Lottery Transaction

To see how a lottery transaction works, let's look at a real-life example of a transaction one of my students handled.

A few years ago, a family won a $6 million lottery. Their prize, paid out over 20 years, worked out to $300,000 a year. As you might expect, $300,000 was more cash than those people had ever encountered at one time. The first year, they couldn't spend it all. They literally didn't know how, because they weren't used to it.

However, by the second year, they had gotten lots of practice, and had figured out how to spend it very well—so well, in fact, that by July they had only $5,000 left of their $300,000 payment.

They panicked.

What do you think they did first?

They ran to their accountant for advice. The accountant asked if they had prepaid their mortgage. ("No.") He asked if they had prepaid their kids' college tuition. ("No.") So, the accountant asked, what had they done with all that money? The family couldn't exactly remember.

Finally, the accountant asked them how much income they really needed each year to maintain a reasonable, though not extravagant, lifestyle. After thinking it over for a moment, the family came up with a number.

The accountant determined that in order to generate that amount of money annually through investments, plus pay off their home, debts, and taxes, they would need a lump sum of just over $1 million. At that point, remember, the family didn't have $1 million; they had $5,000. But the accountant told them he might know someone who could help them. He contacted a cash flow broker.

The accountant gave the broker his client's name and phone number. The broker then called the family to discuss options. He asked them some questions and filled out an informational worksheet. As soon as he hung up the phone, the broker contacted a funding source that specialized in buying lottery payments. He explained to the funding source what the family was trying to accomplish.

The family had collected payments for two years already, so they had 18 years of payments remaining. Because the family needed only $1 million, the funding source proposed a bid for the next eight annual lottery payments, rather than all 18. The funding source made the broker an offer to buy the next eight years of payments for $1,368,465.

The broker called back the family to tell them the good news. He offered them a bid of *$1,320,465* in exchange for the next eight annual payments. At the end of eight years, they would start getting their annual payments of $300,000 again. Needless to say, they eagerly accepted the bid, and the deal closed.

Granted, the family would have received a total of $2,400,000 instead of $1,320,465 over the long run if they had they waited another eight years. But what they needed in order to make some solid financial plans was a *lump sum*.

The family walked away a winner, because they were able to get a lump sum of more than $1.3 million that they could spend and invest. In addition, they knew that after eight years, they would receive 10 more annual payments of $300,000.

The funding source walked away a winner, because over eight years, it made almost $1.1 million in earnings on a $1.3 million investment.

Finally, the broker walked away a winner. *The broker—who sim-*

ply connected the seller with the buyer—made $48,000 on that transaction. And he made it without putting up any of his own capital.

Brokering Lottery Winnings

The primary money-making opportunity for you in lottery winnings is in brokering them rather than buying them. (Lottery prizes simply are too large for most individual investors to buy.) If you broker lottery winnings, you can earn commissions in the tens of thousands of dollars on a *single transaction.* And you can use the same cash flow system to do it. All you have to do is (1) locate lottery winners; (2) explain your services; and (3) connect them with funding sources.

Identifying Lottery Winners

The majority of states—38 in fact—have adopted lotteries as revenue producers. Even states that don't allow gambling have voted to permit lotteries.

Not all states permit the assignment of lottery proceeds. In fact, out of the 38 states that have lotteries, only 16 states permit their assignment. However, the trend is moving toward assignability. It's just a question of time before all states permit the assignment of lottery proceeds. In the Resources section, you will find a list of the states that have lotteries as well as those that currently permit their assignment.

States have discovered the best way to produce big lottery jackpots: start out with a big lottery prize for the first couple of winners, then decrease the size of the awards and *increase* the number of winners. *As a result, there are more winners now than ever before.* Most of those winners have no idea that cashing in their prize for a lump sum is an option in many states. Your job is to get the word out to them.

So how do you go about finding lottery winners? Primarily by networking. If you focus on lottery winnings as a cash flow niche, you should tell everyone you know, in social and business circles, about the service you provide. You can also try networking with professionals likely to come in contact with winners, such as estate planners, accountants, and lawyers.

The truth is, you never know where your referrals will come from.

Take Inger Jensen, for example. Inger first heard about the cash flow industry when she was going to school to study business management. After completing one of my training programs and attending a cash flow convention, she decided to broker lottery winnings.

Inger attended a Black Expo convention and did some networking. That's how she met her first lottery winner—and brokered her first lottery transaction. *That one transaction netted her a $51,500 brokerage fee.* And that amount was only *her half* of the total fee. She had collaborated with another broker to complete the transaction, for a total fee of $103,000.

Another way you can locate lottery winners is by researching stories about them in the media. Check current newspapers and magazines, as a well as previously run stories about new and old winners. Or run a simple advertisement in the classified section of the newspaper to increase your prospects. In your ad, let people know what you offer and how they can contact you.

Finally, you can try to get stories about your service published in a newspaper or newsletter. This will increase interest and awareness, as well as educate the public.

EXPLAINING SERVICES

Generally, people who have recently won a substantial amount of money in the lottery are not inclined to sell their income stream. They tend to be more receptive a few years later—after the initial thrill of winning has worn off and problems have set in. By that time, they realize there is a limit to the amount of money they will receive annually, and they know they have to plan ahead for the year the payments stop coming. They start looking for an opportunity to convert their lottery payments into an investment alternative—after they have paid off and paid for their lifestyle needs. Cashing in all or some of their payments gives them the opportunity to buy a house for cash, fund their children's education, live within a budget, and take care of other financial planning needs.

The point is, when you locate lottery winners, you don't have to do a lot of explaining. They either want a lump sum for their annual payments, or they don't. If they do, all you have to do is collect basic information about the total amount of their prize, the amount of their annual payments, the number of payments they have coming to them, and how much cash they need.

A lottery winner doesn't have to cash in *all* of his or her winnings at one time. Remember the concept of the "partial"? A lottery payment transaction is most often structured as a partial. In that case, a funding source gives the seller a lump sum for five to eight years of payments. At the end of the five- to eight-year period, the winner can choose to cash in more payments or start receiving his or her annual lottery payments again.

Working with a Funding Source

Many of the same funding sources that buy private mortgages and insurance payments (which we'll discuss in the next chapter) also purchase lottery winnings. Their experts understand lottery transactions inside and out; they know all the legal and financial issues involved. Your role is simply to send them referrals; they handle the rest. When the transaction closes (usually three to four weeks later), you earn your fee.

You can structure your fee one of two ways. First, you can negotiate your own fee and build it into the offer you make the lottery payment seller. In other words, if the funding source offers to buy a certain number of payments for $1,800,000, you might offer your client $1,742,000. When the transaction closes, you would earn the difference—$58,000. The most experienced cash flow brokers tend to use this fee structure, because they are more closely involved in the details of the transaction.

Second, you can receive a "finder's fee" based on a percentage of what the funding source offers the seller. That percentage ranges from 3 percent to 5 percent of the amount of money the funding sources advances. Brokers that operate primarily as referral sources typically are paid according to this structure.

Either way, brokerage fees for lottery transactions can add up to astronomical figures, as you can see from the following table:

TYPICAL BROKERAGE FEES ON LOTTERY TRANSACTIONS

Funding Source Pays	You Make
$500,000	$15,000 to $25,000
$1,000,000	$30,000 to $50,000
$2,000,000	$60,000 to $100,000

In my experience, most cash flow brokers don't *specialize* in transacting lotteries, but do keep an eye open for lottery opportunities. The disadvantage of specializing in lotteries is the infrequency of the transaction in the course of a year. The advantage, of course, is the substantial amount of the broker fee, when and if a transaction closes.

On the other hand, lottery transaction can be combined with other cash flow specialties to provide an occasional spike to earnings. My graduates Jim and Shannon Hancock of San Diego, for example, focused primarily on mortgage notes, business notes, and boat notes when they started their cash flow business. Nonetheless, they managed to close a lottery deal as one of their very first transactions. That single transaction netted them $30,000 in fee income.

Clearly, no astute cash flow broker passes up the opportunity for a lottery transaction when it becomes available.

REMEMBER THESE HIGHLIGHTS

- Lottery payments are seldom paid out all at once. Usually, they are paid in yearly installments over 10 to 26 years.
- Many lottery winners find themselves in a financial crisis in the third or fourth year of receiving payments and often seek a way to cash in payments for a lump sum.
- Lottery winners' need to "cash in" lottery payments creates a promising money-making opportunity in brokering those winnings.
- A lottery payment transaction is frequently structured as a partial. The funding source gives the seller a lump sum of cash for five to

ten years of payments. At the end of the five- to ten-year period, the winner can choose to cash in more payments or start receiving the annual lottery payments again.

- Fees for brokering transactions range from 3 to 5 percent of the amount of money the funding sources advances.

CHAPTER TEN

Turn Your Neighbor's Insurance Policy into Profit

INSURANCE. Is it any wonder it has a bad name?

Auto insurance, life insurance, homeowner's insurance—each month we pay out hundreds of dollars in insurance premiums, just for peace of mind. We know if we're lucky, we'll never see that money again. That's how insurance companies make a profit: The money we receive in claims is nowhere near the amount of money we have paid out in premiums over the years—especially when you factor in the time value of money and lost investment income. Those premiums we pay today create investment capital that insurance companies invest for earnings tomorrow.

In the cash flow industry, "insurance" isn't a bad thing. On the contrary, insurance payments offer you a tremendous opportunity to help others and earn a living at the same time.

Why? Because, like many other cash flows in this book, insurance payments are just another type of income stream owed to you and millions of others just like you.

The cash flow industry is opening up a world of financial options related to insurance. Even if you do not pursue these income streams as a cash flow niche, you need to read this chapter. Your knowledge of these options could prove invaluable to both you and your family.

Viatical settlements, annuities, and structured settlements are three types of insurance-related income streams you can broker in many states. All involve payments coming from an insurance company and directed to an individual.

Viatical Settlements

Over the years, Mike, a retired factory supervisor, has paid thousands of dollars into his life insurance policy. Mike knows that the policy isn't intended for his own future enjoyment—it's intended to provide for his beneficiaries.

Recently, Mike was diagnosed with terminal cancer. He has run up a stack of medical bills in the process of trying every possible treatment: surgery, chemotherapy, you name it. Mike's physician, however, has informed him that the treatments aren't working, and he probably has only a year and a half to live.

"There's nothing left to try," the doctor tells him. "So just go home and enjoy the time you have left with your family and friends."

In the meantime, Mike's financial resources are running out. He had to sell off a number of investments just to pay his hospital bills. He's not wondering how to enjoy the next year. He's wondering how he's even going to make it without leaving his wife destitute. In addition to the physical and emotional stress he's suffering, Mike has serious financial concerns.

If only he could get cash now for his life insurance policy, he thinks. He could use the cash to settle his debts and do some estate planning. He could even take his grandson on one last trip, maybe to the Grand Canyon.

✦ ✦ ✦

The truth is, there is a way Mike *can* get cash today for his life insurance policy. It's called a viatical settlement.

A **viatical settlement** is an arrangement in which a terminally ill or chronically ill person sells his or her life insurance benefits for a lump sum payment—thereby receiving cash for an otherwise nonliquid, inaccessible asset. During the past few years, an entire segment of the cash flow industry has risen up around viatical settlements. All types of life insurance policies can now be viated: whole life, term, universal, and even group life insurance from an employer.

In a viatical settlement transaction, a funding source (called a viatical settlement company, or "provider") pays cash to the insured for the right to name itself beneficiary of the policy. The purchase price for the policy is discounted from its face value based on the life expectancy of the insured. Then, the funding source continues to pay future premiums to keep the policy in force, if it is not already paid up. The funding sources makes a profit when the death benefit is collected.

Let's look at the example of Mike again.

Suppose Mike's policy is worth $100,000. After consulting its life expectancy tables, the funding source offers Mike $68,000 cash in exchange for his policy. Mike receives his cash, which he can use for whatever he pleases. In the meantime, the funding source continues to pay Mike's insurance premium. At the time of Mike's death, the funding source receives the death benefit on Mike's policy.

To see how it works, refer to the visual representation on p. 199.

Although the idea of making money from someone's shortened life span may seem unusual—and possibly distasteful—viatical settlements fulfill a very serious need. They provide much-needed money for the terminally ill. That money, in turn, allows men and women to live the balance of their lives with a sense of security, control, dignity, and financial independence. Viatical settlement options can truly lift a burden often borne by those individuals' families.

Why won't life insurance companies allow dying individuals to cash in their policies?

In some cases, they will, if a particular rider is already in place. However, they often limit payment to 50 *percent or less* of the policy's value, and stipulate a physician-certified life expectancy of only six

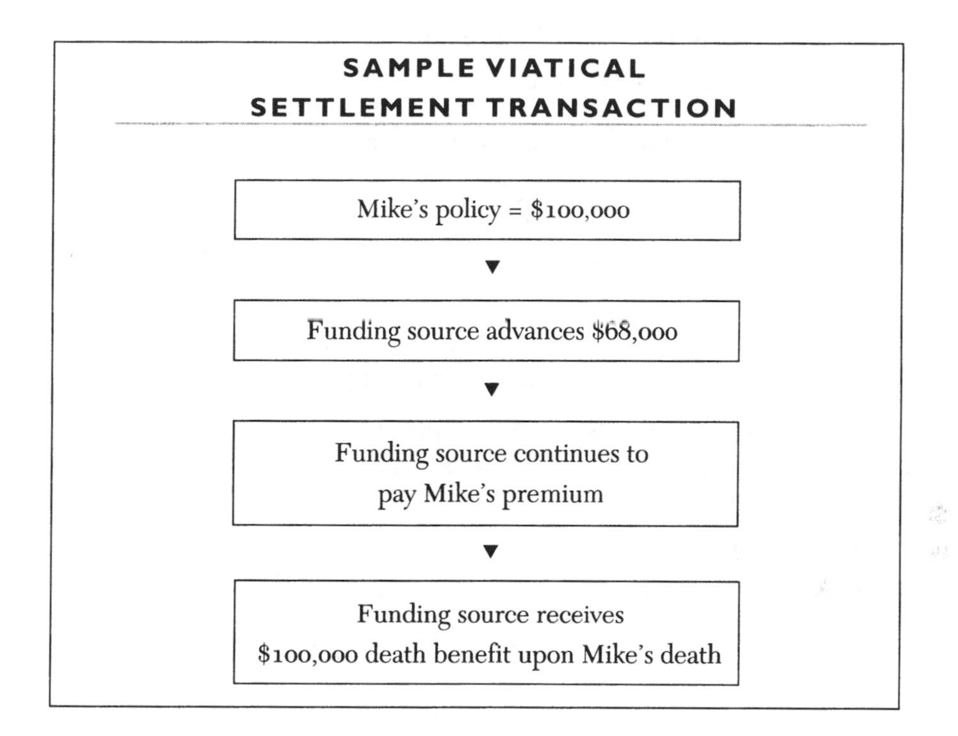

months. In addition, insurance companies sometimes impose restrictions on how the funds can be spent.

Viatical settlement companies, on the other hand, can offer a fair rate of return on the death benefit, because they know they will collect their money eventually—it's just a question of time. Unlike insurance companies, viatical settlement companies can viate policies on individuals with a life expectancy as high as two years. Moreover, viatical settlements carry no restrictions as to the disbursement of funds once they are transmitted to the terminally ill individual.

When a funding source buys life insurance benefits, it performs exactly the same function as an insurance company, but in reverse. A life insurance company prices its policy based on the average life expectancy for a man or woman. When conditions warrant it, a viatical funding source discounts a policy down to present-day value based on that same actuarial scale or a specific medical report. The only difference is the funding source that buys the policy doesn't penalize the individual for cashing it in early.

THE HISTORY OF THE VIATICAL SETTLEMENT INDUSTRY

Viatics, as a separate segment of the cash flow industry, literally emerged because of a radio talk show.

In 1986, Rob Worley, an insurance agent from New Mexico, heard a talk show featuring a terminally ill man who had tried, unsuccessfully, to sell his life insurance policy for *half its face value.* The story intrigued Worley, and he contacted several insurance companies to ask if they ever received similar requests. They did—an average of seven a week, in fact. Worley recognized an opportunity to provide an invaluable service to terminally ill individuals and started a viatical settlement company in 1989.

In the beginning, viatical settlements were used primarily as a financial option for AIDS patients. AIDS victims, with a clear-cut terminal illness, were unable to get the resources they needed for medical and living expenses at a critical time. Eventually, viatical settlement options were extended to victims of other terminal illnesses, such as cancer and leukemia.

Historically, viatical settlements have been the subject of scrutiny by the IRS because they involve a lump-sum payout. In 1996, however, President Clinton signed into law the Health Insurance Portability and Accountability Act, which contained a provision granting terminally ill individuals the right to sell their life insurance policies for a lump-sum payment—*tax free.*

Before the legislation was in place, it was difficult to determine whether the IRS viewed a viatical settlement as a taxable event. Now that the new law has passed, more people will likely consider viatical settlements as a financial option.

BREAKTHROUGHS IN THE VIATICAL SETTLEMENT INDUSTRY

Two recent developments in the viatical settlement industry are increasing public awareness of the viatical option.

In 1996, a handful of viatical settlement companies pioneered a brand-new market—viating life insurance policies for elderly men and women. The practice thus far has been limited to men and women over age 85. However, the option may be extended to those between 75 and 85 who have been diagnosed with certain chronic medical conditions.

The number of American citizens over 75 is significant today, and will continue to multiply according to current aging patterns. Within this rapidly growing market, the need for flexible financial options is widespread. The elderly often have more money going out than they have coming in. They may receive a few hundred dollars each month from Social Security or a private pension plan, but have several thousand dollars a month worth of expenses. They may have generous life insurance policies, but the fact is, they won't ever see their life insurance benefits—their heirs will. *In short, elderly people with chronic illnesses don't need money when they die—they need it today.*

The implications of this development are enormous and far-reaching. As tragic as AIDS, leukemia, or terminal cancer is for its victims and their families, the number of individuals who fall into those categories today is still relatively small. Therefore, the opportunity for viatical settlement companies and brokers to service that market is limited by the size of the group.

However, when you consider men and women over age 75 as an additional group that can benefit from viatical settlements, *the market for viatical settlement transactions increases exponentially.* What began as a $400 million segment of the cash flow industry could well grow into a $100 billion segment by the end of this decade.

The second recent breakthrough is the innovative ALIVE program developed by Affirmative Lifestyles of San Antonio. ALIVE is a viatical settlement program being offered to major companies as an employee benefit.

The ALIVE program allows terminally ill and elderly individuals to sell their life insurance policies for cash, which they can use for living expenses, health care, nursing home care, gifts, or simply peace of mind. What makes the program unique is that it operates on a bidding system, ensuring that individuals will get the highest possible offer on their policy from capital providers.

Peggy Wallace, the founder of Affirmative Lifestyles and the ALIVE program, got involved in the viatical industry because of a friend who was terminally ill and wanted to access his life insurance funds. She views her service almost as a ministry; *her clients see it as a godsend.* She has been recognized industry-wide for her work in the viatical settlement industry.

Affirmative Lifestyles is actively marketing the ALIVE program on three levels—to individuals, health care institutions, and corporate human resources departments. The response to the program is certain to be overwhelming.

THE VIATICAL SETTLEMENT TRANSACTION

The nature of viatical settlements—the assignment of a death benefit—makes it a niche people either love or hate. If your background is in social work, nursing, or health care, insurance, or human resources, you may find the viatical industry especially interesting. If you're a sensitive and compassionate person, and want to earn your income by applying those traits, you can find a great deal of personal fulfillment in it. The viatical settlement industry offers a unique opportunity to use your skills and experience to help terminally ill and elderly individuals and their families solve financial crises.

Because viatical settlements involve the transfer of life insurance benefits, you must be licensed to be a funding source. However, it's entirely feasible to earn a full- or part-time income as a referral representative for this income stream, with no licensing requirements at all.

IDENTIFYING SELLERS

When you broker a viatical settlement, you basically act as a referral agent. You locate terminally ill or elderly individuals and their families and educate them about the viatical option.

How do you find possible candidates for viatical settlement transactions? You can start by contacting professionals who interact daily with terminally ill and elderly men and women, such as social workers, attorneys, physicians, and nursing home or hospice staff members. You can also mention your services to members of support groups for patients with terminal illnesses. You can also locate prospects by giving an informative presentation on viatical settlements to nursing home residents and their adult children.

Explaining Services and Gathering Information

As with every other cash flow, the next step after you've identified a potential client is to explain how the settlement works. In many instances, you work with the insured's family rather than the insured directly. You take down some preliminary information, including how old the policy is, the amount of the death benefit of the policy, the carrier, and so on. Then you obtain a medical release form and authorization form, which allow the viatical settlement company to review your client's medical records and verify details about the life insurance policy.

You must find out exactly what your client's needs are. For example, does he or she want to cash in all of the policy, or just part of it? Your client can sell just a portion of the life insurance policy for cash, so that his or her beneficiaries will also receive a portion at the time of death.

Working with a Funding Source

The next step is to contact a viatical settlement company, which handles the funding for the transaction. When it receives the referral, the funding source contacts your client's attending physician and insurance company to confirm the client's diagnosis and verify the details of the policy. Then, the viatical settlement company makes your client (or your client's family) an offer for the policy.

If your client accepts the offer, the last step is to have the insured assign the policy to the new owner—the viatical settlement company. The viatical settlement company then assumes responsibility for paying future premiums if any are due. The predetermined amount of cash is given to the insured in a lump sum.

The entire settlement process may take anywhere from two to six weeks. When the transaction is complete, the viatical settlement company pays you a finder's fee, typically about 1 percent of the amount of the death benefit. If the policy's death benefit is $100,000, for example, you would earn a $1,000 fee.

THE IMPACT OF VIATICAL SETTLEMENTS ON THE CASH FLOW INDUSTRY

Viatical settlements revolutionized the cash flow industry from several perspectives. First, of course, they provided an opportunity to unleash the cash buried in life insurance benefits that, prior to 1989, had been limited through cash-surrender-value provisions in the policy. On that score alone, viatical settlement companies have provided a valuable service. However, on an even broader level, viatical settlements blew open the door for the opportunity to broker or buy other types of insurance-based income streams, including annuities.

ANNUITIES

An **annuity** is a contract issued by an insurance company that either immediately or at some point in the future provides a stream of payments back to the person designated as the beneficiary. Annuities are backed by the "full faith and credit" of the insurance company issuing them, so they are relatively safe payment streams. They are basically guaranteed for as long as the insurance company remains solvent.

Annuities are very flexible savings vehicles. Individuals and companies can buy annuities and use them for a number of different purposes. Companies, for example, can purchase annuities as pensions for their employees. Individuals can buy them as an estate planning tool—naming their children, grandchildren, a trust, or a charity as the beneficiary. However, the primary reason people purchase annuities is for retirement savings and distribution.

In most cases, an individual buys a retirement annuity with an initial lump sum payment, then continues to make contributions over time. This is called the **accumulation phase.** During the accumulation phase, earnings on the policy grow *tax-deferred.*

After retirement, the individual starts drawing a payout from the policy. This is called the **distribution phase** or **payment phase.** By waiting until retirement to receive payouts, the individual enjoys certain tax advantages, avoids tax penalties, and often falls into a lower tax bracket when the payments start. In addition, in many states, annuities are exempt from attachment, which means they offer excellent asset protection devices.

Annuity sales have been increasing at an average annual rate of about 21 percent since 1973, bringing the inventory of annuities from $1 billion up to $100 billion today. Experts expect the surge in growth to continue, first in the accumulation phase of annuity contracts, then in the payout phase, as American baby boomers enter retirement.

Despite the growth in annuities purchased for retirement, current cash flow opportunities in retirement annuities are somewhat limited at this time. The problem is that cashing in a retirement annuity can result in complicated tax issues. In some cases, however, retirement annuities can be sold for cash, provided the client has a copy of the policy, the carrier is a solvent insurance company, and tax issues do not present a problem.

Structured Settlements

An additional opportunity for brokering annuities in today's market is in the area of structured settlements. Structured-settlement annuities differ from retirement annuities in that structured-settlement payments *are not subject to income tax.* This factor lessens the complexities involved in selling them and makes them more accessible to funding sources.

If you've ever been involved with a lawsuit, you've encountered the settlement concept. It's a way of paying damages to an injured party when a lawsuit is settled. A **structured settlement** is simply a method for paying the plaintiff (injured party) *over a period of time.*

Structured settlements usually result from automobile personal injury, medical malpractice, wrongful death, or other tort cases. In those cases, the parties involved often agree to pay damages to the plaintiff over a period of years rather than in a lump sum. The periodic payments are usually funded in the form of an annuity contract.

For a variety of reasons, individuals receiving structured settlement payments may want to sell all or some of their future payments for a lump sum of cash. Sometimes receiving payments over time is in the plaintiff's best interest at the time of the award. But sometimes the plaintiff's financial circumstances change. He or she made need or want access to future settlement payments in order to pay medical bills, college tuition costs, or settle a divorce.

In many states, structured settlement recipients can get cash for future settlement payments. A cash flow funding source can provide a cash advance on all or certain number of future payments in exchange for a fee.

Here's how it works.

Let's say John was injured by a drunk driver. John was awarded a personal injury settlement of $72,000, to be paid out by the driver's insurance company over ten years. That works out to $600 a month, or $7,200 a year.

Now, John knows that $7,200 a year isn't going to get him very far.

First of all, he's got medical bills due *now,* not ten years from now. Second of all, if he starts to depend on the extra $600 a month of income, he's going to be in trouble when the payments finally stop after eight years. If he had his future payments now, he could use the money to pay off some debts, take a few college classes, and start a strong retirement plan.

John conveys his thoughts to his attorney. He asks her if there's any way to restructure the settlement payments so that he can receive a lump sum now.

Now, suppose you are a cash flow broker, and you had met John's attorney at a networking luncheon a few months ago. When John mentions his situation to her, she recalls you and the service you offer. She locates your business card and gives you a call.

You set up an appointment with John and the attorney. You take down some information and ask some basic questions about the source of this income stream, the amount of the income stream, and so forth, and compile this information on a worksheet. You then contact a funding source that specializes in buying structured settlements and fax them the worksheet about John's income stream.

The funding source offers to buy John's settlement for $58,000—enough to meet his goals. He agrees, and walks away with $58,000. Problem solved.

And what do you get for the time it took you to talk to John, his attorney, and the funding source? *A fee of about $3,000.*

BROKERING STRUCTURED SETTLEMENTS

The most immediate opportunity available to you in structured settlements is in brokering them. Buying structured settlements requires some legal background, so funding sources that purchase structured settlements employ on-staff experts who handle the legal work. Settlement transactions tend to be so large that you would have to have a great deal of capital—as well as legal expertise—in order to fund them. As a structured settlement broker, you operate primarily as a referral source for transactions. You locate people who are receiving structured settlement annuities and explain that you work with funding sources who can buy their future payments for cash.

Identifying Sellers

The first step in a structured settlement transaction is to locate someone receiving payments who wants to cash them in. Most structured settlement leads come from networking and referrals, rather than from direct marketing. And of the leads generated from networking, most result from contact with attorneys and other legal and financial professionals.

Attorneys are the ones responsible for negotiating awards for their clients in the first place, so they know which clients are receiving structured settlements. If an attorney has settled a case for a client, chances are that client will come back two or three years later to ask for a lump sum.

Martin Bender, who founded Barrister Funding of America in New York City, generates most of his leads for structured settlements and other income streams through attorneys. Mr. Bender is a licensed attorney himself, so it was natural for him to target them as referral sources. He communicates his services through direct mail, ads in the *Law Journal*, and networking.

Some attorneys are not aware that structured settlement payments can be assigned to another party; you may have to inform them that your funding source specializes in researching techniques for doing just that.

Other good sources of leads include court reporters, court bailiffs, and other professionals employed by the court system. You can even obtain leads from ordinary citizens in your neighborhood. Just about everyone you meet has heard of at least one acquaintance who has received a settlement.

Explaining Services and Gathering Information

When you've located a potential structured settlement seller, the next step is to explain your service. You simply inform the seller that you have access to funding sources that buy structured settlement payments. As with lottery payments, people either want cash, or they don't. Your primary purpose is not to convince your client to sell his or her payments, but to find the right solution to your client's needs.

One of my colleagues of a major funding source for structured settlements offered this example of the importance of understanding the seller's needs. He said that a young man about twenty-three years old came to him and wanted to cash all of his $60,000 personal injury settlement. The settlement was paying him $500 a month for 10 years.

The funding source pointed out that the amount of money his company could advance on the $60,000 settlement paid over 10 years would be discounted to its present value. He pressed the man about whether or not selling off all his future payments was the right solution to his need. The young man confessed that he really only needed $23,000.

And what did he need it for? To buy a motorcycle!

The funding source ended up convincing the young man to sell only enough of his payments to provide him with $23,000. In five years or so, the man will start receiving his $500 monthly payments again.

In an unrelated situation, a young woman approached a funding source and wanted to cash in a wrongful-death settlement. This woman—also in her twenties—was receiving a lump sum payment every three years. The first payment would be $150,000; the second,

$175,000; and the third, $200,000; for a total of $525,000. She wanted to cash in the full amount of the settlement. However, the funding source pointed out that it would be to her benefit to cash in only the first payment and wait to receive her second and final payment as scheduled.

Obviously, concern for the seller doesn't always get the funding source the biggest profit or you the highest commission. However, it does build trust between you and your clients, and it gives them a reason to refer to you others.

The information you gather from a structured settlement client will depend on your funding source's requirements. In many cases, all you have to do is get the name, address, and phone number of a prospect. Then, you answer a few basic questions about the settlement to determine if it's transactable.

First, you must verify that the structured settlement payments are not your client's sole source of income (most funding sources will not purchase the settlement if it is the client's only ongoing source of money). Second, you have to confirm that your prospect is at least eighteen years old (by law, settlements involving minors cannot be sold to someone else). Finally, you have to make sure that the income stream does not result from child support payments, which cannot be assigned in any state. In addition, you have to gather a few documents for verification, including a copy of your client's drivers license, social security card, and a copy of the annuity policy.

Working with a Funding Source

After gathering information about your prospect's settlement, you introduce your prospect and his or her attorney to the funding source. Then you step aside, and the funding source takes over. They handle all of the legal issues and the paperwork, examining the transaction and making an offer to your client. If your client accepts the offer, the parties proceed with closing the transaction. The entire process generally takes about three to four weeks.

As with lottery winnings, you can structure your brokerage fee for a structured settlement annuity one of two ways.

First, you can negotiate your own fee and build it into your offer. If the funding source offers to buy a settlement for $1,500,000, you might offer your client $1,466,000. When the transaction closes, you would earn the difference—$34,000. The most experienced cash flow brokers tend to favor this fee structure.

Second, you can receive a referral fee based on a percentage of the purchase price the funding source offers the seller. That percentage can be as high as 4 percent to 7 percent of the funded amount, although it tends to be reduced in larger transactions. The referral fee is paid to you directly from the funding source, as broken down below:

TYPICAL BROKERAGE FEES ON STRUCTURED SETTLEMENT TRANSACTIONS

If Funding Source Pays	You Make
$250,000	$10,000 to $17,500
$500,000	$20,000 to $35,000
$1,000,000	$40,000 to $70,000

No single category of cash flow has precipitated such intense retail advertising as the area of structured settlements. Several major funding sources, especially those which started out cultivating retail business rather than broker-driven business, run advertisements on television for "car accident settlements" and other income streams.

Their advertising is having a profound effect on the industry, as it increases visibility for the whole business of brokering cash flows. In addition, it also shows in hard numbers how much more efficient it is for a funding source to work through trained brokers, rather than attempting to attract income stream sellers directly through advertising. *And those factors combined mean even more opportunities for you.*

REMEMBER THESE HIGHLIGHTS

- Viatical settlements, annuities, and structured settlements are three types of insurance-related income streams that can be sold for cash. All involve payments coming from an insurance company to an individual.

- A viatical settlement is an arrangement in which a terminally ill or chronically ill individual sells his or her life insurance for a lump sum payment. The individual can use the cash for living expenses, medical expenses, gifts, or whatever else he or she desires.
- Viatical settlements are receiving increased exposure these days through corporate employee benefits programs. They are certain to become more common as the American population continues to age.
- The emergence of the viatical settlement industry paved the way for brokering other insurance-based instruments such as annuities.
- Annuities, including retirement annuities, can be sold for cash in some cases, provided the client has a copy of the policy, the carrier is a solvent insurance company, and tax issues do not present a problem.
- The primary opportunity for transacting annuities in the secondary marketplace today is in the area of structured settlements.
- A structured settlement is a payment stream that usually results from a personal injury, medical malpractice, wrongful death, or other tort case.
- The brokerage fee for structured settlements is generally between 4 percent and 7 percent of the purchase price of the income stream.

PART III

TECHNIQUES FOR SUCCESS

CHAPTER ELEVEN

WHY THE ENTIRE INDUSTRY *WANTS YOU* TO SUCCEED

SO FAR IN THIS BOOK, I've introduced you to the cash flow business, explained the basics of every cash flow transaction, and described step-by-step how to transact ten of the most profitable income streams in the industry.

At this point, I want to diverge from the technicalities of the cash flow business and talk about the *possibilities* of the business, for you in particular. In the next three chapters, I'll explain why your success in the business is so supported, how the business can take you from well-off to wealthy, and what you need to do to get started as a full- or part-time cash flow specialist. In the final chapter, I'll finish up by presenting you with some basic principles to guide your success—not only in the cash flow business, but in life.

By now, you've got to be considering the possibility of starting a cash flow business on a full- or part-time basis. Right now, you're probably wondering, "Could I be successful as a cash flow specialist?"

The answer, is yes, you can. Why am I so sure? Consider this: The entire cash flow industry *wants you* to succeed.

FUNDING SOURCES WANT YOU TO SUCCEED

First, funding sources in the cash flow industry want you to succeed.

Hundreds of funding companies nationwide have access to billions of dollars of capital. Any one of the largest of these funding sources has access to far more cash than all of the transactions combined for the entire country.

They've got the cash; they need the transactions. If you can find quality transactions for them to fund, they will want to work with you again and again and again.

As a broker, you can provide a tremendous value to funding sources. Your help in locating income stream sellers saves them a great deal of time and money in marketing costs. For that reason, many funding sources that used to market directly to the public now rely exclusively on brokers to bring them transactions. And others, who are just now discovering the brokerage network, are shifting their focus from the public to *you*.

BROKERS WANT YOU TO SUCCEED

Second, your fellow brokers in the cash flow industry want you to succeed. Aren't other brokers your competitors? Not really. The cash flow industry is still in its infancy; there are many more transactions available than there are brokers to handle them. The reality is that less than 2 percent of the $3.8 trillion of available inventory is transacted annually. Less than 2 percent! That leaves more than 98 percent of the inventory untouched, for one simple reason—there aren't enough brokers to find them.

Even cash flow brokers in your immediate geographic area can benefit from *your* success, because *your success will bring more visibility to the cash flow industry . . . and to them.* And the greater the visibility of the industry, the more profit potential for all of its participants.

I'm reminded of my college days at the University of Notre Dame, which is located in the small college town of South Bend, Indiana.

When I was nineteen years old, I moved off-campus with several roommates. Soon after, I went into South Bend to look for a part-time job. My first stop was the town's only fur shop. I had always wanted to learn the fur business, because my Italian ancestors had been fur merchants way back in the eighteenth century. (In 1970, fur was still "politically correct"!).

I walked into the fur shop and told the owner I wanted to work for him. He replied that he couldn't afford to hire me.

"You don't understand," I said. "I'm willing to work for nothing. I just want to learn the business."

"You can't work for nothing," he said. "By law, I've got to pay you minimum wage."

"Okay, I'll work for minimum wage, then," I told him.

"But I can't *afford* to hire you at minimum wage," he said.

"I don't get it," I said. "Business *has* to be good. You're the only fur business in the entire South Bend area."

Then the shop owner shared a lesson—one I've never forgotten.

He said, "*That's the problem. I am the only fur business in South Bend, Indiana.* If anybody in South Bend wants to buy a fur, they drive a hundred miles to Chicago, where there are fifty fur businesses to choose from. The fur business has much more visibility in Chicago. It's thriving in Chicago: it's dying in South Bend."

With visibility comes greater product recognition. And with greater product recognition comes greater access to the market.

A more recent example of this pattern is the cappuccino craze in this country.

Go to any corner of any city in America today, and you'll see a shop that sells cappuccino. Ten years ago, few people even knew what cappuccino was. However, a few pioneers recognized the potential of cappuccino as a product and worked hard to market it. The rise of competitors in the market *helped, not hurt,* those pioneers, because with more competitors, more people learned about the product faster. The result of that trend? Today, you can find a cappuccino bar on every street corner, and gourmet coffee is the most profitable segment of the entire coffee market.

Another good example of the visibility factor is cellular service. Just a decade ago, cellular phones were considered status symbols—only sophisticated businesspeople and wealthy jet-setters owned them. Then, deregulation opened up the market to new competitors in the industry. For the most part, marketing and advertising by competitors didn't *take away* business from existing carriers. On the contrary, the overall effect was a dramatic increase in every carrier's customer base. In many cities today, more than 20 percent of the population owns a cellular phone.

The cash flow industry is just like any other emerging industry—gourmet coffee or cellular service. The more brokers there are educating mainstream America about the existence of cash flow services, the better. Because the better the public understands what the cash flow industry is all about, the more money everybody will make.

And that's exactly why I have written this book. Several of my colleagues told me that there was no value to writing this book, because I had more students in my training programs than I had seats available to train them. But that's not the point. The more mainstream America recognizes that cash flow brokerage is as available to them as real estate brokerage is, the more transactions will take place. And the more transactions take place, the more competitive the services will be, and the more profit will be made by everyone involved.

That's also why I have helped the American Cash Flow Association establish local chapters—so that cash flow brokers nationwide could band together and support each other in their local communities. By collaborating, brokers can increase awareness in their local areas, and even work together on mutually beneficial transactions.

One great example of brokers profiting through collaboration is Coastline Financial Group. About a year ago, Jeff Callender formed Coastline Financial Group along with two partners, Ernie and Rose Marie Zerenner, whom he had met at an American Cash Flow Association convention. Jeff lives in Washington State, and the Zerenners live in Delaware. Working together, the three of them provide factoring brokerage and funding services to companies coast to coast.

As you can see, other brokers are not your competitors; they're your colleagues. And they are as eager for you to succeed as you are.

Sellers Want You to Succeed

Finally, income stream sellers want you to succeed. In other words, your *potential clients* in the cash flow industry want your business to be successful.

Why do they care? Because a cash flow business provides a valuable service to individuals and businesses that need or want cash. When you meet with motivated sellers, you don't have to fight to convince them that your service is beneficial. You just have to tell them your service *exists*.

When individuals and businesses decide to sell an income stream, they have a simple goal: to sell their future payments for the most competitive price possible in the most advantageous way possible. That's it. No hidden agendas, no surprises. As you become more successful in the industry, your relationships with top-notch funding sources will grow more efficient. And the better your relationship with funding sources, the better you can help sellers accomplish their objectives.

Buyers want you to succeed. Brokers want you to succeed. Sellers want you to succeed.

Can you think of any other business in America in which everyone in the industry is pulling for your success?

Remember These Highlights

- Funding sources want you to succeed because they have billions of dollars of capital to invest, and they need people like you to find transactions.
- Brokers want you to succeed, because your participation will bring more visibility to the industry, and with visibility comes increased profits for everyone.
- Sellers want you to succeed, because you provide a valuable cash flow service to businesses and individuals that want or need cash.

CHAPTER TWELVE

GOING FROM WELL-OFF TO WEALTHY: "THE PERPETUAL MONEY MACHINE"

I REMEMBER WATCHING AN INTERVIEW with the actor Arnold Schwarzenegger a while back, when the subject of the capital gains tax came up. The interviewer asked how changes in the capital gains tax would affect the wealthy. Arnold's reply surprised me. He candidly remarked that whether the capital gains tax is 15 percent or 40 percent, it wouldn't make a bit of difference in how he lives his life on a day-to-day basis. He didn't say that in a bragging way. His point was that when you're wealthy, the capital gains tax is irrelevant. Your daily life simply isn't affected by it.

THE DIFFERENCE BETWEEN BEING WELL-OFF AND BEING WEALTHY

If I were to ask you if you wanted to be "well-off" in life, what would you say? Nearly everyone wants to be well-off, right? But being well-off is not the same thing as being wealthy. It's merely a stepping-stone to being wealthy.

So what is the difference between the two?

"Well-off" is having a great lifestyle.

"Wealthy" is having a great lifestyle *without having to work for it.*

Well-off is driven by labor-based income. Most of us are driven by labor-based income. As a long as we work, we earn money. But if we stop working, we earn nothing, or next to nothing. We may have enough money saved up to sustain us temporarily, but sooner or later our lifestyle will be altered. Well-off, in other words, is temporary.

Wealthy, on the other hand, is driven by capital-based income. When you're wealthy, your income is being generated by capital, not by labor. Whether you're working or not, your lifestyle is not affected.

Let me give you an example of what I'm talking about.

As a lawyer, I made a great deal of money. From day one, I was a commercial trial lawyer, dealing with business cases. I never did "car accidents." I never did divorces. I never handled many of the cases that represent the mainstay of the livelihoods of most lawyers in this country. I never wanted to. I wanted to do business—and business only.

When I started my practice at the age of thirty, I quickly ended up representing businesses in court. At that time, I was charging $125 an hour—not bad considering the average fee in 1980 was $100 an hour for a lawyer. Before I retired permanently from the law practice in 1992, I was billing $300 an hour—bringing in about $300,000 a year. (I tell you that not to be boastful, but because it's the only way I can make my point. I do recognize that $300,000 is a lot of money!)

So why did I retire from a practice that was earning me that much each year? It wasn't because I didn't have clients. I had more clients than I knew what to do with.

I retired because I was working so hard to *live well,* I didn't have any time left over *to live.* Sure, I was making a good income—but so what? It doesn't matter how much you make when your income is driven by labor.

Back then, I was a "well-off" lawyer making $300,000 a year. My former college roommate was a government employee making $75,000 a year. My future wife, Janet, was an insurance company administrator making $28,000 a year. But all of us—regardless of income level—were trapped in the same boat.

In order to make my income, I had to be in court or taking depositions or drafting complaints or interviewing witnesses. In other words, I had to be *doing* what lawyers do to make money. For my former roommate to make his salary, he had to kiss his wife goodbye and travel from one correctional facility to another, all across Illinois. For Janet to make her salary, she had to follow her boss's orders, work overtime when her boss needed it, and fill in her timesheet every week.

Our salaries were irrelevant. The issue is that we all were driven by labor-based income. Work, and you get paid. Don't work, and you don't get paid.

Throughout the entire time I was practicing law, I was investing. As I mentioned earlier, I bought my first private mortgage note in the early 1980s. It was the first time I had the opportunity to collect income without working a whole lot for it. My real estate investments had been profitable, but they created more work for me to do. That mortgage note was the first investment I owned that produced income with little to no effort.

As I continued to buy mortgage notes and other income streams, the amount of my debt instrument portfolio continued to increase. As it grew, so did my income. And as my income grew, I was able to buy more instruments. With each dollar I wasn't spending to support my lifestyle, I began investing in as many debt instruments as I could buy.

Sometime in 1994, before our first baby had been born, my wife and I were talking with each other over a candlelight dinner. (We were able to do that in those days!) Janet asked me if we were wealthy. I asked her what she meant. And what she said cut to the very core of the issue.

She said, "I mean . . . if we just cashed it all in now, would we ever have to work again? Would our kids be able to go to college? Would our lifestyle change?"

I hesitated, not because I didn't know the answer, but because I wanted to present it in the right way.

"Janet, I'm not exactly sure when, but as of about a year ago, I have been working because I *want to,* not because I *have to.* And I will work until the day I die, because I love what I do, affecting people's lives. But no matter what happens, our kids won't have to worry. They will have the money they need to get through college and have a decent start in life."

I'm not sure exactly when, but sometime in 1993 or 1994, capital replaced labor as the primary source of our income. Our investments, not our labor, were creating most of our wealth. From that point on, our *future lifestyle*—not just our present lifestyle—was secure.

I share that story with you not to be immodest, but only because it conveys what I want you to understand. If you want to go from being well-off to wealthy, you have to replace labor-based income with capital-based income.

How do you do that?

Whether you're making $30,000 a year or $300,000 a year, the process is the same.

First, you generate income through labor. Then, you set aside a certain amount of that income and invest it. You continue to invest consistently, and eventually, the amount of income you're earning from your investments becomes the primary source of income for your lifestyle. Thereafter, even if you continue to work—as I will until the day I die—it is because you *want to,* not because you *have to.*

You Can Generate Capital-Based Income in the Cash Flow Industry

Doctors—like lawyers—tend to earn a substantial salary. Most earn enough to set aside a portion of their labor-based income to generate capital-based income. But how many doctors actually know what to do with the money they've set aside? Very few. The skills doctors learn and use to produce their labor-based income (diagnosis, surgery, knowledge of the body) are entirely irrelevant for producing capital-based income. That's why doctors are notorious for making bad investments.

The cash flow industry is unlike any other income-producing opportunity, in that it allows you to generate capital-based income *using the very source of your labor-based income.*

You can start out in the industry as a broker, learning the business earning a fee on every transaction. The income you earn brokering debt instruments sustains your current lifestyle. What you don't use to support your lifestyle, you set aside and invest in exactly the instrument that allowed you to make money in the first place.

Suppose your niche is in private mortgage notes, for instance. When you broker a mortgage note, you earn a commission. That's labor-based income. You work, you earn. When you buy a mortgage note, on the other hand, you can use the skills you've learned as a broker to make an investment that will continue to generate income long after the deal closes. That's capital-based income. You don't work, you still earn.

One sustains your current lifestyle; the other provides for your future lifestyle.

We all want to exchange our labor income for capital income. Right now, most of us are accustomed to receiving income based on what we do. Whether it's with mental muscle or physical muscle, one way or another we're exchanging labor for income. What we would like to be able to do is to exchange capital for income.

The cash flow business is a way to move from one to the other using the same skills.

When you focus on generating capital-based income, something exciting happens. You multiply your resources faster and faster over time. The more money you invest, the more income you produce. That, in turn, creates an even greater buying opportunity, which again, produces more income. It continues to cycle until the income generated from the capital actually exceeds our current requirements to live.

That is what I call the "perpetual money machine."

STRATEGIES FOR MOVING FROM WELL-OFF TO WEALTHY

Obviously, the key to moving from well-off to wealthy in the cash flow industry is to make the shift from broker to *investor.* With my experience in the cash flow industry, buying debt instruments for my own portfolio as well as observing the best and the brightest in the field, I've found a number of strategies you can use to reach your goal.

Buying a Partial

One of the best ways to make the progression from broker to investor—particularly in private mortgages—is by buying partials.

As I discussed in Chapter Six, buying a partial means buying just a portion of a note. If a note holder is receiving payments on a note for 20 years (240 months), he or she may decide to sell only four years' (48 months') worth of payments for a lump sum of cash. After the four years are up, the payments revert back to the seller, along with the remaining principal still left on the loan.

Partials are an incredibly flexible, simple, and very secure way for a small investor to obtain a big investor's yield on a limited amount of cash. If you've got a small sum of capital—$10,000 or $15,000 saved up—you can buy a partial for your own portfolio rather than brokering it to a funding source. Over time, the partial will generate interest income. But don't touch that income. Look to your brokerage fees to provide money to maintain your lifestyle.

Instead, allow that partial to continue generating more income over time. Then, the next time you come across a partial, you buy that one. And then you buy a third, a fourth, and so on.

Structure a Tail

A second way to gradually become an investor is to structure a "tail."

Suppose you broker a mortgage note with 160 payments. Instead of offering the full 160 payments to your funding source, you offer the funding source only 144 payments, intending on keeping the balance of 16 payments for yourself. Once you obtain your quote from the funding source, you negotiate a purchase price with the seller, allowing you to obtain not only a fee for the transaction, but the ability to receive the last 16 payments for yourself. Your payments may not come due for 10 or 15 years, or they may come due in two or three years if the note gets refinanced or paid off. Either way, sooner or later they *will* come in.

A tail is like a pension that costs you nothing. And if you turn around and invest that tail in a retirement account, the earnings on your contribution could be tax-deferred. With this technique, you're never at risk. You've already earned your commission; the payments you structure as a the tail are just a bonus. The tail strategy will work with just about any income stream, not just private mortgage notes.

Use Leverage

Leverage means risking or spending something in order to get greater returns. But when you borrow money to buy an investment that produces an income stream, your risk is dramatically reduced.

The way you use leverage in the cash flow industry is to borrow money at one interest rate to buy an income stream that will generate even higher returns. Rather than brokering an income stream to a funding source, you borrow money to buy it yourself. You collect the income coming from the payor, then you cut a check to the bank for the monthly payment on the loan.

Suppose, for example, you locate a high-quality note for sale. The note will generate sixty payments of $550 each. The seller needs $25,000 in cash for the note. You don't have $25,000 on hand to buy the note, but you do have collateral you could use to secure a $25,000 home equity loan from the bank. So, you finance $25,000 for sixth months, due in payments of $460.

Now, each month you're making a $460 loan payment to the bank. However, you're *receiving* a $550 payment from the payor of your note. The $90 difference you get each month is pure profit, which you can use to reinvest in other notes or partials.

The process of using leverage operates the same regardless of what the collateral is. In this example, you borrowed the $25,000 against your home with a home equity loan. However, the process also works—and works even better—when you are able to post as collateral the very note that you bought.

Let me give you an illustration of what that looks like. Suppose the note you want to buy has a $50,000 balance secured by a piece of real estate worth $70,000. You want to purchase the note for $43,000, and the seller agrees to do that. However, you have one small problem—you don't have the $43,000. So you go to the bank requesting a loan for $43,000 to be secured by the $50,000 mortgage you intend to buy. The bank hands you a promissory note, which you execute to the bank, along with the $50,000 mortgage (if you assign it as additional collateral), all supporting the repayment of the $40,000 loan to you.

The process I just described to you is called **hypothecation,** a fancy term that simply means buying an income stream with borrowed funds, collateralized by the very income stream you're buying. It's a tongue-twister, but it works.

Shorty Williams of Birmingham, Alabama, has mastered this technique to the tune of several million dollars. The first note he ever bought using hypothecation netted him a *positive cash flow* of $3,000 per month (the difference between how much he was collecting from the payor and how much he was paying to the bank on his loan). In a recent conversation, Shorty commented to me that if he had learned these strategies ten years ago, it could have meant a seven-figure—and possibly eight-figure—difference in his net worth.

Hypothecation using a collateral-based instrument is the same exact process that a small factor uses when he or she starts out as a broker.

One of my former students, Bill Goetschel, of Nerstrand, Minnesota, used this strategy to switch from being a broker to operating as an investor almost immediately after entering the cash flow industry. The only difference was that the collateral he offered to the bank were the accounts receivable he was purchasing.

When Bill first started his cash flow business as a broker, he quickly came across a prospective client whose invoices were too small for the traditional factors. He went from one factor to another and kept getting turned down, because the invoices were below minimum buying parameters. He looked at the situation, recognized that the invoices were strong, albeit small, and decided to fund them himself.

That simple decision transformed Bill Goetschel into a national factor working out of his home with his wife and daughter—earning this past year about $300,000 in net income. Not a bad journey in less than three years.

Going to the bank for financing is just one way of leveraging to buy income streams. You can tap other sources of capital as well. You can borrow against your retirement account, for example, or actually buy cash flow instruments with your retirement program.

CONSISTENCY IS THE KEY

One of the most important factors that will allow you to move from well-off to wealthy is consistency. First, be consistent as a broker. As often as possible, set aside a portion of the income generated from your brokerage fees to buy good quality income streams. Second, be consistent as an investor. When your income streams start producing revenue, set aside some—and possibly all—of that revenue for buying other income streams to add to your portfolio.

I know many professionals in the cash flow industry who have successfully made the transition from broker to investor. One such success story is Rich Wood of Henderson, Nevada.

Rich got started in the cash flow industry about four years ago after attending one of my training programs. He had owned a construction company, and had used factoring services to maintain cash flow in his company. He recognized the enormous potential of factoring construction receivables.

Rich got trained and certified as a broker, then set a goal for himself: In two years, he wanted to be making $100,000 a year. He accomplished that goal in six months, not in two years. Today Rich's company, AeroFinancial, has completed over $200 million in transactions, and is going public.

If you move from mainly brokering to mainly investing, at some point, you'll be in complete control of your own money and your own destiny. You won't have to deal with stockbrokers or money managers. Your money will be working entirely for you. And ultimately, you won't have to work at all for your money. It will flow in automatically as steady earnings from your cash flow investments.

Cash flow is powerful—not only because it provides current income, but more importantly because it offers the opportunity to create a "perpetual money machine," a base of capital sufficient to sustain your lifestyle regardless of whether or not you work. In the cash flow industry, your decision to work can be driven by choice—not circumstance. And *that* is the benefit of being wealthy.

REMEMBER THESE HIGHLIGHTS

- "Well-off" is having a good lifestyle. Well-off is driven by labor-based income.
- "Wealthy" is having a good lifestyle without having to work for it. Wealthy is driven by capital-based income.
- The key to moving from "well-off" to "wealthy" is to move from creating labor-based income to creating capital-based income.
- The cash flow industry is unique in that you can generate capital-based income using the very source that produces your labor-based income. You do that by progressing from broker to investor.
- When you broker income streams, you earn money to maintain your current lifestyle. When you invest income streams, you earn yields that support your long-term financial needs.
- Several ways to progress from broker to investor include buying partials, structuring a tail, and hypothecating.
- If you want to use the cash flow industry to move from well-off to wealthy, the key is consistency—both as a broker and an investor.

CHAPTER THIRTEEN

HOW TO GET FROM *HERE* TO *THERE*

IN THIS BOOK, I'VE REVEALED how thousands of people are making hundreds and *hundreds of thousands* of dollars in the cash flow business by putting willing sellers together with willing buyers. They don't have to buy inventory. They don't have to set up offices. They don't have to hire employees. And there's absolutely no limit on the money they can make.

If you're seriously considering a career in the cash flow industry, you must be thinking, "So how do I get from *here* to *there*?"

So far, I've given you all this information about a substantial full- or part-time income opportunity. Now, let me give you some steps for making the journey from where you are today—at exactly this moment in your life—to *where you want to be.*

1. Find your cash flow niche.

Within the cash flow industry there are hundreds of different areas you could service. But don't try to tackle all of them; instead, choose a specialized niche. It will make a huge difference in your level of success. If you can position yourself as an expert in an area in which no one else has specialized, then you'll have an entire market to yourself.

My friend Archie Adams, for example, first got into the cash flow industry as a private mortgage broker and investor. Later, however, he put his knowledge of the used car business to work and carved out a niche brokering automobile notes. Today, he is one of only a few cash flow specialists nationwide who broker and buy this type of debt instrument.

So which area of the cash flow industry should you pursue? That's something you have to decide based on your skills and interests. Take a moment to examine the experience and skills you already have acquired. Then, consider how you could translate that knowledge into a cash flow opportunity.

Suppose, for instance, you have worked in the construction industry. Could you use your knowledge of that field to broker construction receivables? Or perhaps your background is in health care. Could you use your understanding of the health care industry to broker medical receivables? Maybe you've worked in life insurance. Could use your experience to broker insurance settlements?

One of the graduate advisors I employed at my training organization, Mark Combs, was fascinated with the viatical segment of the cash flow industry, because he had been on the other side of the table for so long—selling life insurance policies. For him, the opportunity to give *value* out of a life insurance policy, rather than trying to sell a life insurance policy, made all the difference in the world.

Even if you have no practical experience that seems to lend itself to the cash flow industry, you still can be successful. The fact is, many people who get into the industry as brokers and investors had no prior experience in it.

One of my students, for example, had worked in geological science for thirty years before starting his cash flow business. His former job had involved working primarily with scientists, geologists, and Mother Nature.

He recently told me that getting into the cash flow industry was a real adjustment, because it's totally people-oriented. But his *sincere interest* in working with people compensated for his lack of past experience, and he has become quite successful brokering and investing in private mortgage notes.

If your past experience seems irrelevant, simply evaluate your personal interests. Are you interested in helping individuals or businesses? Do you want to work with real estate? Or boats? Or antiques? Your interest level can very often drive your decision about which debt instruments to focus on.

The following list details possible debt instruments you could transact based on your prior experience or current interests. These, of course, are merely suggestions. The choice is ultimately up to you.

TRANSLATE EXPERIENCE AND INTERESTS INTO CASH FLOW OPPORTUNITIES

Your experience or interest in:	Could translate to opportunities in:
Antiques and collectibles	Collectibles notes, retail installment contracts
Automobiles	Automobile note and leases
Banking	Accounts receivable, business notes
Collections	Bad debt, commercial and consumer judgments
Construction	Construction invoice factoring, private mortgage notes
Engineering	Any income stream
Entertainment	Royalty payments, commissions
Farming	Farm production contracts, equipment notes and leases
Health care	Medical receivables
Heavy equipment	Equipment notes and leases
Human resources	Viatical settlements
Insurance	Structured settlements, viatical settlements
Law	Bankruptcy receivables, accounts receivable, structured settlements
Manufacturing	Accounts receivable (invoices), equipment leases

Mortgages	Private mortgage notes, business notes
Professional sports	Sports contracts
Property management	Commercial leases
Real estate	Private mortgage notes, mobile home notes, tax liens, business notes
Retailing	Accounts receivable (invoices), retail installment contracts
Sales	Any income stream

2. Determine your career objective.

Next, develop an action plan based on your career objectives.

Can cash flow be a full-time professional career for you? Certainly. Can it be a part-time source of additional income? You bet. The number of hours you work your cash flow business is entirely up to you. I have seen cash flow specialists:

- Start the business part-time, and go full-time
- Start the business part-time, and stay part-time
- Start the business full-time and go big-time.

In Chapter Twelve, I mentioned Bill Goetschel. What I didn't tell you was that Bill was a full-time airline mechanic making $4,000 a month when he got started in the cash flow industry. He decided to switch his mechanic's schedule to night hours and work his cash flow business part-time during the day.

Bill's entire objective was to work the business part-time until he could earn an income equal to what he was making as an airline mechanic. It took him a full year to do that, but, when he did start making $4,000 as a part-time factoring broker and factor, he quit his night job and started working his cash flow business full-time.

Bill's net income today? In excess of $25,000 a month!

I recently saw Bill when he visited Orlando. I asked him what it's like to have been an airline mechanic—never having made more than $48,000 a year—and now making *$25,000 a month.* Bill said that for the first time in his life, he has the opportunity to *give money away.*

Give money away. Not *spend* it. To Bill, and his wife, Carolanne, the opportunity to give money away and participate in the ministry of his church are the best rewards of all.

Getting wealthy? That's fine. But having the opportunity to help his fellow church members over tough financial straits continues to help Bill "ease through the eye of the needle" every day of his life.

3. Determine your income objective.

Some people are making a few hundred dollars a month in the cash flow industry. Others are making several thousand a month. And a dedicated few are making half a million dollars a year in this industry.

Whether you go into cash flow part-time or full-time, you've got to identify your income objective in advance. In other words, you've got to decide exactly how much money you want to make. Some people enter the industry intending to make an extra $500 a month. Others come into the industry planning to make $1,000, $2,000, $3,000, or $10,000 a month.

It doesn't matter how high or low your income objective is, because there is no right answer. What is relevant is that you identify an objective, so you can choose a niche and establish a work pattern that will make it possible for you to achieve your goal.

4. Decide when you want to get started.

Next, decide when you want to get started in the cash flow industry. Is your goal to start today? A month from now? A year from now? Maybe you want to get started right away. Maybe you plan to wait a year or two when you retire from the military, have children, or leave the corporate world.

Even in this area, there is no right answer. I have graduated individuals from my training institutes who were literally ready to get started the Monday after the five-day training was over. On the other hand, many others have had to clean up life circumstances or complete current assignments, jobs, and the like before they could take a stab at being successful in the cash flow industry.

Whatever your time frame is, decide . . . and get on with it!

5. Get training.

If you start out in the cash flow industry as a broker, your value is in bringing transactions to the table. *The more transactions you bring, the more money you make.* The way to "get good" at locating and structuring transactions is to get training. Training is the threshold way you set yourself apart from other brokers.

Training opportunities abound in the cash flow industry. In addition to my organization, there are several others that provide seminars from as short as one day to as long as five days (check the Resources).

Training gives you an opportunity to develop initial professional skills and expand on those skills. In addition, it allows you to get a handle on the full scope of the industry before you decide to pursue it.

From the vantage point of a newcomer to the industry, all of the information in this book might appear daunting. However, in just one short week, and in some cases even less, you can get your arms around the full extent of the industry, develop a comfort level with it, and walk away with a plan of action for Monday morning.

6. Continue your training.

After you get started in the cash flow business, allow yourself the opportunity for continuing education.

Would you go to a doctor who went to medical school twenty years ago and hasn't been back since? Would you go to a real estate broker who got licensed fifteen years ago and hasn't been to a seminar since?

The cash flow industry is no different. The more you know, the more you grow, and the more you grow, the more money you make.

One way to stay on top of the latest trends in the cash flow industry is by attending industry conventions. Every spring, for example, the American Cash Flow Association holds the largest convention in the nation focusing on the cash flow industry. The convention features lecturers from all segments of the industry and draws as exhibitors virtually every major funding source.

In addition, the American Cash Flow Association also publishes the *American Cash Flow Journal,* which keeps you up to date on what's happening in the cash flow industry. (For information about attending the national convention or subscribing to the *American Cash Flow Journal*, refer to the Resources section.)

7. Show a commitment to service.

No matter what niche you choose, show your clients true commitment to service. While professional competency is important, demonstrating a genuine concern for your seller's needs is the way you set yourself apart in the cash flow industry.

My friend Kevin Clancy, a private mortgage and structured-settlement broker in Jupiter, Florida, understands the value of service. In every transaction he completes, Kevin's focus is meeting the needs of the seller. He says he spends less time describing his services and more time simply *listening* to the seller's needs and concerns. Much of Kevin's marketing involves talking to his clients about their jobs, families, successes, and personal interests. That curiosity not only is a reflection of who Kevin is and how he views his role, but also demonstrates to his clients where his heart is.

If you're willing to take these seven steps, you can move from where you are today to where you want to be in the cash flow industry. Your background doesn't matter. Your education doesn't matter. And the amount of capital you have doesn't matter. What matters is your willingness to succeed and your desire to apply proven strategies to get there.

REMEMBER THESE HIGHLIGHTS

- To get on the road to a career in the cash flow industry, you've got to take seven action steps:
- First, find your cash flow niche based on your interests and past experience.
- Next, determine your career objective.
- Then, determine your income objective.
- Next, decide when you want to get started in the cash flow industry.

- At that point, get training in your niche area.
- Then, continue your education through training, reading, networking with other cash flow professionals, and attending industry conventions.
- Finally, show a consistent commitment to service.
- Following these steps is the key to moving from where you are today into a successful full- or part-time career in the cash flow industry. From here, your achievement depends only on your willingness to succeed and your desire to apply proven strategies to get there.

CHAPTER FOURTEEN

Seven Attributes of a Millionaire

You may think it's a little "cheesy" to talk about becoming a millionaire. Maybe it sounds too impossible for you to consider seriously. Or maybe you have no intention of becoming a millionaire; you simply want to live a successful and self-satisfied life.

Regardless, this chapter is for you. Even though I've titled this chapter "Seven Attributes of a Millionaire," the attributes I will describe are appropriate for any aspect of successful conduct, whether it is related specifically to business activities or life in general.

I believe these attributes allow us to develop certain attitudes that make us better people when we learn them and apply them. The description of these attributes, for some readers, might turn out to be a refresher of what you know already—and sometimes forget. For others, this may be an opportunity to take a good, hard look at how you operate in life and determine how you should modify your conduct to achieve more successful results.

Whether you want to be a millionaire, or simply want to be more successful overall, I hope my thoughts and observations about these attributes will be helpful to you.

Professional Competency

The first essential attribute of a millionaire is a commitment to professional competency, which means possessing an exhaustive knowledge of whatever business you're involved in. It means that whatever you're doing—whether you work in corporate America or you're self-employed in the cash flow industry—you know your business like the back of your hand.

I've been involved in a number of different businesses over these past years. Right after law school, I started a firm that did legal research and writing for lawyers. After a while, I added on some additional publishing houses as clients, and I started researching and producing legal newsletters.

Then, I got into the sporting goods business with my dad. We took a sporting goods business from one retail unit up to nine retail stores and then franchised those out. Later, I was even involved in seven different restaurants. And to top off those pursuits, I was a commercial litigator for fourteen years.

No matter what business I was in, whether it was retail sporting goods, restaurants, or law, the first essential requirement for success in that business was professional competency—knowing the business.

I don't know what your background is, or what your history is. It doesn't matter. If you intend to become a millionaire in this country, the first thing you need to do is learn the business—and learn it very, very well. Whatever your business is, you've got to know your trade.

In this book I've introduced you to an industry that has made me a great deal of money over the years. If you have succeeded in another business, you can succeed at this business. Even if you have failed in another business, you can certainly succeed in this business. But first, you have to demonstrate a commitment to professional competency. If you can learn this business like the back of your hand, there's no reason you can't produce a six-figure income on an annual basis for the rest of your life—and become a millionaire in the process.

Let's consider two requirements for professional competency.

The first requirement for professional competency is learning your business right from the start. Most people think that the way to get involved in self-employment is to go out and start or buy a business. The part they leave out is *training* for the business. It doesn't matter how well you understand self-employment, if you don't understand *your business,* you can't succeed. Initial training launches that process.

The second requirement for professional competency is to *continue* to educate yourself about your business. People who are striving to know their business are not satisfied with initial training, they seek ongoing training. They simply can't get enough.

In every business I've started, I have always taken two steps to continue my education. First, I subscribed to everything I could read relating to that particular business. And second, I went to the major national industry conventions, wherever they were.

Whatever business you decide to pursue, commit to reading and learning as much as you possibly can. The more, the better. Every single time you learn more material, you're going to get that much better at your business.

SINGLE-MINDEDNESS OF PURPOSE

The second essential attribute for becoming a millionaire is what I call a commitment to single-mindedness of purpose, which is what drives an individual to go from zero income and zero assets to a six-figure income and seven-digit assets in decades or less.

Chances are the billionaires you read about in the newspapers didn't start off in five or ten or twenty businesses. They started making money by concentrating on one business, not a dozen. You simply cannot make a lot of money tackling half a dozen different things.

An old expression goes, "You can only be a master of one." If you're not a master of one, you are the opposite—a jack of all trades. And a jack of all trades seldom makes money. The only way to make serious money in this country is to be single-minded of purpose. Whatever your purpose is, approach it exclusively.

I've got a friend who has made money operating a restaurant. That's the only business he's worked. He started off as a chef when he was seventeen years old. Later, he became a maître d', and eventually he opened his first restaurant, a little hole-in-the-wall. Then, he opened another restaurant, then another, then another. He demonstrated single-mindedness of purpose.

I'm not saying you have to start pursuing your goals as a teenager. What I am saying is when you find a business that suits you, pursue it with single-mindedness of purpose. One business is all you need to know to make a serious amount of money in this country.

Another friend and former client of mine, Mr. Khan, from Kissimmee, Florida, also has demonstrated the incredible single-mindedness of purpose that it takes to become a multi-millionaire in this country. Mr. Khan is a very humble, respectful Pakistani who made a little bit of money in the Blackpool district of London as a shoe merchant before coming to this country. He arrived here in 1980, with just enough money to buy a few tiny T-shirt shops and a home for his young family just east of Disney World.

Over the years, I watched Mr. Khan's T-shirt shops increase from an average size of 600 square feet per store to 18,000 square feet per store. I saw him buy shopping centers, hotels, campgrounds, and more stores. After fourteen years, he became the largest retailer—and probably one of the wealthiest individuals—in the Central Florida tourist area.

Mr. Khan had the opportunity for some local fame when he sold his 30,000 square-foot house to Shaquille O'Neal, then the center for the Orlando Magic. The closing, held at my office, attracted unquestionably the largest congregation of real estate brokers, mortgage brokers, insurance agents, well-wishers, and "Shaq O'Philes" I had ever seen.

When the closing was over, Mr. Khan and I were walking out to get a bite to eat, and a local television station pointed a camera at Mr. Khan.

"Mr. Khan," a reporter asked, "how did you manage to amass so much wealth in such a short period of time in this country?"

Mr. Khan looked directly at the camera, held up his right digit finger and said, "One T-shirt at a time."

One T-shirt at a time. *That* is single-mindedness of purpose.

On the other hand, I once got a call from a very different individual who had taken one of my cash flow training courses.

"Larry," he said, "I was so impressed with your training and so impressed with your cash flow system."

"I really appreciate you calling and telling me that," I said.

He paused, then said, "Can I ask you something?"

Then, he proceeded to tell me about a multi-level long distance telephone service he wanted to sell me. After listening to his pitch, I answered, "You know, my friend, our company has just about the cheapest long-distance service you can imagine. We negotiate pretty well—we kind of know what we're doing—so the chances are not very strong that you can offer us a service that makes economic sense. So, let me ask *you* something. How many other things are you involved in? Because you obviously haven't applied anything you learned from your cash flow training yet."

This student told me he was involved in a multi-level long-distance service, a multi-level herbal products program, multi-level vitamins, multi-level cleansing formulas, and five or six other activities. That poor guy truly lacked single-mindedness of purpose.

At length, I said to him, "I don't want to be personal, but let me ask you a simple question. How much money do you make a month?"

"Gee, Larry," he said, "I feel kind of embarrassed."

"I can appreciate that, and you don't have to answer. But I'm curious. How much money do you make a month?"

He said, "Well, last month was my best month so far."

"So far in terms of what?" I asked.

"So far since I started my own business after leaving my job," he said.

"How long ago was that?"

"About two years ago."

I asked, "Okay, last month, how much did you make?"

"$1,200," he blurted out.

"Two years later," I said, "you've made $1,200 a month. And during this entire two years is this the stuff you've been doing?" He confessed he'd also tried to represent a few other products.

I said, "You know what you are, my friend? You are a starving man picking up crumbs when you've got a feast—a banquet—over here waiting for you. As long as you keep picking up crumbs, the most you're ever going to make is $1,200 a month. Let me make a suggestion to you; stop nibbling off of all these other tables and go for the banquet that's waiting for you."

Let me make the same suggestion to you.

If you are making $1,000 a month, $2,000 a month, $3,000 a month, or even $4,000 a month by dabbling in a little bit of this and little bit of that, whatever you're dabbling in, pack it up, stick in a box, and put it in your garage. In the cash flow industry, you've got at your disposal an opportunity to make a very significant amount of money. Allow yourself to develop focus and determination, and let the cash flow industry take care of the rest.

Personal Responsibility

The third attribute of a millionaire is a commitment to personal responsibility. Personal responsibility means realizing there is only one person who can produce outcomes in your life—and that's *you*. You are the cause of everything that happens in your life.

Think for a minute about all of the outcomes that have occurred in your life. Who do you think caused them? *You* are the only constant in your life. You are responsible for every outcome—whether positive or negative.

Personal responsibility means you stop trying to find scapegoats for your failures. Likewise, you mustn't credit "luck" for your successes. If it happened, it's because *you did it*. If it didn't happen, *it's because you didn't*. If it's going to happen in the future, *you've got to do it*.

If you start a cash flow business—or any other kind of business—let me make a suggestion to you. Don't worry about what everyone else thinks. Maybe your friends or relatives have tried different systems to make money. They may come to you and say, "You can't make money that way. You'll never make money that way." Those individuals have no bearing on your success or failure. Remember, only one person can produce results in your life—you.

When you operate with a sense of personal responsibility, your life becomes much cleaner. If you see an outcome you like, you simply repeat the behavior, and you'll get the same outcome. If you see an outcome you don't like, change your behavior, and you'll get a different outcome next time. But you'll never be able to provide that type of objective response to a negative outcome unless you recognize that you are the person who created the original outcome to start with.

Personal responsibility is not burdensome, it's empowering. It allows you to move from being a victim of your circumstances to being a creator of them. If you want to become a millionaire, take personal responsibility for both your successes and your failures.

COMMITMENT TO EFFECTIVE CONDUCT

The fourth essential quality for becoming a millionaire is a commitment to effective conduct. A commitment to effective conduct means evaluating your goals and using specific techniques to reach them.

If you listen to motivational speakers, you might think you can just "will" your way into effective conduct. It's not that easy. I have yet to meet a millionaire who willed his or her way into effective conduct. It takes more than positive thinking to be effective.

A commitment to effective conduct requires action, not hype. Whether your goal is to make $100,000 in one year, or $1 million at the end of three years, you've got to determine what type of conduct is going to produce that—and then *do it*.

Effective conduct requires three components on your part. First, you have to have an *objective* understanding of where you are in the present time. Second, you have to understand *clearly* where you want to be in the future. Third, you've got to have a *specific implementation plan* that will take you from where you are now to where you want to be.

Effective conduct occurs when those three elements are working in tandem. However, when any of the three is missing, you will produce ineffective results.

Let's look at those components in more detail.

Understand Where You Are

The first requirement for effective conduct is to understand objectively where you are right now. "Objectively" means seeing your situation exactly for what it is.

Let's say you have $500 in the bank. Maybe you're thrilled to have $500 in the bank. Or maybe you're alarmed to have only $500 in the bank.

Understanding your present position objectively means that if you have $500 in the bank, you've got $500. It's neither good nor bad; it just *is*—it's a fact. Whether you feel good about it or bad, when you are finished "feeling," you still have only $500 in the bank. Your attitude doesn't change your circumstance one bit.

In the final analysis, it doesn't matter if you have one dollar in the bank right now. If you have one dollar, but you have an effective system for producing $10,000, you can make $10,000 in no time at all. But you've got to start with an objective understanding of where you are.

Know Where You Want to Be

The second component of effective conduct is to understand clearly where you want to be in the future.

What is your goal? To make money? That's not very clear. To make a lot of money? That's not any clearer.

How about to earn an extra $10,000? That's clearer, but it still doesn't hit the mark. How about to make $10,000 by the end of the first three months after you begin working this business? That's clear.

The issue of clarity simply suggests that you have to be able to recognize "when you get there." In order to know whether you've reached your goal, you first have to know what your goal is.

Implement a Plan for Getting There

The third component of effective conduct is to develop a specific action plan that will take you from where you are now to where you want to be. How do you plan on making $10,000 in the next three months? I'm not talking about a general answer like, "I'm going to get into the cash flow business," or "I'm going to work for it." I'm talking about using specific techniques to implement your plan.

You have $500 right now. You want to make $10,000. What are you going to do *today*? What are you going to do *tomorrow*?

What are your timelines? Benchmarks? Due dates? What plan do you have to self-correct in the event you're off course, and when you do self-correct, what do you do to make sure you get back in line again?

A navigator who flies between New York City and Orlando will provide the pilot with more than 200 navigational corrections to make sure the plane arrives safely at the airport. How many times are you self-correcting to make sure you reach your destination based on the course you've planned?

If you're starting off in one place, and you want to end up in another, you've got to use a road map to get there. Effective conduct means following a "road map"—a specific day-to-day plan for achieving your goals.

PERSEVERANCE

The fifth attribute that millionaires possess is perseverance. What do I mean by "perseverance"? I'm not talking about trudging through the desert on a camel. I'm talking about giving yourself the chance to be *successful*. I have met so many people who, if they only gave themselves the chance, would be so much more successful than they are. Every time they are about to break free, they hit a minor resistance point and head in another direction.

Take an acquaintance of mine, Ken, for example. Every time I see Ken, he's doing something different. Every now and then I run into him downtown at the cappuccino-espresso shop.

"Hi, Ken. How are you doing?" I say.

"Larry, man, I'm doing great." (He's always doing "great.")

"So, Ken, what are you doing now?" I ask. Ken's answer always varies.

"Larry, I am representing a printing company right now. This is the most *outrageous* printing company I've ever seen. This company does eighteen-color photography." (Ken lives in the superlative).

"Eighteen colors? Ken, there are only six colors out there."

"I know. I know," he says. "I'm not sure where he found those extra colors. But it *is* the most amazing printing company you've ever seen. Can I come by sometime and show you their work?"

"By all means, Ken, show me their work. You know how much printing I do!"

Three months later, I pass Ken on the street again. "Hey Ken, how are you doing?"

"Larry, I'm doing great. I'm just fantastic."

"That's great Ken, you're always doing so very well. . . . Printing, right?"

"Printing? Nah, forget about that. . . . Can I talk to you about something else, Larry?"

"Sure. Of course you can, Ken."

"Have you ever taken—," he says, taking a glass out of his pocket. (In downtown Orlando, he's got a glass in his pocket.) "Have you ever taken a glass, filled it up in your kitchen sink, and held it up to the light? Have you ever looked at the grime, the grease, the toxins—just polluting your body? Have you ever done that, Larry?"

"No, Ken, I don't examine the water. I drink the water."

"Larry, I've got a little machine that I can put right underneath your sink so that the next time you decide to drink water, it's going to be as a clean as a Colorado spring. Can I come show you how it works?"

"Any time, guy. Any time you want to come show me, you show me, okay? Take care of yourself, Ken." (Of course, he never comes to demonstrate it. I didn't expect him to.)

Three months later I see him again on the street. "How are you, Ken?"

"Larry, let me tell you—if I were any better I couldn't stand it."

"Water purifiers, right?"

"Nah, forget about that." He says, "Larry, can I ask you something?"

"Of course, Ken. You always ask me something."

"I've got something new—something so powerful, you're not going to believe it. Have you ever heard of this company? It's called . . . it's called . . . Amway."

And on and on it goes.

Now, I don't have a problem with Amway. I don't have a problem with water purifiers. I don't have a problem with being a printing broker. I couldn't care less what he does.

But, Ken, for heaven's sake—just do it. Every single time you start to get some traction in your life, you run off in a different direction.

Can you build momentum driving your car on a downtown city street? Stop signs. Pedestrians. Red lights. Green lights. Traffic. No, if you want to build momentum, you get on a highway.

If you want to build momentum in your life, get on a highway, put your foot on the gas, and forget about the exit ramps. You see, if every single time you meet resistance, you go in a different direction, your life will be about going in different directions.

What do you do with resistance points? You simply sidestep them. How many times have you reached what you thought was an obstacle, but when you took a close look at it, it was nothing more than an inconvenience—a resistance point. Forget about the resistance points. Forget about the obstacles. And forget about the exit ramps.

At this point, you know a little about the cash flow industry. Do you want it to put you over the top? Do you want to be making $100,000 a year? Do you want to be a millionaire? If you've got the tools, you've got the technique, and you've got the five attitudes I've mentioned so far, all it's going to take is perseverance—allowing yourself the time to make it happen.

I have given lectures on self-employment and the cash flow industry to more than one million people. As I've traveled across the country, I have come across so many people who, like Ken, don't need to be at those lectures at all. They had already found their niche a long time ago, they simply needed to stay on the highway and persevere. Instead, they come back, time and time again, searching for something new, something different, something better. And all the while, the answer is right there waiting for them. They simply have to make it happen.

This point is so very personal to me, because the effects are so insidious. If every single time that you're about to seize on something you go in a different direction, somewhere deep down inside your soul you begin to believe you are not successful as a person. But it isn't that you're not successful as a person, it's just that you haven't given yourself the opportunity—the chance—to be successful.

Do you want to join me in the cash flow industry? If so, here's my challenge to you. *I want you to stay in the cash flow industry until such time that you have made a success of it.* Because if you do, and you then decide to something else, you will bring into that experience the success you achieved in this.

I know, based on my experience with countless graduates across the country, that if you stay in the cash flow industry long enough, you will be successful. My goal is to make sure that you understand the industry on the front side and keep you in it long enough on the back side to become successful. The industry will take care of the rest.

After you've become successful, start a ministry. Go into the Peace Corps. Do whatever you want to do. But until then, persevere. Stay in the game. Don't change your mind and take an exit ramp until you have stayed in the industry long enough to succeed at it.

No one in this country became a millionaire working for two weeks. No one in this country became a millionaire working for six weeks, three months, or six months. Millionaires become millionaires because of perseverance; they give themselves the chance to become successful.

INTEGRITY

The sixth attribute of a millionaire is what I call the "Human Manifestation of an Absolute—Truth." On the absolute level, it's called Truth. On the human level, it's called Integrity. Truth represents a perfect reflection of itself. Integrity represents living consistently with our highest truth.

To the same degree that a building without structural integrity will eventually collapse, an individual without integrity sooner or later will fall apart. You can't be successful, or a successful millionaire, without integrity. At least not in the long term.

Several years ago I was talking with my father about a cover story in the *Orlando Sentinel* that day. A top-notch, wealthy individual in Orlando had been indicted. My father was shocked, but I knew the man. I wasn't surprised. I said, "You know what, Dad? 'Even the mighty, so shall they fall,' It's only a question of time."

Once in a while you may cross paths with people who are millionaires. But if they don't have integrity, it's only a matter of time before they'll fall and lose everything they have.

The fact is, it won't do you any good to focus on money alone if, in the meantime you end up losing your soul. And I don't mean that in a religious sense; I mean it in the human sense. We are human beings first; we are businesspeople second.

Commit yourself to live by the highest level of integrity. It's a vital attribute for becoming—and staying—a millionaire.

LOVE AND CARING

The seventh attribute of a millionaire is the business application of the Absolute Principle, Love. What does "love" mean in terms of business? Just simple caring.

There are only two ways to operate in life, and thus two ways to operate in business. First, you can operate by being self-serving. Or second, you can operate by being other-serving. Self-serving or other-serving. That's it. You're either going to serve yourself, or you're going to serve somebody else. You can't serve two masters.

If you are self-serving, you use the knowledge, skills, and competency you've gained to serve yourself. You manipulate circumstances.

If you are other-serving, you use your knowledge, skills, and competency to benefit other people.

Can you be other-serving and still make a profit? Of course you can—by making a value-for-value exchange. In this book, for example, I give you information in exchange for a fair price. That's a value-for-value exchange.

The issue isn't whether or not you make a profit. The issue is your motivation for doing that. Do you intend to serve yourself, or do you intend to serve others? That's the question. If you serve yourself, you'll make a profit, in the short term, and maybe even in the long term. If you serve others, you may even leave some money on the table once in a while. But does it really matter? When you serve yourself, only one person can prosper, but when you serve others, we all prosper. Let me suggest that we allow ourselves to operate in a way which gives to the entire community, not just to ourselves.

Hence, it's not about making a profit. Or about producing income. Or about becoming a millionaire. Operating with genuine caring is simply a method of being. Let's care for the people whom we serve. If you care for others, they can tell. If you don't, they can tell.

By communicating with you in this way, I can share what we at my training organization call our "core values." Our core values are the seven attributes I have indicated in this chapter. In order to be employed by us, and to continue that employment, it is not sufficient to have only one. Our employees must have all of these attributes. Hence, publishing them in this book gives me a chance to extend to you what we consider to be at the "core" of our existence as a company.

I also want you to recognize that when we value these seven attributes, and we truly attempt as a group to work within them, any mistakes we make will be mistakes of application, not errors of intention.

Finally, I want you to be able to talk in these terms with me. By discussing these issues myself, I have given you the chance to speak about these things in the future with me. Clearly, our relationship can be business-based, but we have the chance to discuss things far more important than just business—a chance to be real, a chance to be personal, a chance to be human.

If we should come across each other at some point in the future, wherever and whenever that might be, I hope that you take seriously my invitation to treat this as a relationship founded not on being in business, but on being human. There is nothing that I could aspire to more than the opportunity to influence you in that very real way.

Remember These Highlights

In my personal experience, I've identified seven attributes I believe are critical to becoming successful. They are:

- Professional competency—Know your business inside and out.
- Single-mindedness of purpose—Get focused and stay focused.
- Personal responsibility—Accept that you are the cause of everything that happens in your life.
- Commitment to effective conduct—Evaluate your goals and use specific techniques to reach them.

- Perseverance—Give yourself the time and the opportunity to be successful.
- Integrity—Live consistently with your highest truth.
- Loving and caring—Operate by being other-serving; use your knowledge, skills, and competence to benefit other people.

PART IV

RESOURCES

Sources of Additional Information

The cash flow industry at this time represents a loose-knit organization of about 20,000 individuals, very much like you, across the country. Cash flow professionals fall into four basic categories: funding sources, master brokers, certified brokers, and service providers.

Needless to say, these pages are far too limited to include all 20,000 practitioners. However, on the following pages I have listed the names, addresses, and telephone numbers of key players in the industry whom you may contact for additional information about the cash flow industry and your participation in it.

Funding Sources

The database of funding sources (buyers) primarily directed toward broker-driven business is comprised of more than 600 capital providers nationwide. Listed below you will find some of the major funding sources in the income stream categories described in this book.

Most funding sources expect brokers dealing directly with them to understand the components of a cash flow transaction thoroughly and have skills in negotiating, structuring, packaging, presenting, and closing transactions.

Some funding sources can assist beginning brokers in those areas; however, their internal resources are dedicated primarily to funding transactions. The funding sources below prefer to deal with competent, trained brokers, but are willing to provide the assistance new entrants require.

Funding Source	Contact Regarding
Affirmative Lifestyles 10010 N. San Pedro, Suite 650 San Antonio, TX 78216 (800) 876-2991 Contact: Chris Stuart	Viatical settlements
Alliance Capital Factoring Group PO Box 23834 Ft. Lauderdale, FL 33307 (561) 367-9558 Contact: Melton Elliott	International factoring
The Associates Financial Services, Inc. Private Mortgage Operation 1187 Thorn Run Road Extension, Suite 140 Coraopolis, PA 15108 (412) 262-4898 Contact: Purchases	Private mortgages notes
Express Business Funding 3326-10 Del Prado Blvd. Cape Coral, FL 33904 (941) 945-3863 Contact: Jack Wiadro or Kurt Church	Factoring and purchase orders

First National Acceptance Company of North America, LC 435 E. Grand River PO Box 4010 East Lansing, MI 48826 (517-333-0665) Contact: Rebecca Anderson or Doug Barcy	Provides lines of credit to brokers for the purchase of private mortgage notes, business notes, and/or mobile home notes
Goetschel Funding Company PO Box 83 Nerstrand, MN 55053 (800) 663-6031 Contact: Bill Goetschel or Terry Bailey	Factoring and commercial leases
Medical Capital Corp. 140 S. Chaparral Court Suite 110 Anaheim Hills, CA 92808 (800) 824-3700 Contact: Joseph Lampariello	Medical accounts receivable
Metropolitan Mortgage & Securities Co. 929 W. Sprague Avenue Spokane, WA 99204 (509) 838-0224 Contact: Central Negotiating Center	Private mortgages notes, business notes, mobile home notes, structured settlements, annuities, sports contracts, and lottery winnings
Quantum Corporate Funding, Ltd. 1140 Avenue of the Americas 16th Floor New York, NY 10036 (800) 352-2535 Contact: Howard Chernin	Construction receivables factoring

Settlement Capital 15851 Dallas Parkway, Suite 740 Dallas, Texas 75248 (800) 959-0006 Contact: James Lokey	Structured settlements, lottery winnings, annuities, estate settlements, and farm production contracts
Singer Asset Finance 1800 Old Okeechobee Road, Suite 200 West Palm Beach, FL 33409 (800) 407-4446 Contact: Stacy Blum	Structured settlements, annuities, and lottery winnings
Stone Street Capital 4550 Montgomery Ave., Suite 650-N Bethesda, MD 20814 (800) 586-7786 Contact: Purchasing	Structured settlements, annuities, lottery winnings, class action awards, law firm receivables, and royalty payments
Sun Capital 1615 Forum Place, Suite 1B West Palm Beach, FL 33401 (800) 880-1709 Contact: Jay Atkins	Factoring and purchase orders

MASTER BROKERS

The American Cash Flow Association awards the designation of Master Broker to brokers who exhibit a high level of expertise and skills in particular areas of the cash flow industry. Master Brokers close as many as 50 cash flow transactions each month. In addition, many of them also fund cash flow transactions.

Following is a list of Master Brokers who specialize in income streams identified and discussed in this book. If you have an income stream you are interested in selling, or if you have located a transaction and would like to refer it to a Master Broker (in exchange for a referral fee), you might want to contact the individuals below.

Name/Company	Contact Regarding
Edward Adams Adams Mortgage Investments 5100 East Skelly Drive, Suite 590 Tulsa, OK 74135 (918) 663-0859	Private mortgage notes
Archie Adams ADA Business Credit Corp. PO Box 2266 Bonita Springs, FL 34133 (941) 498-5088	Automobile notes
Jeff Armstrong Armstrong Capital PO Box 4003 West Hills, CA 91308 (800) 845-3055	Capital
Pamela Benson-Smith ICF Funding Services 455 Don Diego Dr. Los Angeles, CA 90008 (213) 292-1449	Factoring
Bill Bordelon Advance Funding Co. 1551 Rue Desiree Baton Rouge, LA 70810 (504) 769-8398	Private mortgage notes
Evelyn Braby Advance Funding Services 8913 Heely Court Bakersfield, CA 93311 (805) 644-0219	Factoring

Kevin Clancy
American Funding Group
4047 SE Barcelona, #3
Stuart, FL 34997
(561) 221-0037

Private mortgage notes

Bob Daniels
MIC Financial, Inc.
6084 Apple Tree Drive, Suite 5
Memphis, TN 38115
(901) 794-4555

Automobile notes
Equipment leases

Ben Dean
MCA
27700 Franklin Road, No. A-3
Southfield, MI 48034
(810) 352-4330

Private mortgage notes

Mike and Merle DeSherlia
Advance Funding Services
8913 Heely Court
Bakersfield, CA 93311
(805) 664-0219

Factoring

Rick Ganster
Ganster Funding Services
2430 Juan Tabo NE, Suite 242
Albuquerque, NM 87112
(505) 332-3958

Private mortgage notes

Marty Granoff
Granoff Enterprises
3145 Maple Lane
Davie, FL 36715
(954) 370-1806

Lottery winnings

Laurie Javier Advance Capital Healthcare Financing 8 Heavenly Way Mill Valley, CA 94941 (415) 388-2228	Medical receivables
Dee Jones DD Jones Funding 7332 Antoine Drive, Suite 234 Houston, TX 77088 (281) 448-1791	Private mortgage notes
Scott and Joyce Joosten JJ Capital Ventures, LLC 9610 E. 29th Street Tucson, AZ 85748 (520) 722-5999	Private mortgage notes
Rick Jowers Southland Equities Corp. PO Box 8025 Atlanta, GA 30306 (404) 892-4747	Private mortgage notes
Ed Lisogar National Capital Corporation 3605 N. 68 St. Scottsdale, AZ 85251 (602) 370-5670	Business notes
John Marth J. Carl Marth & Associates PO Box 534 West Bend, WI 53095 (414) 338-3045	Private mortgage notes

Judy Miller
American Note Investments
75 Digital Drive, Suite 200
Novato, CA 94949
(415) 883-6611

Annuities
Structured settlements
Private mortgage notes

Mike Morrison
MCA
3211 Bramer Drive, Suite E
Raleigh, NC 27604
(919) 876-4940

Private mortgage notes

Michael Morrongiello
Sunvest International
PO Box 271596
Tampa, FL 33688
(813) 935-3553

Private mortgage notes

Helen O'Boyle
Texas Funding Specialists
6804 Highway South, Suite 399
Houston, TX 77083

Factoring

Wayne Palmer
National Note of Utah
1549 West 7800 South
West Jordan, UT 84088

Private mortgage notes

William Shaw
Professional Financial Service
663 S. Bernardo Avenue, Suite 241
Sunnyvale, CA 94087

Factoring

Marilyn Singer
Capital Funding Group
59 Linwood Avenue, Suite 3
Buffalo, NY 14209
(716) 884-8889

Delinquent debt

Herb Spencer Capital Growth Tax Liens 22647 Ventura Blvd., Suite 233 Woodland Hills, CA 91364 (818) 372-4400	Tax liens
Dow Stanley Sunbelt Funding Company PO Drawer 769 Conway, SC 29526 (803) 248-5791	Mobile home notes
Bill Tan National Note of Southern California 7720-B El Camino Real La Costa, CA 92009 (619) 634-0492	Private mortgage notes
Lynda Vaillancourt Western Capital Investments 230 River Front Road Durango, CO 81301 (970) 259-7922	Private mortgage notes
Victor Wagner Flexible Mortgage Co. 3 Dunwoody Park, Suite 103 Atlanta, GA 30338 (770) 700-1334	Private mortgage notes

Certified Brokers

The American Cash Flow Association has certified more than 19,500 brokers to date. That list of brokers is proprietary to the Association. However, if you have an income stream for sale and would like to work with a broker in your community, feel free to contact the Association at (407) 843-2032 for a referral.

SERVICE PROVIDERS

Trainers

Diversified Cash Flow Institute®
PO Box 4916
Orlando, Florida 32802
(800) 713-6901

International Factoring Institute®
PO Box 3787
Orlando, Florida 32802
(800) 348-0158

National Capital Institute
PO Box 3787
Orlando, FL 32802
(800) 809-7601

National Mortgage Investors Institute
PO Box 2069
Orlando, Florida 32802
(800) 543-1211

Pino Training Organization
PO Box 1511
Orlando, Florida 32802
(407) 649-8488

Consumer and Business Credit Reporting Services

Dun & Bradstreet
(800) 234-3867

Equifax Credit Information Services
(888) 202-4025

Experian (formerly TRW Information System and Services)
(800) 520-1221

Membership Organization

The American Cash Flow Association
PO Box 2668
Orlando, Florida 32802
(407) 843-2032

Periodicals

The American Cash Flow Journal
PO Box 2668
Orlando, FL 32802
(407) 843-2032

The Cash Flow Connection
(800) 499-9444

Glossary of Cash Flow Terms

Account Debtor. In a factoring transaction, the company that bought the goods or services from the client and received the invoice; the customer.

Assignability. Ability to assign (or sell) an income stream to another individual or business.

Cash Flow Industry. The buying, selling, and brokering of privately held debt instruments in the secondary marketplace.

Collateral. Tangible assets used to secure an income stream.

Collectibility. Measure of the ability to collect future income stream payments once they are purchased.

Commercial Debt. Debt owed from a business or government to another business as a result of a commercial transaction.

Consumer Debt. Debt owed from by consumers to businesses as a result of a retail transaction.

Debt Instrument. Evidence of monies owed from one person or entity to another. Also called a *cash flow instrument.*

Factoring. The process of purchasing accounts receivable, or invoices, from a business at a discount.

Funding Source. Individual or company that specializes in buying debt instruments. In a cash flow transaction, the funding source is also called the *buyer* because it purchases debt instruments.

Hypothecation. The process of buying a debt instrument with borrowed funds, using that very same debt instrument to collateralize the loan.
Income Stream. A payment or series of payments that is owed sometime in the future.
Loan to Value Ratio (LTV). A measure of the amount of equity invested in a property in relation to its current value. LTV is calculated by dividing all loans outstanding by the value of the property and multiplying by 100 percent.
Mortgagee. The person or institution that receives mortgage payments on a piece of real estate.
Mortgagor. The person who owes mortgage payments on a piece of real estate.
Non-performing Debt. Debt that is more than 120 days delinquent, and thus eligible for a write-off.
Payee. Person or business that holds a debt instruments and is receiving regular payments on that debt instrument. In a cash flow transaction, the payee is also called the *seller,* because it is the person who is interested in selling future payments.
Payor. The person or business that is making payments on a debt instrument. The payor is important in a cash flow transaction, because funding sources base their debt instrument purchases, in part, on the payor's credit history.
Performing Debt. Debt that is no more than 30 days delinquent.
Privately Held. Describes a debt instrument that is held by a private individual, company, or business, as opposed to a lending institution.
Promissory Note. Debt instrument created in the sale that involves collateral (real estate, automobiles, mobile homes, businesses, etc.). The promissory note is the buyer's written promise to pay the seller the balance owed, plus any interest, over time.
Sub-performing Debt. Debt that is from 30 to 120 days delinquent.
Time Value of Money. A financial principle that addresses the way the value of money changes over a period of time. It determines how much a future payment is worth in today's dollars and therefore how much a funding source will pay now for a money it plans to receive sometime in the future.

Debt Instruments by Category and Estimated Inventory

Our training organization actively monitors the growth of inventory within each of the six income stream categories. (Inventory refers to the dollar amounts of income streams available in the market waiting to be transacted.) The following list shows each of the six income stream categories, along with an estimate of the amount of inventory available today within each group based on our research.

Business-Based Income Streams
$2.4 Trillion Estimated Inventory

Accounts receivable (invoices)
Chapter 11 reorganization plans
Bankruptcy receivables
Commercial judgments
Equipment leases
Commercial leases
Purchase orders
Equipment timeshares
Partnership agreements
Letters of credit
Contracts
Aerospace leases
Commissions
Commercial deficiency portfolios
Sports contracts
Automobile leases

Collateral-Based Income Streams
$950 Billion Estimated Inventory

Privately held mortgage notes
Condominium assessments
Equipment notes
Collectibles notes
Mobile home notes
RV and business vehicle notes
Warehouse inventory lines
Business notes
Aerospace notes
Marine notes
Automobile notes
Tax liens/certificates
Private instrument securitizations

Consumer-Based Income Streams
$175 Billion Estimated Inventory

Health/country club memberships
Retail installment contracts
Credit card debt/charge-offs
Consumer deficiency portfolios
Cemetery pre-need contracts
Unsecured non-performing or delinquent debt
Time-share memberships
Prizes and awards
License impounds
Student loans
Inheritances, trust advances, and probates

Contingency-Based Income Streams
$25 Billion Estimated Inventory

License fees
Corporate charitable contributions
Consumer judgments
Royalty payments
Franchise fees
Commercial judgments

Government-Based Income Streams
$75 Billion Estimated Inventory

Tax refunds
Lottery winnings
Farm production flexibility contracts

INSURANCE-BASED INCOME STREAMS
$165 Billion Estimated Inventory

Annuities
Funeral purchase assignments
Workers' compensation awards
Structured settlements
Viatical settlements

DOCUMENTS THAT SECURE REAL ESTATE

THE DEBT INSTRUMENT THAT SECURES REAL ESTATE is most often called a "Mortgage." However, in some states, real estate is secured by a document called a "Deed of Trust." In others, both a Mortgage and Deed of Trust can be used. The following list below shows which instrument is used in each state to create an interest in real estate.

State	Debt Instrument	State	Debt Instrument
AL	Mortgage	FL	Mortgage
AK	Deed of Trust	GA	Mortgage
AR	Both	HI	Mortgage
AZ	Deed of Trust	IA	Mortgage
CA	Deed of Trust	ID	Deed of Trust
CO	Deed of Trust	IL	Both
CT	Mortgage	IN	Mortgage
DC	Deed of Trust	KS	Mortgage
DE	Mortgage	KY	Both

State	Debt Instrument	State	Debt Instrument
LA	Mortgage	OH	Mortgage
MA	Mortgage	OK	Mortgage
MD	Both	OR	Deed of Trust
ME	Mortgage	PA	Mortgage
MI	Mortgage	RI	Mortgage
MN	Mortgage	SC	Mortgage
MO	Deed of Trust	SD	Mortgage
MS	Deed of Trust	TN	Deed of Trust
MT	Deed of Trust	TX	Deed of Trust
NC	Deed of Trust	UT	Deed of Trust
ND	Mortgage	VA	Deed of Trust
NE	Deed of Trust	VT	Vermont
NH	Mortgage	WA	Deed of Trust
NJ	Mortgage	WI	Mortgage
NM	Mortgage	WV	Deed of Trust
NV	Deed of Trust	WY	Mortgage
NY	Mortgage		

Tax Lien Certificate and Tax Deed States

NOT ALL STATES ISSUE TAX LIEN CERTIFICATES. Some states handle delinquent property taxes by offering actual properties or *deeds,* at their county tax sales. In states where deeds are offered, the property owner is generally three to five years overdue in paying his or her taxes. Listed below are states which issue certificates and those which auction deeds. For more information about investing in tax lien certificates or buying tax deeds, contact the local Tax Collector's Office in that county.

Tax Lien Certificate States

Alabama	Georgia	Kentucky
Arizona	Illinois	Louisiana
Colorado	Indiana	Maryland
Florida	Iowa	Massachusetts

Michigan
Mississippi
Missouri
Montana
Nebraska
New Hampshire
New Jersey
North Dakota
Oklahoma
South Carolina
South Dakota
Vermont
West Virginia
Wyoming

TAX DEED STATES

Delaware
Idaho
Kansas
Minnesota
New York
North Carolina
Ohio
Oregon
Pennsylvania
Tennessee
Utah
Washington
Wisconsin

STATUTE OF LIMITATIONS FOR COLLECTING DELINQUENT DEBT

Each state has legislation limiting the length of time during which creditors may *sue* to recover delinquent debt. Once the statute of limitations has passed, creditors may still attempt to collect debt; however, they cannot sue in order to do so. The table below shows the statute of limitations in years for each U.S. state and the District of Columbia.

STATUTE OF LIMITATIONS FOR COLLECTING DELINQUENT DEBT

State	Years	State	Years
Alabama	6	Connecticut	6
Alaska	6	Delaware	3
Arizona	6	DC	3
Arkansas	5	Florida	5
California	4	Georgia	6
Colorado	6	Hawaii	6

State	Years	State	Years
Idaho	5	New York	6
Illinois	10	North Carolina	3
Indiana	10	North Dakota	6
Iowa	10	Ohio	15
Kansas	5	Oklahoma	5
Kentucky	15	Oregon	6
Louisiana	10	Pennsylvania	6
Maine	6	Rhode Island	15
Maryland	3	South Carolina	10
Massachusetts	6	South Dakota	3
Michigan	6	Tennessee	6
Minnesota	6	Texas	4
Mississippi	3	Utah	6
Missouri	10	Vermont	6
Montana	8	Virginia	5
Nebraska	5	Washington	5
Nevada	6	West Virginia	10
New Hampshire	3	Wisconsin	6
New Jersey	6	Wyoming	10
New Mexico	6		

Lottery States

Although lotteries are legal in most states, lottery payments are not *assignable,* or saleable to funding sources, in all states. The lists below show which states hold lotteries and which states allow for the legal assignment of lottery winnings.

States That Hold Lotteries

Arizona
California
Colorado
Connecticut
District of Columbia
Delaware
Florida
Georgia
Idaho
Illinois
Indiana
Iowa
Kansas
Kentucky
Louisiana
Maine
Maryland
Massachusetts
Michigan
Minnesota
Missouri
Montana
Nebraska
New Hampshire
New Jersey
New Mexico
New York
Ohio
Oregon
Pennsylvania
Rhode Island
South Dakota
Texas
Vermont
Virginia
Washington
West Virginia
Wisconsin

STATES IN WHICH LOTTERIES ARE ASSIGNABLE

Arizona
California
Colorado
Connecticut
District of Columbia
Iowa
Maine
Michigan
Montana
New Hampshire
New York
Oregon
Pennsylvania
Vermont
Washington
West Virginia

ACKNOWLEDGMENTS

THE THOUGHTS, OBSERVATIONS, INSIGHTS, and recollections you have the opportunity to read in this book would never have been possible were it not for the incredible contributions to its evolution by some very significant people.

To the students who have graduated from my training programs and tackled the cash flow industry—oftentimes based only on trusting in me that something out there awaited them—I can only express my profound gratitude. I am humbled when I see what they have accomplished in their professional careers and personal lives. I could not even hope to list them all here, but you will see many of their stories reflected in the pages of this book.

To the industry pioneers, who have blazed a trail in establishing—most often, case by case—what have become the protocols, standards of conduct, and guiding principles of the industry, I owe the very substance of what is in this book. Their stories, too, you will find within these pages.

Moreover, I must express my sincere gratitude to Debbie Bracknell, until recently the Executive Director of the American Cash Flow Association, who has boldly, deftly, and intelligently helped to lead the cash flow industry in a direction that serves the interests of all professionals, and to Karen Knott and Cathy Simmons, without whom this book simply would not have been completed.

In addition, to my publisher, Simon & Schuster, and to my editor, Fred Hills, I offer my sincere gratitude for their faith in me, as well as in the subject of my book, and for the gentle, yet insightful guidance I received throughout as we slowly shaped this book—together—into the very best it could possibly be.

Finally, my thanks to you, the reader, for committing the time and effort to learn these strategies, digest them, and process them into the mainstream of the economy.

When I look back at the themes my life has reflected, I have so much I want to share. I look forward to sharing some of those discoveries with you today.

INDEX

Access, 21, 23
Account debtor, 144
Accountants, 69, 151, 152, 191
Accounts receivable, 46, 75, 139, 175
  due diligence, 159
  factoring, 140, 142
  see also Invoices
Accounts receivable purchasing, 27, 29
Accumulation phase, 204, 205
Adams, Archie, 231
Adams, Rich, 92
Advertising, 69, 91–92, 119–20, 121, 154, 210
Aerospace notes and leases, 46
Akers, Jeff, 122
ALIVE program, 201–02
American Cash Flow Association, 30, 31, 71, 100, 235–36
  conventions, 235
  local chapters, 218
American Cash Flow Journal, 30, 235–36
Annuities, 46, 53, 59, 63, 71, 197, 204–05, 210, 211
Appreciation, 80
Assets, 17, 18, 205
Assignability, 72, 73–74, 78, 191, 208
Assignment, 65
Attorneys
  see Lawyers
Automobile leases, 47
Automobile notes, 39, 46, 53, 59, 69, 72, 101, 122, 231

Background, 39–40
Bad debt, 61–62
  as good investment, 176–86
Bank officers, 112
Bankers, 151, 152
Bankruptcy receivables, 47
Banks, 60–61, 81, 108, 135, 138–40
Baronoff, Peter, 136
Bender, Martin, 207
Blankemeyer, Frank, 122
Boat notes
  see Marine notes
Brennan, Mike, 151
Broker(s), 24, 31, 65, 66, 78
  certified (list), 263
  consistency by, 228
  factoring, 144, 175
  fee models, 75–78
  funding sources and, 216
  making money: bad debt, 179–82, 186
  making money: business notes, 111–15
  making money: factoring, 145–48, 160
  making money: mobile home notes, 118–20
  making money: private mortgages, 31, 85–86
  master brokers (list), 258–63

Brokers *(cont.)*
profit as, 67, 68
starting as, 224, 235
and success, 216–18, 219
Broker network, rise of, 27–29
Broker–to–investor transition, 99, 115
strategies for, 224–28, 229
Brokering, 66, 68, 78, 107, 132
business notes, 110–11
commercial lease payments, 171–72, 175
factoring, 148–60
lottery winnings, 191
structured settlements, 207–10
Brokering process, 68–72, 96
flow chart, 72*f*
Business brokers, 111–12
Business calculator(s), 100
Business invoices
see Accounts receivable; Invoices
Business–based income streams, 52, 63, 75, 132
Business notes, 47, 59, 63, 69, 71, 75, 101, 131, 132
to avoid, 116–17
collateral, 79, 107
specifics on, 113
what to look for in, 115–16
Business sales
owner–financed, 108–10
cash flow concerns, 16, 29, 60
mid–sized, 148–49
Buyer, 65, 78
Buying delinquent notes, 101, 104–05

Callender, Jeff, 39, 151, 218
Capital, 11, 37, 67, 68
available, 66, 78
Capital–based income, 221, 223, 224, 229
generating, in cash flow industry, 223–24
Career objective(s), 233–34, 236
Cash flow, 15, 17–18, 24, 30
business of the future, 32–42
concept of, 15–18
factoring and, 136, 138, 141–42, 147–48
power of, 228–29
and profits, 142–43
see also Transaction(s)
Cash flow brokers
see Broker(s)
Cash flow business, 15–24
differs from start–up business opportunity 36–38
possibilities of, 215–19
Cash flow concern(s), 16–18, 24
businesses with, 16, 29, 60
solving, 12, 24
Cash flow industry, 10–12
accommodates anyone, 38–42
action steps to career in, 236–37
beginning of, 25–31
definition of, 19–21
generating capital–based income in, 223–24
getting started in, 234, 236
growth of, 30–31
impact of viatical settlements on, 204
inventory in, 53–55
making money in, 144
power of, 77–78
Cash flow opportunities, 31
experience and skills and, 232–33*t*
Cash flow revolution, 42
Cash flow specialist(s), 10, 11, 23–24, 29, 37, 117, 118, 171
building wealth as, 66–68
skills and experience for, 45
Cemetery pre–need contracts, 47
Charitable contributions, 47, 53
Chee, Winston
Clancy, Kevin, 236
Client(s), 65, 67
in factoring, 144, 145, 146–48, 149–50*t*
as referral source, 91, 154
structured settlements, 208–09
Club memberships, 47
Coastline Financial Group, 218
Cold calling, 154–55
Collateral, 73, 75, 79–131, 132, 138–39, 226
mobile home notes, 118
specifics on, 70, 93, 113
Collateral–based income streams, 53, 63, 170
Collectibility, 72, 73, 74, 78

Collectibles notes, 47
Combs, Mark, 231
Commercial debt, 52, 176, 185, 186
Commercial deficiency portfolios, 47–48
Commercial factoring, 137
Commercial judgments, 48
Commercial lease payments, 175
  brokering, 171–72
Commercial leases, 48, 52, 61, 63, 132, 170–74
  defined, 170–71
  future in, 174
Commercial transactions, 132–33
Commission(s), 48, 60, 65, 67
  commercial leases, 173
  delinquent debt, 182*t*
  factoring, 145, 146–47, 159, 160
Computer programs, 100
Condominium assessments, 48
Consistency, 228–29
Construction receivables, 167–68, 231
Consumer–based income streams, 53, 63
Consumer debt, 48, 71, 176, 177–85, 186
Consumer deficiency portfolios, 48
Consumer factoring, 136–37
Contingency–based income streams, 53, 63
Contractors, 167–68
Contracts, 48, 51, 149, 167
Core values, 251
Corporate donations, 39
Corporate employee benefits programs, 62, 211
Corporate expatriates, 39
Creating notes, 101, 105–06, 115
  mobile home, 121–22
Credit–card charge–offs, 48, 53, 178, 183
Credit card transactions, 136, 156
Credit insurance, 163–64
Credit protection
  in factoring, 161–63
Credit report(s), 159, 163, 184
Credit reporting services (list), 264
Credit restoration, 184–85, 186
Creditworthiness, 55, 159, 162–63, 173
Customer(s), 144

Debt
  types of, 177
  uncollected, 47–48
  see also Bad debt; Delinquent debt
Debt collection, 61
Debt instruments, 19, 20–21, 25, 30, 31, 38–39, 42, 232–33*t*
  by category/by estimated inventory, 54–55*t*, 268–70
  investing in, 35–36
  involving collateral, 79–131
  kinds of, 45–52
  profitable, 58–63
Debt investing, 42
  equity investing versus, 32–35
Delinquent debt, 176, 180–81
  reasons for buying, 183–84
  statute of limitations for collecting, 275–76
Delinquent notes
  buying, 101, 104–05
Discount/discounting, 86–87, 94–95
Discount transactions, 82
Discounted purchase(s)/sale(s), 137–38
Distribution/payment phase, 205
Diversified Cash Flow Institute training program, 38
Documentation
  income stream, 70, 93, 114
Documents
  private mortgage notes, 95
  securing real estate, 271–72
Due diligence, 158–59
Education, continuing, 235–36, 240
Effective conduct, commitment to, 244–46, 251
Elliott, Mel, 168
Employees, 11, 36
Equipment, 11, 36
Equipment notes and leases, 48–49
Equity investing, 42
  versus debt investing, 32–35
Experience and skills, 12, 45, 224, 231–33, 232–33*t*, 235
Expertise, 66, 78
  legal, 207
Explaining services and gathering information, 68, 69–70, 72, 78
  bad debt, 180–81
  business notes, 113–14
  commercial leases, 173

Explaining Services *(cont.)*
factoring, 148, 155–57
lottery winners, 192–93
mobile home notes, 120
private mortgage notes, 87, 92–93, 96
structured settlements, 208–09
viatical settlements, 203

Factor(s), 144
knowledge needed by, 161
Factoring, 25, 27, 28–29, 31, 77, 132–70, 175
advantages of, 156–57t
benefits of, 140–42, 156–57
different from loan, 137–38
facts about, 134–36
forms of, 161–63
making money in, 143–48, 160–61
players in, 144
purpose, of, 137
time value of money in, 164–65
Factoring brokerage/broker, 29, 31
Farm Production Flexibility Contracts, 49, 53
Fee models, 75–78
Fees, 65, 66, 67, 71
business notes, 111, 114–15
in factoring, 143, 163–64
lottery winnings, 193–94, 194*t*, 195
mobile home notes, 118–19, 120
private mortgage notes, 86, 96
structured settlements, 207, 209–10, 210*t*, 211
viatical settlements, 204
Feldman, Clifford, 153–54
Financial planners, 69, 90–91
Foreclosure, 105, 115, 124
Franchise fees, 49
Full-time work, 233, 234
Funding source directories, 71
Funding sources, 20, 24, 30, 31, 65, 66, 73, 74, 78
buying bad debt, 62
factoring, 29
fee, 75–76
information about, 255–58
private mortgage notes, 85, 86
relationships with, 219
structured settlements, 206–07
and success, 216
viatical settlements, 198, 199
see also Working with funding source
Funeral purchase assignments, 49, 53
Future payments
buying and selling of, 18–19, 20, 23, 29, 107
cash advance on, 206

Geography
limiting market by, 150–51
Goals, 244, 245
Goetschel, Bill, 227, 233–34
Government–based income streams, 53, 63
Government contracts, 149, 167

Hancock, Jim, 194
Hancock, Shannon, 194
Head, Winston, 115
Health Insurance Portability and Accountability Act, 200
Helping others, 196, 202, 234
Henk, Don, 153
Hilton, Mike, 39
Hypothecation, 227, 229

Identifying a seller, 68, 69, 72, 78
bad debt, 180
business notes, 111–13
commercial leases, 172
factoring, 148–55
lottery winners, 191–92
mobile home notes, 119–20, 121
private mortgage notes, 87, 88–92, 96
structured settlements, 207–08
viatical settlements, 202–03
Income objective(s), 234, 236
Income stream categories, 63
Income streams, 12, 31, 64, 77
buying, 24, 228
categories of, 52–53
connections between, 29–30
considerations affecting, 72–74
defined, 19
documentation on, 70, 93, 114
financing for buying, 227–28
and identifying sellers, 69
insurance–related, 210

payee/payor, 56–58*t*
selling, 219
specifics on, 69
turning into cash, 25
why people buy/sell, 21–23, 24
Industry
limiting market by, 150, 151
Inflation, 22, 23, 26, 34, 74, 80, 87
Information
see Explaining services and gathering information
Inheritances, 49
Insurance agents, 151
Insurance-based income streams, 53, 63
Insurance payments/policies, 39, 49, 52, 62, 71, 75, 193, 196–211, 231
Integrity, 249–50, 252
Interest, 21–22, 23, 68
Interest rates, 74, 76, 80, 81
International factoring, 168–69
Inventory, 36, 59, 61, 63
cash flow industry, 53–55
private mortgage notes, 84
Investing, 66, 78
Investment
bad debt as, 176–86
earning from, 222–23
Investment strategies
private mortgage notes, 101–06
Investor(s), 24, 86
building wealth as, 67–68
consistency by, 228
making money: bad debt, 182–83, 186
making money: business notes, 115
making money: mobile home notes, 121–22
private mortgage notes, 27–28, 84, 99–101
profit as, 96–98
transition from broker to, 99, 115, 224–28, 229
see also Funding sources
Invoices, 21, 38, 46, 52, 60–61, 63, 76, 132–70, 175
and other income streams, 29
see also Accounts receivable
Irish, Cindy, 41

Javier, Laurie, 150, 166
Jensen, Inger, 192
Jones, Dee, 41, 97–98, 104
Jooston, Joyce, 41–42, 90
Jooston, Scott, 41–42, 90
Jowers, Rick, 40, 91–92, 104

Kelso, Dan, 154
Khan, Mr., 241

Labor-based income, 221, 222, 223, 224, 229
Lampe, Diane, 38
Lawyers, 90–91, 191, 207–08
Leasing agents, 151
Legal professionals, 207
Legal-related debts, 183
Legislation, 74
Lending institutions, 60–61
Letters of credit, 49
Leverage, 147, 226–28
delinquent debt, 183
tax lien certificates, 125, 131
Levitan, Howard, 39
License, 11, 202
License fees, 49
Life circumstances, 41–42
Lifestyle, 221, 223, 224, 225, 228, 229
Lisogar, Ed, 59
Lisogar, Sheba, 59
Loan-to-value ratio (LTV), 99–101
Long-term investment(s)
private mortgage notes, 99
Lottery prizes, 39, 49, 53, 62, 63, 69, 71, 72, 73–74, 75, 187–95
Lottery states, 277–78
Love and caring, 250–51, 252

Making money
opportunities for, 66–68
principle for, 144, 170
in private mortgage industry, 84–86
without using your own, 45–63
see also under Broker(s); Investor(s)
Marine notes and leases, 20–21, 50, 69, 122
Market(s)
narrowing, 150–51
Marketing, 69

Marketing *(cont.)*
multi–level, 36, 38
through referral sources, 151–54
Medical receivables, 166–67, 183, 231
Metropolitan Mortgage and Securities Company, 95
Mikkelson, John, 153
Mikkelson, Peggy, 153
Miller, Judy, 92
Millionare(s), attributes of, 238–52
Mitchell, Steve, 89, 103
Mobile home notes, 50, 53, 59–60, 63, 75, 131, 132
buying, 121
collateral, 79, 117–22
creating, 121–22
defined, 118
Mortgage brokers, 89–90, 112
Mortgage notes, 71
see also Private mortgage notes
Mortgagee, 85
Mortgagor, 84
Multi–level marketing, 36, 38
Mutual funds, 32, 33

Needs/desires (cash), 21, 29, 83
Needs of seller
concern for, 236
importance of understanding, 208–09
Negative cash flow, 16, 80
Network marketing, 36
Networking, 69, 91, 191, 192, 207, 237
Networking opportunities, 61
Newman, Elinor, 152
Newspaper classifieds, 112–13
Niche(s), 29, 42, 58, 61
commercial leases, 174
factoring, 148–49, 150, 166–69, 175
finding, 12, 230–33, 236
limiting, 150–51
lottery winnings, 191
Non–performing debt, 177, 178, 180, 186
Non–recourse factoring, 162–63

Objectives, 40–41, 66, 78
career, 233–34, 236
income, 234, 236
Overhead, 11, 141
Owner financing, 25–26, 31, 81–82, 99
advantages of, 82–84
business sales, 108–10

Partial(s), 97, 101–03, 115, 225, 229
lottery payments, 193, 194
Partnership agreements, 50
Part–time [work], 12, 233, 234
Patterson, Ben, 41
Payee, 55–58, 63
Payor, 55–58, 63, 64, 71
credit history, 95
creditworthiness, 73
information on, 70, 93, 113
Performing debt, 177, 186
Perpetual money machine, 220–29
Perseverance, 246–49, 252
Personal injury settlements, 69, 205
Personal responsibility, 243–44, 251
Plan(ning), 245–46
Political unrest, 74
Presentations, 152–54
Private mortgage industry
history of, 81–82
making money in, 84–86
Private mortgage notes, 17, 21, 26, 27–28, 31, 38, 50, 53, 58–59, 63, 72, 75, 127–28, 131, 132, 193, 224
benefits of investing in, 98
brokers specializing in, 31, 69
collateral, 79–107
defined, 81
specifics on, 93
strategies for investing in, 98–99
why individuals sell, 83
why investors buy, 84
Private mortgages
and other income streams, 29–30
Privately held income streams, 19
Prizes and awards, 50
see also Lottery prizes
Professional competency, 236, 239–40, 251
Professional relationships, 151–52
Professionals in transition, 39–40
Profit, 65, 66, 68
cash flow and, 142–43
in factoring, 164–65
love and caring and, 250–51
Progress billing, 168

Promissory notes, 48–49, 81
collateral–based, 106–07
Properties to target
commercial leases, 172–73
Property acquisition
with tax liens, 130–31
Provart, Ron, 40, 147
Public relations, 154
Purchase orders, 50
Purchasing agents, 151

Rate of return, 23, 137
Real estate, 16–17, 26, 32, 33–35, 42, 58–59, 79–81, 101
Real estate agents, 69, 89
Real estate investors, 60, 61
Real estate professionals, 172
Recourse factoring, 161–62
Recreational vehicle and business vehicle notes, 50, 101
Referral sources
business notes, 111–13
marketing through, 151–54
mobile home notes, 119, 121
private mortgage notes, 88–91
Referrals, 207
lottery winners, 192
Resaleability, 116
Research, 69, 92, 192
"Researchers," 124–25
Reselling
bad debt, 182–83
private mortgage notes, 99
tax liens, 130
Resistance points, 248
Retail installment contracts, 39, 50–51, 53, 77, 179, 183
Retail transactions, 132–33
Retirees, 12
Risk, 71, 73, 114
bad debt, 183
commercial leases, 174
in factoring, 160, 162
leverage and, 226
tax lien certificates, 125–26
Risk tolerance, 66, 78
Rothman, Jessica, 92
Rothman, Neil, 92
Royalty payments, 51, 53, 72

Safety
annuities, 204
tax lien certificates, 125
Sales commissions, 53
Scruggs, Lonnie, 122
Seasoning, 99, 100, 101
Secondary market, 19, 20, 86
annuities in, 211
bad debt in, 186
commercial leases in, 171
tax lien certificates in, 125
Secured non–performing or delinquent debt, 51
Security
private mortgage notes, 84
Self–employment, 12
Self–serving(ness), 250
Seller(s), 65, 66, 67, 71, 75, 78
motivation, 70, 93, 114
and success, 219
see also Identifying a seller
Seller–backed financing, 81–82
Selling, 11, 37
Service, commitment to, 236, 237
Service providers (list), 264
Service to others, 250
Services
see Explaining services and gathering information
Shaw, Bill, 40
Singer, Larry, 181
Singer, Marilyn, 181
Single–mindedness of purpose, 240–43, 251
Size
limiting market by, 151
Skills
see Experience and skills
Small loan/business loan officers, 112
Spencer, Herb, 129
Sports contracts, 51
Stanley, Dow, 40–41, 59
Start–up business opportunity
cash flow business differs from, 36–38
Steinberg, Fred, 155, 160–61
Stocks, 32, 33
Structured settlements, 51, 73–74, 197, 205–11
Structuring, 82, 94, 95

Structuring a "tail," 101, 103–04, 115, 225–26, 229
Student loans, 51, 178–79, 183
Sub-performing debt, 177, 186
Success in cash flow industry, 215–19

Tax benefits, 80, 125
Tax lien certificate and tax deed states, 273–74
Tax lien certificates, 60, 63
  collateral, 79, 123–31
  defined, 123–24
  benefits of, 125
  making money with, 124–25
  pros and cons of investing in, 126–28
  risks in, 125–26
  ways to build wealth with, 130–31
  what you need to know to buy, 128–30
Tax liens, 51
Tax Reform Act of 1986, 34–35, 80
Tax refunds, 51, 53
Time value of money, 72, 74, 78, 196
  in factoring, 164–65
Timeshare memberships, 51, 53
Title and escrow officers, 90
Tort cases, 205
Training, 29, 38, 235–36, 237, 240
Transaction process
  private mortgage notes, 87–96
Transactions
  bad debt, 179–80, 185
  basics of, 64–78
  brokering commercial leases, 171–72
  brokering: factoring, 148–60
  business notes, 110–11
  collateral-based promissory notes, 106–07
  factoring, 135*f*, 136–37, 145*t*, 146–47, 170
  lottery prizes, 189–91, 194
  players in, 64–66, 66*f*, 78
  principle of, 117
  steps in, 68–71
  training and, 235
  viatical settlements, 198–99, 199*f*, 202

Viatical settlement companies, 198, 199, 200–01, 203–04
Viatical settlement industry
  breakthroughs in, 200–02
  history of, 200
Viatical settlements, 52, 53, 62, 63, 197–204, 210, 211, 231
  impact on cash flow industry, 204

Wallace, Peggy, 202
Warehouse inventory lines, 52
Wealth building, 115
  as cash flow specialist, 66–68
  with tax liens, 130–31
Wealthy
  going from well-off to, 220–29
Well-off
  difference between wealthy and, 220–23
  strategies for moving from, to wealthy, 224–28, 229
Williams, Shorty, 227
Win-win-win situation, 18, 66, 134, 172, 185
Wood, Rich, 228
Work(ing), 221–23, 229
  full-time/part-time, 12, 233, 234
  at home, 12, 37
Workers' compensation awards, 52
Working with a funding source, 69, 70–71, 72
  bad debt, 181–82
  business notes, 114–15
  commercial leases, 173–74
  factoring, 148, 157–60
  lottery winnings, 193–94
  mobile home notes, 120
  private mortgage notes, 87, 94–96
  structured settlements, 209–10
  viatical settlements, 203–04
Worksheet, 70, 93, 96, 114, 173, 206
Worley, Rob, 200

Yield, 21–22, 23, 24, 66, 68, 71
  commercial leases, 174
  in factoring, 163–64, 166
  private mortgage notes, 84
  tax lien certificates, 125

Zerenner, Ernie, 218
Zerenner, Rose Marie, 218